HEALTH CARE POLICY IN THE UNITED STATES

edited by

JOHN G. BRUHN
PENNSYLVANIA STATE
UNIVERSITY-HARRISBURG

A GARLAND SERIES

Health Care Policy in the United States
John G. Bruhn, editor

GENDER JUSTICE AND THE HEALTH CARE SYSTEM

KAREN L. BAIRD

GARLAND PUBLISHING, Inc.
A MEMBER OF THE TAYLOR & FRANCIS GROUP
NEW YORK & LONDON / 1998

Copyright © 1998 Karen L. Baird
All rights reserved

Library of Congress Cataloging-in-Publication Data

Baird, Karen L., 1961–
Gender justice and the health care system / Karen L. Baird.
    p.   cm. — (Health care policy in the United States)
Includes bibliographical references and index.
ISBN 0-8153-3056-1 (alk. paper)
    1. Women's health services—Government policy—United
States. 2. Women's health services—Moral and ethical aspects.
3. Social justice. 4. Sexism in medicine. 5. Sex discrimination in
medicine. I. Title. II. Series: Health care policy in the United
States (New York, N.Y.)
RA564.85.B35 1997

                                                          97-35313

Printed on acid-free, 250-year-life paper
Manufactured in the United States of America

Contents

Acknowledgments

I would like to thank the American Association of University Women Educational Foundation for providing me with an American Fellowship that facilitated this work when it was in the dissertation stage. Malcolm Goggin and Donald Lutz provided invaluable time for the discussion of ideas, as well as academic and personal support, and put incredible faith in my project. I will forever be indebted to them. I am grateful to Kathleen Knight and Cynthia Freeland who also provided assistance, time, and support. I would like to thank Zehra Arat, my "research support group," and the Department of Political Science of Purchase College, State University of New York, for their academic and personal support. My family deserves special mention for their endless patience and encouragement.

Gender Justice and the Health Care System

CHAPTER 1

Introduction:
Women, Justice, and Health Care

The following issues are now glaringly undeniable truths:

- Women will constitute the larger population and will be the most *susceptible* to disease in the future.
- Overall, women have *worse* health than men.
- Certain health problems are more *prevalent* in women than in men.
- Certain health problems are *unique* to women or affect women *differently* than they do men.

These words are from the Executive Summary of the Report of the National Institutes of Health: Opportunities for Research on Women's Health (U.S. DHHS, NIH 1992, 7). Women live longer than men and thus experience more of the health problems that accompany old age—for example, osteoporosis and Alzheimer's disease. But even in their younger years, the quality of women's lives is affected more frequently and more deeply by their health than is the case for men. Women have more acute symptoms, more chronic conditions, and more short- and long-term disabilities arising from health problems. In addition, more women than men die from strokes; women have a higher incidence of mental disorders than men; more women than men acquire sexually transmitted disease; and women are the fastest growing population with AIDS. But despite all of this, women have been systematically excluded from most medical studies. One example is the widely published study reporting that one to two aspirins a day could reduce one's chance of having a heart attack (Ameswith 1990). That study used 22,000 male subjects and not a single female subject, even though heart disease is the number one killer of men *and* women in the U.S.

Women also disproportionately constitute the poor or near poor and thus account for 60 to 70 percent of Medicaid recipients (many of the rest are their dependent children). Women are disproportionately segregated into lower-paying, lower-status, part-time jobs that are less likely to have health insurance as a benefit. The consequence of this is that women have to devote a disproportionate share of their income to health care costs. Women are also far more likely to provide care in the home to children, spouses, and parents. Unfortunately, the costs of health care fall disproportionately on women. The U.S. health care system results in many injustices for women.

1992 was labeled the "Year of the Woman." The nation elected 24 new female representatives and five new female senators to the United States Congress.[1] This is the largest increase ever in U.S. history. The nation also elected Bill Clinton as president, and by so doing the country gained the most powerful and active first lady. Hillary Rodham Clinton was appointed head of the President's Task Force on Health Care Reform, a group that labored for months to produce recommendations for improving our health care system. The resulting report and legislation, the Health Security Act, called for radical changes to the way we finance and deliver health care in the United States.

Since Clinton was inaugurated, the Family Leave Act was passed, mandating employers to provide up to twelve weeks leave to parents to care for newborn or ill children, as well as other family members. The "Gag rule," which mandated that workers in Federally funded clinics could not give information about the availability of or procedures associated with abortions to patients, has been lifted. RU-486, which has been banned in the U.S. for years, is finally being tested for approval by the Food and Drug Administration (FDA), and the new female condom was approved in April 1993. Furthermore, the FDA, which had a policy forbidding the use of women of childbearing age in medical drug research, announced that any research submitted by drug manufacturers for new drug approvals will need to include data regarding effects on women. Moreover, in 1996, the Health Insurance Portability and Accountability Act limiting pre-existing condition exclusions and increasing the portability of insurance when one leaves a job, and the Newborns' and Mothers' Health Protection Act allowing women to stay in the hospital at least 48 hours after giving birth, were passed.

In 1990, the National Institutes of Health (NIH) established the Office on Research on Women's Health, with the goals of strengthening and enhancing research related to diseases, disorders, and conditions affecting women and to ensure that women are appropriately represented in biomedical and biobehavioral research studies. In 1991, the Women's Health Initiative was created, a 14-year $625 million effort, to study 150,000 women at 45 clinical centers across the U.S. It is the largest clinical study ever undertaken in this country on the health of either men or women.

Health care is currently a very important issue. Costs have risen dramatically. In 1991, the nation spent 13.2 percent of national income on health care (Starr 1994). In 1970, we spent about 7 percent of our Gross National Product (GNP) and in 1980, about 9 percent, for health care; costs for 1992 were approximately $800 billion, 14 percent of our GNP (White House Domestic Policy Council 1993). Health care costs are growing at a dramatic and unbearable rate. Furthermore, we have 40 million uninsured people in the U.S. Approximately one-half of these are employed and one-quarter are the children of the uninsured employed. In addition, we have some 23 million underinsured. These problems have been well-documented in the last few years and many reform proposals have been put forth to address these difficulties.

The President's Task Force on Health Care Reform and President Clinton prepared legislation for overhauling the United States' health care system—the Health Security Act. The nation's 40 million uninsured and 23 million underinsured were the main focus of the proposal, but new financing and distribution of costs and price controls were also main areas of concern. The bill did not pass, but it was the largest effort in decades to change the problematic health care system of the U.S. If such a reform ever does occur, the nation would experience fundamental changes in the way health care is delivered, paid for, and regulated.

In November 1994, many Republicans were elected to the House and the Senate, putting both under the control of the Republican party. This Republican victory was partially in response to the Democrats failed health care reform . Newt Gingrich became the Speaker of the House and proposed, along with other Republicans, the "Contract on America." This "Contract" called for balancing the federal budget, limiting welfare programs, cutting the capital gains tax, revising Medicare, and so forth, but major health care reform was not included. Though the Republicans have proposed major changes in the Medicaid program by requesting that it, along with AFDC, be put in a block grant and distributed to the states, as well as dramatically cutting costs in Medicare, the health care system as a whole has been left intact and no major changes have been advanced.

Even though no longer a politically viable proposal, the Health Security Act called for a radical reform of the health care system. With many women in top positions in government and Hillary Clinton as the leader of the reform group, as well as the obvious support for women's reproductive needs shown by President Clinton, one would hope that the newly envisioned system would dramatically improve health care for women. Would the new system finally institute justice in terms of health care? Would women's specific health problems receive adequate attention, study, and funding? Would the costs of health care be distributed so as not to disproportionately burden women? Would women's reproductive needs be adequately addressed and included in a basic health care package? Would Medicaid and Medicare be restructured so as to be more beneficial to women? How successful would NIH be in including women in medical studies so that diseases, disorders, and treatment of and for women can successfully be analyzed? These are just some of the issues that are important for women with regard to the health care system.

This book will focus on gender justice and the health care system. It will be divided into two parts. In Part One, a framework of gender justice will be developed. What is gender justice? What would a gender just public policy look like? What criteria should such policies meet? In Part Two, the framework will be applied to the area of health care policy, specifically medical research and health care financing and delivery. An analysis of past policies will be made, as well as an analysis of the recently enacted and proposed changes.

PART ONE: GENDER JUSTICE

To date, there is no agreed upon theory of justice for addressing gender inequities, inequalities, discrimination, and differences between the two sexes. Various theories abound, both within traditional political theory and feminist theory, but they differ widely. Gender has been addressed by traditional theorists as far back as Plato but, most often, is discussed only in the context of the proper roles and worlds for each sex—the public world of politics and business for men and the private world of the family for women—or gender is ignored all together.[2] Even contemporary theorists "have largely bypassed the fact that the society to which their theories are supposed to pertain is heavily and deeply affected by gender, and faces difficult issues of justice stemming from its gendered past and present assumptions" (Okin 1989b, 8). Sometimes gender is not mentioned explicitly, but is thought, at least by its author, to be implicitly addressed in the larger framework. But whether gender is excluded from analysis or included in a myriad of ways, no consensus has been reached about justifiable standards or the proper methodology for addressing gender issues. The literature is lacking a framework of gender justice. Developing and justifying such a framework is the subject matter of Part One of this book.

Justice

But what does it mean when one speaks of gender justice? What do we mean by justice? We speak of many things as being just and unjust. As stated above, this book is concerned with justice between the sexes and what a gender just public policy would encompass. So what do we mean when we speak of justice in this manner?

Generally, justice is a criterion by which we judge an action or an outcome of an action. If something is just then it is good, right, fair, and so forth, or if it is unjust, it is bad, wrong, and unfair. More specifically, it is a criterion that we use to judge human matters. We do not speak of just or unjust weather because we have no control over and make no decisions about the weather. Furthermore, justice helps guide and is a criterion by which we judge human *decisions*. For example, death is a human matter but is something about which we do not usually make decisions. Thus, we do not usually speak of just and unjust deaths, even though some deaths may be tragic, unfortunate, or unexpected. Also, we do not usually speak of the activities of animals as just or unjust. We do not think animals are rational beings who can *decide* things; they act on instinct. Generally, justice is a concept that is considered part of the realm of human decision making.

David Miller (1976) notes that there are three principles involved in social justice, which is defined as giving each their due, and "their due" can be defined by *rights* (justice is getting what one is entitled to by a defined set of rights), *deserts* (justice is getting what one deserves through merit, efforts, work, personal characteristics, input, etc.) and *needs* (justice is getting what one needs). Justice also falls into the realm of human obligation—it is what we should feel obliged to do, not what we could do if we so wanted, had the extra resources, or were feeling generous. If there is a problem and two solutions are proposed and when analyzed one is found to be just and the other unjust, we feel obligated to choose the just solution. Morally, it is not a matter of choice after such evaluations are determined. This example also shows the sense in which people speak of justice as a primary good. Justice is the highest of our various moral goals and will always overrule any other goals. As John Rawls (1971) states, "[A]n injustice is tolerable only when it is necessary to avoid an even greater injustice" (4).

Since justice applies to human decision making, it follows that it applies to conflicts or problems that need a resolution. If there are an infinite quantity of resources for a group of people or a society, then we would not usually talk of how the resources are distributed as just or unjust. We do not think of justice as "getting everything one wants." Issues of justice arise when there is a finite amount of something and it has to be distributed in some manner. This is the well-known form of distributive justice, which is the form one most often deals with in making public policies. Theories of distributive justice attempt to articulate principles that specify just distributions of benefits and burdens. As noted above, a just distribution is usually thought of as one in which each person receives what is due to them. The controversy or discrepancy occurs in deciding what is due to each person.[3]

Since Aristotle, one of the main components of justice is treating equals equally and unequals unequally in proportion to their relevant differences. We still have the problems discussed above, but with Aristotle's definition we at least have a starting point by which to begin to untangle the problem of "to each according to what is due to them." Initially, one should assume that all should be treated the same and receive the same benefits, bear the same burdens, experience the same rights, receive the same amount of any good, and so forth. But many times this is not what one would call just. A person with a heart disease requires more medical treatment than a healthy person. It would be just to give each what she or he *needs* in terms of health care; it would be just to treat the two unequals unequally. But we must remember that they only get treated unequally with respect to the one attribute that differentiates them. They should still, presumably, get treated equally with regard to all other matters.

This situation raises the problem of when do differences matter? People are different in almost every conceivable way: health, talents, intelligence, personality, preferences, tastes, wit, beauty, size, physical capabilities, etc. And we do not want everyone treated the same in every way. From the time children are very small, we set up reward systems to give extra benefits and recognition to those who accomplish more. There are many differences we wish to celebrate.

So when do differences turn into something that we call unequal and unjust? Giovanni Sartori (1987) states that we want to address an inequality when the issue becomes relevant, unjust, and remediable (348). These three characteristics are inextricably interwoven. When would a difference be relevant? Why would we care about one difference but not another? We would care about a difference when it is seen as unfair or unjust, meaning when it affronts our moral values. People dying of starvation is seen as relevant and unjust because it is against our value that all people have the right to some basic minimum necessities and our value that people should not needlessly suffer. So, a difference is seen as relevant when it is perceived as unjust, unfair, and against our moral standards. But this has not moved us very far forward in our analysis; we have just restated the question.

The characteristic of a situation being remediable is closely connected with the other two, but provides us more information. Situations are seen as unjust when we think we can control or have some influence over them. As stated above, the weather is not a topic of concern for justice because we have no control over it. This is regardless of the fact that hurricanes and tornadoes kill hundreds and thousands of people. Fatal illnesses that we cannot stop fall into the same category. Such situations are described as unfortunate, terrible, or sad, etc., but they are not described as unjust. But when we can control or influence the progression of an illness and we have to make a decision about such an intervention, issues of justice do arise. So, justice only applies to the realm of human problems that are seen as potentially remediable. This is very similar to the discussion above about finite resources and distributive justice; justice is a concept that is applied to conflicts or problems that need and are amenable to a resolution.

So, with regard to treating equals equally and unequals unequally, and determining when differences do make a difference, people should be treated the same when there are no differences that are perceived as affronting our moral values. Different treatment is warranted when there are differences between people that result in situations or actions that are against our moral standards and are something we can potentially control or influence.

Gender and Justice

Let us now turn our attention toward gender and justice. Gender is one particular way in which people differ.[4] Not that gender is a small difference; many say gender is the most pervasive sociological and psychological facet of any human being. It describes us from the moment we are born and influences every experience in our lives. So, when should this difference matter? It would be simple to state that we should treat men and women the same—equally. Treat them equally and they will be equal. But I, as well as others, contend that the differences between the sexes do matter sometimes and warrant differential treatment so that the differences do not result in injustices. But what this different treatment should be, under what conditions it should be called upon, and on what moral principles it should be based are areas of widespread disagreement. These problems are the subject of Part One of this book.

Historically, two approaches have been used to address the difference problem as it relates to gender, or to the social consequences which many times result in sex discrimination. One approach tries to transcend the concept of gender and create systems, laws, and policies in which no gender distinctions are made—making the theoretical assumption that men and women are basically the *same* and they should be treated as such. People are treated as citizens, employees, taxpayers, social security recipients, and even "non-pregnant persons" but never as men and women.[5] It assumes that people are equal in terms of gender, or at least that it is not an important characteristic, but different in terms of ability, education, intelligence, skills, vigor, and so forth, and that the differences have no relation to one's gender. Or, on a slightly different note, some adherents to such an approach believe that even if the differences are sometimes related to gender, the best way to remove this correlation is to treat people *as if* their gender does not matter; thus, in time, it truly will not matter. This approach has been called "equal treatment," "formal equality," "symmetrical," "assimilation," or the "sameness" model (Littleton 1987a). It is also a tenet of liberal political theory and a type of feminist theory called liberal feminism.

The other common approach to gender discrimination stresses the *differences* between women and men. On the one hand, this approach divides the world into "his" world of politics and business—the public world—and "her" world of home and family—the private world. Each sex has its innate, natural, but different, traits that cause him or her to fulfill their respective "natural" roles. The just social order is the "natural" order. On the other hand, another variant of this approach asserts that women are more nurturing, caring, and sensitive and that their special functions and qualities have been devalued in society. is needed so that their special functions do not result in less power in society. Reform is needed so that their special functions do not result in less power in society. Even though there are two varieties of this strand, both are usually biologically based in women's reproductive capabilities and assumptions about the family. This approach has variously been called "asymmetrical," "sex-conscious," and "difference" models, and on a more negative tone, "essentialism," "special treatment," "protection," and reverse discrimination. Within feminist theory, approaches that validate and glorify women's differences are usually called radical feminism (Tong 1989).

Many scholars address the above-described problem using the term "equality." Some of these authors will be discussed in later chapters, but I want to note here why the concept of justice is a better choice. Equal can mean many things, but it usually includes things being the same, similar, or equivalent. Equality in terms of the law and public policies has usually meant treating everyone the same, as described above. This is precisely the problem that women are now addressing; women and men have different needs sometimes and to treat them as if they are the same means women's needs go unaddressed.

Jane Flax (1992) states that "precisely because equality as currently understood and practiced is constituted in part in and by a denial and ranking of differences, it is less useful as an antidote to relations of domination than is justice" (193). She continues by stating that the necessity of justice arises in political theory out of the recognition of differences—people have different skills, qualities, or claims, and so forth. Somehow, all the people with these various differences must find a way to harmoniously live together.

Justice, as a concept and as a theory, tries to find answers to this problem, and it involves much more than treating people "equally." Wendy Williams (1982) pointedly puts the question: "Do we want equality of the sexes—or do we want justice for two kinds of human beings who are fundamentally different?" (200). Justice is a broader and more complex concept, and it is more useful for handling the problem, than equality.

This issue raises the larger question of whether men and women are basically the same (and any differences are just the result of socialization) or, are there important biological differences? And, if there are significant differences, how do they manifest themselves and what are the appropriate ways to handle them so that we have justice for all concerned? These questions are examined from various angles in many academic fields: biology, psychology, philosophy, law, anthropology, sociology, political science, and women's studies, to name only a few. How these issues relate to the state and its laws is the subject of an area of study called feminist legal theory or feminist jurisprudence. Since there are no specifically feminist theories of public policies or policy-making, writings from this area of legal studies that address whether laws should be gender-neutral (treat everyone as if they are the same) or gender-specific (treat people differently according to their differences) will be examined. Neither approach is adequate to truly address issues of gender justice. Both of these approaches focus on males; women and their needs are measured in relation to men.

Formal Equality

Legal thinking on sex equality is rooted in our Aristotelian heritage: the sexes should receive similar treatment to the extent that they are similarly situated (Rhode 1989). With the rise of the women's movement in the 1960s and the passage of the Civil Rights Act of 1964, the legal doctrine and philosophy behind efforts to better women's position in society came to be called "formal equality" (Rhode 1989). The law should be sex-blind and not differentiate in any way between men and women. This belief was expressed in the fight for the Equal Rights Amendment, just as it was the thinking behind the passage of the nineteenth amendment to the Constitution many years before.

As Littleton (1987a) and others point out, formal equality was also developed in response to analogies between the situation of

African-Americans and women. In the late 1800s and again in the 1950s and '60s, the argument was made that African-Americans were human beings and should be treated equally with any other person and as specifically stated in the Fourteenth Amendment to the Constitution.[6] It was just a logical extension to apply this same argument to women. Women are human beings just like men, and they deserve to have the same rights and to be treated the same.

The formal equality model has been widely used in court cases involving sex discrimination. In fact, the very definition of sex discrimination implies that one is being treated differently only because of her or his sex. The first Supreme Court case to rule that a law that discriminated on the basis of sex was in violation of the equal protection clause was *Reed v. Reed* (404 U.S. 71, 1971). The case struck down an Idaho statute that gave automatic preference to males as executors of estates. The court stated that "all persons similarly circumstanced shall be treated alike." Next, in *Frontiero v. Richardson* (411 U.S. 677, 1973) the Supreme Court ruled that the military regulation that automatically provided dependent benefits to wives of males officers but only in certain instances to husbands of female officers, was unconstitutional discrimination against females. Then in 1976, the Supreme Court ruled in *Craig v. Boren* (429 U.S. 190, 1976) that an Oklahoma statute prohibiting the sale of 3.2 beer to males under the age of twenty-one and females under the age of eighteen was unconstitutional. Oklahoma failed to show that the statute was necessary; it did not meet the standard (at that time) for sex-based classification: that they be "substantially related" to "important" governmental objectives (Rhode 1989).

The formal equality model has also been used for many laws. The Equal Pay Act of 1963 (an amendment to the Fair Labor Standards Act) forbids discrimination in wages on the basis of sex (and other categories) for those engaged in the same work, and Title VII (7) of the Civil Rights Act of 1964 prohibits discrimination on the basis of sex in employment. Title IX (9) of the Higher Education Amendments forbids discrimination in schools and colleges that receive federal aid. And the Equal Rights Amendment (ERA), which was not passed at the federal level but has been passed in many states, provides that "equality of rights under the law shall not be denied or abridged . . . on account of sex." Furthermore, the recently passed Family Leave Act that allows a "worker" to take up to twelve weeks of unpaid leave for the birth of a child, to care for a family member, or for their own serious health condition, employs gender-neutral language that makes the assumption that a man or a woman can care for a newborn or sick family member.

These cases and laws, and many others, are examples of reasoning that men and women are basically the same and that similar people deserve similar treatment. Formal equality under the law has been successful in many ways. Women have gained access to many things from which they had previously been excluded. But a problematical situation for the formal equality model is the fact that women get pregnant and give birth. This, in varying forms, incapacitates (some) women for varying lengths of time. How do we treat women the same as men if men do not get pregnant and give birth? This issue brings to light many of the problems with the formal equality model.

In the first of a series of pregnancy-related decisions, the Supreme Court ruled in *Geduldig v. Aiello* (417 U.S. 484, 1974) that a California program that excluded pregnancy from insurance coverage did not violate the equal protection clause. The justices found that the insurance company did not "discriminate against any identifiable group or class" and that gender was not even at issue; the issue was a physical condition—pregnancy. "While it is true that only women can become pregnant, it does not follow that every legislative classification concerning pregnancy is a sex-based classification" (496, n. 20, quoted in Eisenstein 1988, 66). Pregnancy is not related to sex because non-pregnant persons are both males and females. "The program divides potential recipients into two groups—pregnant women and non-pregnant persons. While the first group is exclusively female, the second includes members of both sexes" (497, also quoted in Eisenstein 1988, 66) Because men do not get pregnant, the Supreme Court justices did not know how to treat men and women equally in this case. As Zillah Eisenstein more fully explains in *The Female Body and the Law* (1988), "(t)he court has conceptual difficulty dealing with 'different' women seeking 'similar' treatment" (98). In *Geduldig*, the court chose to use the male body as the standard; the court would grant women the same rights that men had. And in many instances, this type of reasoning works.[7] But because "pregnancy rights" (for lack of a better term) have not been something for which men have asked, the Supreme Court had no prior granted right to which they could refer and thus give equally to women.

In response to this case, in 1978 the Pregnancy Discrimination Act (PDA; 42 USC, sec. 2000 e[k]) was passed. It states that "women affected by pregnancy, childbirth, and related medical conditions shall be treated the same as other persons not so affected but similar in their ability or inability to work." An employer cannot refuse to hire or terminate a pregnant women, nor can they force her to take maternity leave. Pregnancy is to be considered a temporary disability and benefits that apply to other nonoccupational temporary disabilities (of men and non-pregnant women) are to apply to pregnancy also; pregnancy is to be treated "equally" or the same as other illnesses. But treating pregnancy the same as other bodily conditions is fraught with its own problems. And, in the end, it does not give women what they need to really be equal in ways that count. As Deborah Rhode (1989) notes, "This is one of the contexts in which equality in form has not yielded equality in fact" (119).[8]

One court case that exemplifies many of the problems with the PDA and the reasoning behind it is *California Federal Savings and Loan Association et al v. Mark Guerra et al* (479 U.S. 272, 1987). Cal. Fed. did not allow Garland to return to work for seven months after her (two month) pregnancy leave. She was told that her old job had been filled and that there were no similar positions available. In this case, Cal Fed argued that the California statute requiring them to grant up to four months of unpaid leave with job security for pregnant workers (but not other temporary disabled workers) conflicted with the federal law (PDA) requiring them to treat pregnant workers like any other employees that are temporarily disabled.

The important issue in this case is how pregnancy should be treated. Should pregnancy be treated as an illness? If so, is it to be treated the same as any other illness or should it be treated differently? Alternatively, should pregnancy even be viewed as an illness, or should it be seen as a natural, though temporary, condition? Excluding the possibilities of pathologies associated with pregnancy which would be treated as illnesses, is pregnancy simply a particular class of need specific to women and deserving of coverage?

Various feminists organizations filed briefs arguing both sides of the case. N.O.W. and the A.C.L.U. Women's Rights Project argued against allowing states to require disability leaves only for pregnancy; they argued that the statute should include all workers disabled for four months or less. "Women will secure equality, equity and greater tangible benefits when legal distinctions based on sex and pregnancy are eliminated, and when the similarities in the rights and needs of both sexes are seen to override their differences" (as cited in Eisenstein 1988, 106). If employees cannot be terminated for temporary disabilities than pregnant women cannot be terminated either. This gives equal treatment and, in this case, means protecting the pregnant woman's job just as a man's job would be protected under similar, or as best as can be equated, conditions.

Other organizations such as the Coalition for Reproductive Equality in the Workplace, Planned Parenthood, Equal Rights Advocates, and International Ladies' Garment Worker's Union, AFL-CIO argued that statutes such as California's should be permissible. They argued that the California and federal law implicitly recognize the real differences in the reproductive roles of men and women. "These biological reproductive sex differences must be taken into account if the goal of equal employment opportunity for pregnant women is to be attained" (as cited in Eisenstein 1988, 106). They argued that it is not protective legislation to recognize the real biological differences accompanying reproductive roles; protective legislation is based on false stereotypical notions of female roles. We cannot treat men and women the same in this case because men have no comparable state to pregnancy. They have illnesses or can be hurt, but pregnancy and childbirth are not illnesses. They are natural, common, positive, and physically demanding occurrences that keep the human race from becoming extinct.

We see in this case some of the problems with formal equality. First, men are the standard with which women are compared. Men do not get pregnant, so to speak of treating men and women "equally" with respect to pregnancy is, in a way, ludicrous. Under formal equality, pregnancy has to seem similar to something males experience—disability—in order to gain some protection. Pregnancy has to be looked at as something like a hernia to gain legitimacy. Formal equality treats similarly situated people similarly. Usually, such analysis looks at women to see if they are similarly situated to the prevailing norm, which is usually male-defined. Under formal equality the best that women can hope for is to be treated like the workers that are already there, which are mostly men, and to be given the same male-defined rights and privileges. Once again, the issue of pregnancy seems to disrupt this paradigm.

This leads to a related critique. "(E)quality analysis defines as beyond its scope precisely those issues that women find crucial to their concrete experience" (Littleton 1987a, 1306). Pregnancy, childbirth, and child-rearing might be a few things that many women find important. Precisely because they are associated with women, the male defined world of rights, liberties, and employment does not know how to fit them in to the prevailing mode of thinking. As Littleton notes, given the way employment is structured in this country, pregnancy makes a women unable to work for a few days to a few months (1306). For the most part, pregnancy makes her unable to breast feed after giving birth. And it certainly makes her unable to fully participate in the raising of her children. But this is a structure of the workplace, not reproduction and child-rearing as such. It is conceivable to have a woman work for money, be pregnant, breast feed, and more fully participate in her children's lives than most employment structures now allow. Part-time work is just one possibility. And with regards to pregnancy, Littleton states, "(W)hat makes pregnancy a *dis*ability rather than, say, an additional ability, is the structure of the work, not reproduction. Normal pregnancy can make a woman unable to 'work' for days, weeks, or months, but it also makes her able to reproduce. From whose viewpoint is the work that she cannot do 'work,' and the work that she is doing *not* work? Certainly not hers" (1306).

When the women who are like men get treated like men, this is called "equality" and "non-discrimination." But it is not neutral with regards to sex or gender; it is androcentric. For example, a job or employment is designed with the expectation that one will not be pregnant, not be breast feeding, not have small children to care for, and will not need to miss work when children are ill. So a third critique of formal equality is that gender-neutral policies and institutions are, many times, not so neutral upon closer examination. Women cannot use formal equality to challenge workplace rules that were designed for male employees but, when applied to women, disadvantage them because they have different needs.

A fourth critique is that under formal equality, difference is found to be in women; in the case above, women get pregnant and are thus different from the "normal" worker. But really difference is found in relationships; it is found when you compare two or more items. Difference is not inherent in any one thing. Women are not inherently different; wheel-chair bound people are not inherently different. But they *are* disadvantaged in a world that was designed for people unlike themselves. Many institutions, norms, and practices have been designed in ways that only take into account the lifestyles and needs of a portion of the human race—the adult, white, able-bodied males who are not the primary caretakers of young children.

It is this fundamental premise which is called into question by feminist theory in examining the complex issues involving gender and justice. Feminist theory claims that women, children, and the disabled are relegated to a second, substandard class where they are far too often unjustly disadvantaged by this simplistic, monochromatic system. Many feminists agree that for far too long, far too many injustices have occurred to allow this system to continue unchallenged and unchanged. Fairly meeting the complexity of needs in a fully representational society is the goal of a gender just theory, they cannot be fairly met by the simplistic paradigms of the past.

In summary, the formal equality model treats women the same as men. But we live in a gendered society that treats women as different. And in some respects, women are different and they have different needs and need different treatment. In some circumstances, similar treatment is really a form of discrimination. But at other times, similar treatment is just what women want and need. How can we know the difference? Under what circumstances should we treat men and women the same and when should we treat them differently? We have to be very careful in deciding which cases fall into each camp. And on what basis do we make the distinction? And who gets to decide?

The formal equality model is inadequate to truly address gender injustice. It only opens the status-quo large enough to allow women to have what men have had. Formal equality cannot address the issue of why more women do not apply to be firefighters, welders, construction workers, etc. Sometimes systematic discrimination is so effective that women will not even apply for traditionally male jobs (Becker 1992, 105). This is similar to the problem we have with equal pay and comparable worth. Formal equality grants equal pay for women who obtain the same education, apply for the same jobs, and work at the same jobs that males do; we should give women the same as we have given men. But trouble arises with the idea of comparable worth. When education, job titles, and job requirements are not *exactly* the same, we do not know what to do. If formal equality cannot be granted, many times nothing is.

The Difference Model

The other main approach to eradicate sexual inequality, injustice, and discrimination is to treat the sexes as if they are different and thus deserve different treatment. In the past, this method of reasoning has been used to legitimize the private world of women and the public world of men. This tradition started with Aristotle who viewed everything as having a nature and a function. The polis and the family exist by nature, and it is woman's function to reproduce and continue the family, and it is man's function to participate in the polis. Such a society is properly ordered in accordance with nature.[9]

But in present feminist theory, differences between men and women are used to show why the formal equality model is inadequate, and in feminist legal theory, the differences show why formal equality is inadequate. As Elizabeth Wolgast (1980) argues, women cannot be men's equals because equality by definition requires sameness. Wolgast and others argue that there are inherent differences between men and women; this is a fact and is not the problem. The problem is that women and their values, special qualities, and activities have been devalued in the male-defined society; the feminine voice and body have been excluded from the system. Reform is needed so that their special functions do not result in less power in society. This type of feminist theory was spurred by the research of Carol Gilligan in which she found that women think about moral issues, and justice in particular, in different ways than men do. When viewing moral or ethical problems, women focus more on relationships, care, responsibilities, and the context in which the events are taking place. Thus, women speak "in a different voice" (Gilligan 1982).[10]

This version of feminist legal theory draws heavily upon feminist moral and ethical theories. Feminist moral theories can be divided into two categories: feminine ethics and feminist ethics. Feminine ethics suggests that traditional ethics fails to fit the moral experiences, values, and intuitions of women and that the discipline must be modified to include women. Feminist ethics applies a specifically political perspective to traditional ethics and suggests that it must be revised if it is to evaluate the dominance and oppression of women. Such oppression is morally unacceptable. This approach recognizes women's moral experiences and values, but it also includes a critique of the social system in which women's experience takes place. For example, a feminist moral theorist might say that women are more caring, but they have developed that trait because they have been valued by men according to the care that they give. Their specifically feminine characteristic is really just a result of patriarchy. Most writings in feminist jurisprudence include some of both of these perspectives, even though some are certainly more political than others.

Recognition of difference in policy and legal issues has been termed the special benefit or special protection rule. Some present policies that adhere to the differences approach are the Bona Fide Occupational Qualification (BFOQ);[11] the unique physical characteristic exception under the proposed ERA;[12] sex conscious relief in particular litigation; and affirmative action.

Adherents to such an approach point out instances in which sex-neutral policies have actually hurt women. One such area is in divorce law. Regarding child custody, judges used to assume that it was in the best interest of the child to award custody to the mother. Most states have replaced this presumption with one in favor of joint custody. Though there may be many positive effects of this change, it has also entailed many negative consequences for women. For instance, such a change makes it easier for judges to discriminate against women who do not conform to traditional norms; lesbians and women who have had extramarital affairs, for example, can suffer in custody disputes. Having or not having a career can also hurt women in custody disputes. If a mother has a career, her working interests can be seen to conflict with her domestic duties. Of course, no such prejudice holds for fathers. But if mothers do not work outside the home, they are unable to provide the financial security a father could and can be seen as a less qualified parent. Also with the changes in custody presumption is an increase in the father's bargaining power. Since most mothers still want custody, fathers have more leverage to get mothers to make property and economic concessions to avoid a custody dispute (Rhode 1989, 157; Becker 1992, 108-109). And the new rules have not caused any great restructuring of parental roles. Women still get custody in about 90 percent of divorce cases, and there is little research and no definitive evidence that fathers are more involved with their children under joint custody arrangements. Furthermore, many fathers seek joint custody in order to reduce child support obligations (Rhode 1989, 156).

Also, with the changes in alimony laws and the way child support is calculated, women disproportionately suffer economic consequences after divorce. Alimony, if allowed at all, is granted only for a year or two in which it is presumed that the mother will get training and a job. But most women cannot obtain jobs that pay as well as men's jobs. Child support is calculated on the basis that both parents will have jobs and both parents will contribute to their children's welfare. Men and women are equal in the marketplace, the reasoning goes, because we have Title VII and the Equal Pay Act. So, judges must treat men and women equally in economic terms in a divorce. But they are not equal. A woman with custody of children rarely has enough money after a divorce to maintain a similar standard of living to the one she and her children had during the marriage, even if she actually receives the child support (Weitzman 1985). Many studies have shown that the economic status of men rises after divorce, whereas the status of women and children declines dramatically.[13] In 1980, the per-capita income of divorced women was only 62 percent that of divorced men (Okin 1989b, 161). As Okin (1989b) notes

> The basic reason for this is that the courts are now treating men and women more or less as equals. Divorcing men and women are not, of course, equal, both because the two sexes are not treated equally in society and . . . because typical, gender-structured marriage makes women socially and economically vulnerable. The treatment of unequals as if they were equals has long been recognized as an obvious instance of injustice. (162)

Thus, many argue, the change to sex-neutral policies in divorce law has had grave consequences for women. This is an area in which sex-neutral is really gender specific. These sex-neutral policies have very different effects on men and women: men are advantaged and women are disadvantaged.

In the case described above, *Guerra*, the Supreme Court upheld the disputed California law allowing it, in a sense, to treat pregnancy differently from other disabilities. Many argue that this was a victory for women. No longer are only women—by virtue of the fact that only women get pregnant—going to have their jobs taken away because they get pregnant. If this was allowed, this would be sex discrimination. Women need to be treated differently, in a sense, in order to be the same. Because of their difference from men in their biological make-up, women need different treatment so as not to be treated unjustly. Why should women, or only pregnant women, disproportionately bear the burden of pregnancy? Why should such biological differences result in vastly different social and economic consequences for men and women? This would be unjust.

Many argue that an approach that recognizes women's special needs is an improvement over formal equality. But many also worry that different treatment will only serve to reinforce existing sex roles and stereotypes. Special treatment has been used to burden as well as benefit women (Becker 1992, 107). Under past special treatment rules that were supposedly recognizing women's special needs, women were "protected" from owning property, voting, having certain jobs, working too many hours, and earning too much money. Rhode (1989) states that the difference-oriented approach "verges on tautology. It allows different treatment for those who are different with respect to legitimate purposes, but offers no criteria for determining which differences matter and what counts as legitimate. On a practical level, the focus on difference has failed adequately to raise, let alone resolve, the problems it seeks to address" (81). She continues to state that

> (s)ex related characteristics have been both over- and undervalued. In some cases, such as those involving occupational restrictions, courts have allowed biology to dictate destiny. In other contexts, such as pregnancy discrimination, they have ignored women's special reproductive needs. (82)

The formal equality model is inadequate, and the difference model gives us insight to needed changes. But it is also inadequate to address gender inequalities. Both formal equality and the difference model focus on males; either women get what men have received or their differences from men become the focus of laws or policies. In either approach, men are the center and women are measured in relation to them. What is needed is a new theory of gender justice that focuses upon women and their needs. A new approach is needed that focuses less on how women are the same as or different from men and more on how women, as a diverse group, are disadvantaged by certain policies or the absence of specific policies. The development of such an approach is the focus of Part One of this book.

In Part One, some contemporary theories of justice will be examined. The most important and widely read contemporary political theory of justice is Rawls's *A Theory of Justice* (1971). Okin (1989b) states that "John Rawls's *A Theory of Justice* has had the most powerful influence of any contemporary moral and political theory" (89). She also notes that the scope of Rawls's influence is indicated by the fact that other contemporary theorists, such as MacIntyre (1988), Nozick (1974), and Walzer (1983) all respond to Rawls, either in agreement or disagreement. Kymlicka (1990) states, "It is generally accepted that the recent rebirth of normative political philosophy began with the publication of John Rawls's *A Theory of Justice* in 1971. . . . His theory dominates contemporary debates, not because everyone accepts it, but because alternative views are often presented as responses to it" (9).

Thus, the exploration of gender justice will begin in Chapter Two with an analysis of Rawls. What implications do his ideas of the original position, veil of ignorance, and principles of justice have for gender? What other aspects of Rawls are important for analyzing gender justice? How does his theory, as a whole, address gender inequalities and discrimination? Rawls's critics will also be examined to ascertain what implications they have found in Rawls's theory for gender justice. Though Rawls has received much attention, little analysis has been done regarding the application of his theory of justice to gender. Chapter Three will address utilitarianism. Utilitarianism can be described as a theory that proposes the greatest good for the greatest number of people. It is a commonly used idea of justice, even if not explicitly, in public policy making because we usually want to help the most people that we can with any given policy. "Justice as fairness" and "the greatest good for the greatest number" will both be examined for their usefulness or applicability to gender issues. What do both of these theories tell us about good and bad policy regarding gender?

Chapter Four will turn to theorists who directly address the concept of gender justice and whom, either fully or partially, reject the formal equality/difference paradigm. The theories of Eisenstein (1988), Littleton (1987a, 1987b), MacKinnon (1987, 1989), Minow (1990), Okin (1989a, 1989b, 1990), Rhode (1989, 1992), and Young (1990) will be reviewed. MacKinnon presents a theory of "gender as dominance;" Young advocates a "politics of difference;" Okin calls for a "humanist justice;" and Rhode looks at "gender as a disadvantage." All of these theories directly address views of justice and gender and provide new frameworks or ideas on this matter. A theory of gender disadvantage "in which women as a group are not disadvantaged in controlling their destiny" will be advanced as the most promising and will be the basis upon which I will build (Rhode 1989).

Chapter Five will further analyze what such a theory of gender disadvantage might encompass. Similarities and differences between Rawls, utilitarianism, and feminist theorists will be presented. Common themes will be drawn and a synthesis of the various theories, a theory of gender justice, will be proposed that focuses on gender disadvantage. Most importantly, criteria and questions will be developed that we can apply to public policies to judge how they are treating women.

The above-mentioned theorists will be examined with regard to two main questions. First, what does their theory tell us or imply about gender justice? And second, how can we apply their theory, as it relates to gender justice, to policy or law? In the end, any moral or normative theory is irrelevant unless we can use it to judge phenomena of our everyday world. In this work, the theory will be applied to public policy, and specifically health care policy.

A grand, all-encompassing theory of gender justice will not be proposed herein. Many critiques have been made about such types of theories. General statements about gender justice will certainly be made, but it is realized or not realized in specific contexts and instances. Certain policies can institute equality, equity, justice, and fairness or they can result in unjust, unfair outcomes that advantage one group over another. And of course when policies are instituted again and again that advantage one group over another, the result can be that one group is systematically disadvantaged and oppressed; but this occurs out of specific instances and events.

PART TWO: HEALTH CARE

In Part Two of the book, the theory of gender justice will be applied to health care. The importance of developing a theory of gender justice is to have a tool by which to judge various policies and practices. Recent and important governmental policies and proposals that promise to improve health care for women will be analyzed in light of the framework of gender justice developed in Part One. Included in this inquiry will be the NIH's and FDA's medical research policies regarding women and policies to reform the health care insurance and delivery system. The NIH and FDA recently enacted policies to ensure that women are adequately represented in medical and drug research. With regard to the health care system, managed care has revolutionized how health care is paid for and delivered in the United States and it, along with changes in the Medicaid program, will be explored. Moreover, many health care reform proposals call for universal coverage and a standard benefits package. Since these proposals appear to be, if implemented, very beneficial for women, they too will be explored. These policy changes are the most comprehensive advances that have occurred in the recent past regarding women and health care. They arose, at least partially, from the recognition that there are fundamental and systematic inequities in the health care system, and they seek to resolve some of these problems.

Office of Research on Women's Health, the NIH

In 1990, the NIH established the Office of Research on Women's Health (ORWH). ORWH Director Dr. Vivian Pinn states that the first priority of ORWH is to increase the understanding of women's health by ensuring enforcement of already existing NIH policy—all research conducted and supported by NIH must include women subjects, particularly in clinical trials. This was also mandated by the 1993 NIH Revitalization Act. ORWH will supplement existing research projects to expand study populations to include women and will encourage specific NIH institutes to promote research about women's health. When ORWH was established, a substantial amount of NIH funded research was performed only on males. Furthermore, in 1987, only 13.5 percent of the NIH budget was devoted to the broadly defined category of women's health issues. ORWH sought to remedy these inequities. ORWH will also devote some funding to encourage more women to become scientists, mainly through organizing national conferences.

Women's Health Initiative

In 1991, the NIH also established the Women's Health Initiative, a 14-year $625 million effort, to study some 150,000 women across the United States. It has two closely related goals. One is to decrease the prevalence of cardiovascular disease, cancer, and osteoporosis among women. The initiative will develop recommendations on diet, hormone replacement therapy, diet supplements, and exercise. The second goal is to evaluate the effectiveness of various strategies for motivating older women to adopt health-enhancing behaviors. Again the establishment of the ORWH and the

Women's Health Initiative are two very important advances for women in terms of health care.

Research and Funding

As stated above, women's health concerns and diseases have not been funded in proportion to men's issues and diseases. Furthermore, women have been systematically excluded from many medical studies. These issues will be explored further, along with the recent ORWH policy changes. Also, in 1993 the FDA announced a new policy for the inclusion of women in drug research. Previously the FDA had recommended that women of "childbearing potential" be excluded from large-scale clinical trials until further testing on animals was complete. The exclusion of women in earlier phases of drug testing led to their exclusion in later phases also. Obviously the past has been unjust, but will the proposed remedies ensure justice in the future with regards to medical research and women? This is the topic of Chapter Six.

Health Care Insurance

We finance, and thus allocate, much of health care through private and public insurance. How gender just is this system? This issue entails many areas of concern. One issue is employment because more than 90 percent of people with private insurance were insured through an employment-based plan; this raises issues of inequality in pay, job status, and labor force participation. Also, it is important to closely examine what services insurance will cover. Will it cover mammograms and abortions? Furthermore, with the feminization of poverty, Medicaid has increasingly become a women's issue; women and their children form the largest group of recipients—nearly 70 percent—of those receiving Medicaid (U.S. DHHS, HCFA 1997a).

The issue of costs is related to the issue of finance. With the rising costs of insurance and medical services, the burden disproportionately falls onto lower income groups who now have to devote an increasingly burdensome percentage of their income to health care. Many just go without health insurance. These topics are covered in Chapter Seven.

Managed Care

Managed care organizations are revamping the U.S. health care system at an alarming pace. About one-half of the insured are enrolled in either a health maintenance organization (HMO) or a preferred provider organization (PPO). More women than men are enrolled in managed care and many ideas for reforming the system propose to increase enrollment in managed care organizations. Furthermore, Medicaid has enacted many changes in the last few years and although the changes vary state-to-state, most states have either required or encouraged enrollment in managed care.

The growth of managed care can have many positive and negative consequences. It can help physicians and hospitals provide more efficient care and higher quality care in that it emphasizes primary and preventive services; it also facilitates coordination of the array of services often needed by patients with chronic illnesses. Moreover, for people without a regular source of care or who use emergency rooms for routine care, it can provide a path into the health care system. But managed care can become a mechanism for cutting costs without regard for access and quality. Financial incentives reward plans and providers who offer fewer and less expensive services, resulting in substandard care. For some patients, it may create new barriers to care and for patients who use and need more medical services—namely women—managed care may not serve them well. These issues are discussed in Chapter Seven.

Universal Coverage and a Basic Benefits Package

Two common health care reform proposals are universal coverage and a standard basic benefits package. Universal coverage is designed to eradicate the problem of the uninsured. Of course, universal coverage is a proposal that anyone could agree with if costs were not a concern. Thus the important issue becomes how the universal coverage will be achieved. In other words, who will pay for it? The Clinton Health Security Act called for universal coverage: all people would be enrolled in a health plan, either through their employer or on their own. Insurance would be much cheaper and subsidies for lower income families would be provided. Insurance would be jointly paid for by employers and employees. Clinton's plan for universal coverage will be discussed and used as the basis of analysis of how women will fare under universal coverage proposals.

A well-defined basic benefits package is also an important topic and has been incorporated into many reform proposals. A set benefit package is designed to reduce the problem of insurance not covering many needed health care services and charging too much for others. Proposals usually include a focus on primary care and preventive services and limited co-pays and deductibles. It is also important to determine what they cover: do they cover contraception, abortion, mammographies? Again, the benefits package in the HSA will be used as the example for analysis of how such reform proposals treat women. This will be discussed in Chapter Seven.

Health care offers a unique opportunity for the application of a theory of gender justice. Regarding most issues, it is very difficult to discern whether there are any differences between men and women. And if there are differences, are they inherent, natural differences or only derived from socialization; are they even significant? But, biologically, there are clear differences, and these result in men and women needing different treatment in the health care system. Health care policy offers a unique opportunity for analysis because it encompasses many clear differences and similarities between men and women. In those areas in which it is clear that the sexes need different care, are women receiving their needed care? Or are they receiving the care that men receive or little care at all? Are women disadvantaged in terms of health care financing? Are women disadvantaged because of their need for services but lack of payment ability?

The medical research policies of the NIH and FDA, managed care, changes in Medicaid, and reform proposals for universal coverage and a basic benefits package will be investigated and analyzed according to the framework of gender justice developed in Part One. The past policies will be shown to be unjust and enacted or proposed changes will be examined for their adherence to gender justice. Will the recent policy changes at the NIH and FDA result in a more just system for women, and if so, in what ways? In what ways has managed care affected health care and thus justice for women? These and other questions will be explored.

RECOMMENDATIONS

In Chapter Eight, the book will conclude with a summary and recommendations. Recommendations for change in the health care system so that we will have a more gender just system will be presented. Elements of a gender just system that recent reforms have contributed will be highlighted, and ideas for further reform will be discussed. A vision of a gender just health care system for women will be presented.

NOTES

1. Actually, four were elected in 1992, and the fifth, Kay Bailey Hutchinson of Texas, was elected in 1993 in a special election.

2. See Okin (1979) and Elshtain (1981, 1982).

3. The concept of justice is usually divided into distributive and rectificatory justice. To rectify is to right a wrong or to make equal, good, or whole again when one has been hurt or had an injustice committed against them. This notion of justice is fundamental to our civil and criminal legal systems. Another form of justice that modern legal scholars discuss is "procedural justice." This form deals with the fairness of rules. We think that if the rules or procedures are set up so as to be unbiased and treat all the same or, more correctly, treat likes alike, then the outcomes of such procedures will also be just. It is a focus on procedures or processes as a methodology for deciding if the outcome is just. This form is also part of our legal system. We have laws that apply to all; if one is thought to have broken the law, then there is a trial to determine one's guilt or innocence. There is a set of procedures that everyone has agreed are fair that guide the trial. As long as the rules are followed, whatever outcome results from the trial is thought of as just.

4. In this book, I will use the usual distinction of sex and gender. I will use sex when referring to straight biological differences between men and women and gender when referring to the social ramifications of these sexual differences. Of course, sometimes it is difficult to keep the these distinctions pure. For example, I will use the common phrase of "sex discrimination," even if it might be more appropriate to use gender instead of sex. But it is my intention to try to use the terms in the described manner.

5. In *Geduldig v. Aiello*, 417 U.S. 484 (1974), a case upholding the constitutionality of a California program that excluded pregnancy from insurance coverage, but included disabilities affecting only men, Justice Stewart stated that this case did not even involve "gender as such;" California had just made a distinction between "pregnant women and non-pregnant persons."

6. The fourteenth amendment states, "[N]or shall any State . . . deny to any person within its jurisdiction the equal protection of the laws."

7. But, many argue, because of our patriarchal heritage, this means granting women access to whatever men have had, whether or not it is what women want or need.

8. Much of this discussion of the PDA is taken from Eisenstein (1988) and Williams (1985).

9. See Okin (1979) for a full discussion of Aristotle, as well as Rousseau, and their thinking on the family, the private and public spheres, and men's and women's roles within them.

10. Gilligan's research has incited much discussion and criticism. See Becker 1992, 77-78, n. 14, for a list of such literature. Gilligan's work is also discussed herein in Chapter Two.

11. BFOQ is an exception to Title VII of the Civil Rights Act of 1964, 42 U.S.C. $2000e-(2)(e), that permits sex to be a job qualification when it is a valid one.

12. The leading interpretation of the proposed federal ERA would permit a "unique physical characteristic" exception to its otherwise absolute embargo on taking sex into account.

13. Weitzman's (1985) study found that in the first year after divorce, the average standard of living of divorced men, when adjusted for household size, increases by 42 percent, while that of divorced women falls by 73 percent (Okin 1989b, 161).

PART ONE

The Problem of Gender and Justice

CHAPTER 2

Rawls, Gender, and Justice

Will Kymlicka (1990) states, "It is generally accepted that the recent rebirth of normative political philosophy began with the publication of John Rawls's *A Theory of Justice* in 1971. . . . His theory dominates contemporary debates, not because everyone accepts it, but because alternative views are often presented as responses to it" (9). Susan Moller Okin (1989b) notes that "John Rawls's *A Theory of Justice* has had the most powerful influence of any contemporary moral and political theory" (89). She also notes that the scope of Rawls's influence is indicated by the fact that other contemporary theorists, such as Nozick (1974), Walzer (1983), and MacIntyre (1988), all respond to Rawls, either in agreement or disagreement.

But despite the importance of Rawls's theory, not much detailed analysis of its implications for gender have been performed until very recently. Okin (1989b) addresses Rawls's treatment of the family and briefly outlines some other important issues for women in a Rawlsian theory of justice. She then notes that "there are likely to be further feminist ramifications" and that "the feminist *potential* of Rawls's method of thinking and his conclusions is considerable" (105, 108). Besides some brief treatment of Rawls by Benhabib (1987), Benhabib, et al. (1995), Kittay (1997), Pateman (1989), Shanley and Pateman (1991), and Young (1990), this potential has not been developed.

The exploration of gender justice begins in this chapter with an analysis of Rawls's "justice as fairness." What does Rawls say or imply about gender and justice? Does Rawls's theory of justice result in gender justice? Can Rawls help us, and if so in what fashion, create a society or provide the basis for policies that would result in justice for women? The implications of the original position, veil of ignorance, and principles of justice for women will be examined and it will be argued that if Rawls's theory is corrected to include gender issues, if we amend his theory, it has some constructive implications for a theory of gender justice.

"JUSTICE AS FAIRNESS" FOR WOMEN?

John Rawls (1971) calls his theory "justice as fairness" because the principles of justice are agreed upon in an initial situation that is fair. This simply means that the parties making the voluntary agreement are free, equal, and have no knowledge about their particular place in society or particular personal characteristics. This last condition, the veil of ignorance, is really just a condition of impartiality. Rawls assumes that people are self-interested, but since the parties in the original position do not know what their specific interests are, they have no ability to design the initial agreement in favor of themselves or their particular conception of the good.

This brief description of the conditions of fairness raises many points. One characteristic that people do not know is their sex. On the one hand this seems very positive. If women and men were truly free, equal, and impartial, and if they could be empowered to debate and arrive at principles of justice in the original position, this would be a very good situation for women. Criticism abounds in feminist writings that the present system and laws have been made *by and for* white males, meaning that they are biased because they were not made by all people nor were the concerns of all people taken into account. So the inclusion of women as fully empowered participants in the design of the basic institutions of society and the removal of bias—in this particular case sexism—would certainly be a great improvement.

But this raises two further questions. One, as written by Rawls, are men *and* women free, equal, and impartial parties to the initial agreement? And secondly, has the removal of the knowledge of one's sex removed sexual bias (I will call this sexism) and really insured that the design of society will be made from a condition of sexual impartiality?

Men and Women as Free, Equal, and Impartial "Parties"?

Rawls calls the people in the original position "parties," not individuals or men and women. These "parties" are to be thought of as "representing continuing lines of chain," "deputies for a kind of everlasting moral agent or institution," "heads of families," "continuing persons," or "representatives of families" (128, 146; see also Okin 1989b, 91-92). Rawls says he has to include this description of the parties as heads of families so that it is assured that each person in the original position will care about the well-being of some of those in the next generation (128). This is important to stipulate because, given other limitations such as the parties being self-interested and not willing to have their interests sacrificed to others, the parties in the original position could derive principles of justice that only benefit their generation and no future ones. Since Rawls is concerned with how to create a stable and lasting society, he needs the stipulation about families so as to have a society that lasts longer than one generation—so that each generation saves for the next generation (284-92).

This issue has been examined by Jane English (1977). In exploring some of the plausible interpretations of the meaning of "heads of families," English says that Rawls could not mean that the parties in the original position are self-interested individuals that just happen to be heads of families. Then they might choose principles that only benefit heads of families and this would be contrary to Rawls's goals (93). Rawls must intend that the heads of families "care" about the welfare of their family members. But the heads are still disinterested with respect to members of other families. Thus, heads of families bring the interests of all family members with them to the bargaining table. But, we should ask, how are the interests of the family members represented by the head in the original position? Is there a causal connection between the fact that the head of the family "cares" about the family members and knowing and representing the interests of the rest of the family, the children as well as the spouse?

Also, we do not usually think of a family as having two heads. The use of the word "head" implies one, the top of a hierarchy, the leader, or the sole place of beginning or ending, but it does not imply partnership, one person or the other (meaning the mother or the father and it does not matter which one fills the role), or equality. So what does Rawls mean when he speaks of the head of the family? One assumes the typical family of a mother, father, and children; who gets to be the representative of such a family in the original position?[1] And he uses the head of the family construct so as to ensure that anyone in the next generation has someone that cares about him/her in the present generation. This idea could apply to all parents but, in Rawls's formulation, there is only one head or representative of the family.[2] Furthermore, what about when the interests of the family members conflict? Why would Rawls not assume that family members' interests would conflict since he so strongly emphasizes that societal members hold differing views about the good, political beliefs, and religious beliefs, for example, and provide for such a situation? Why such a vast shift in assumptions?[3]

Add to these problems the references to fathers and sons in the section entitled "The Problem of Justice Between Generations:" "[n]evertheless, since it is assumed that a generation cares for its immediate descendants, as fathers say care for their sons"(288), and "[t]hus imagining themselves to be fathers, say, they are to ascertain how much they should set aside for their sons by noting what they would believe themselves entitled to claim of their fathers" (289). In addition, there are no references to mothers, daughters, or mother and daughters in the same section on justice between the generations. As written, it is difficult to posit that men *and* women are free, equal, and impartial parties to the initial agreement.[4]

So let us examine one possible different conception of the parties in the original position. What if the parties in the original position were conceived of as parents or potential parents so that each cared about someone in the next generation? This satisfies Rawls's need for consideration of other generations and removes the problems of having the parties being heads of families, as noted above. This helps ensure that men *and* women are parties in the original position since men *and* women are parents or potential parents. It does not make families obsolete; the institution can exist just like every other basic institution Rawls describes. Also, English (1977) suggests that we remove the present time of entry constraint in the original position. Rawls requires that the parties in the original position be contemporaries; they all live together in the same time period. It is not clear why he requires this. The only support offered is that if we thought of the original position as containing all those who could ever live, it would "stretch fantasy too far; the conception would cease to be a natural guide to intuition" (Rawls 1971, 139). But as English points out, this is a very weak argument considering all the other facts, such as our era in history, our specific culture, our sex, and our own conception of the good that we must forget when under the veil of ignorance.

Removing the present time of entry constraint allows us to remove other problematical tenets of the theory. If people do not know when they will be living in the society, they will be motivated to care for all generations throughout time. This removes the need for a just savings principle, as Rawls himself already notes (291-92). People will already want to design society so that any generation will save for future generations.[5] Furthermore, we no longer need to view participants in the original position as heads of families (English 1977). Note that Rawls requires this so that anyone in the next generation has someone who cares about him/her in the present. With the present time of entry constraint removed and thus the participants in the original position not knowing to which generation they will belong, and with all the parties conceived of as parents or potential parents, the motivational assumption becomes that everyone would care about every generation. And as English (1977) notes, this precludes any injustices that might arise within the family under Rawls's "heads of families" scenario. This seems to be a reasonable, and perhaps better, alternative to Rawls's formulation.

Sexual Impartiality?

The second question noted above is: has the removal of the knowledge of one's sex removed sexual bias—sexism—and really insured that the design of society will be made from a condition of (sexual) impartiality?

One important issue involved in this question is if people can really accomplish such a task; can people remove the knowledge of their sex? There are two closely related points involved in this question. One, can people actually not know what sex they are—just somehow lose this knowledge? This, of course, does not actually seem possible but Rawls does address this.[6] Secondly, even if people could lose this knowledge, has the prior knowledge of themselves and treatment as a man or woman become so inextricably tied to who they are—their thoughts, values, and concerns—that the question of whether they could lose their present identification with a sex really moot? In other words, just because I do not know if I am a man or a woman today, this does not mean that I am not a gendered person in my values, goals, thought processes, ideas, etc. The question becomes "can a man think like a woman and a woman think like a man?"

This is an important issue for the original position, veil of ignorance, and principles of justice because if it is impossible not to be a gendered being, then the issue of being impartial certainly becomes questionable. Furthermore, it is possible that men and women may not agree on what should be the guiding principles of justice for their society. Of course this a complex topic, involving many psychological and sociological issues, and I will only touch on some of them here.

First, it is important to clarify what Rawls means. As Susan Moller Okin (1989b) notes, the veil forces people to "think from the perspective of *everybody*, in the sense of *each in turn*" (101; see also Kohlberg 1981, 199). Seyla Benhabib (1987) describes this as the "generalized other." "The standpoint of the generalized other requires us to view each and every individual as a rational being entitled to the same rights and duties we would want to ascribe to ourselves. In assuming the standpoint, we abstract from the individuality and concrete identity of the other" (Benhabib 1987, 87). Okin (1989b) does not believe that Rawls asks people to think from the position of *"nobody*, as is suggested by those critics who then conclude that Rawls's theory depends upon a 'disembodied' concept of the self" (101).[7] So, Rawls is asking the parties to be impartial in a particular sense. It is an impartiality that involves more that just being a judge or a jury member and trying to be fair and unbiased towards the evidence, witnesses, victim, and defendant; Rawls asks the parties to think, act, and feel *as if* they were the witness, victim, and defendant. Rawls asks one to allow the possibility that they could be anyone in the society and how would they think and feel if they were any one person in particular and then take turns at being each person in society.

In the above noted question of can a woman think like a man and vice-versa, what we are really asking is does one's sex indelibly influence the way one thinks in general, and specifically in making moral judgments? In other words, in the original position, can individuals *truly* not allow their maleness or their femaleness to influence their thinking and can they *really*, in an intellectual sense, become and think, act, and feel like a member of the opposite sex for a brief period of time? Many questions have been raised in the last decade regarding genderized thinking and moral judgments, starting with the study of Carol Gilligan (1982).

Gilligan found that women speak "in a different voice" from men, expressing different concerns. Women, she found in her study, focus more on relationships and see them as part of a web of interconnectedness; focus more on care, responsibilities, and bonds of attachment; and generally consider moral dilemmas in a more contextualized fashion as opposed to applying universal rules of justice and rights. Her work has prompted a voluminous body of literature about women and moral theory and development in particular, and about women and their differences from the universal male "individual" in general.

Some of the early feminist scholarship in this area emphasizes women's roles as mothers—emphasizing both aspects of physically giving birth and emotionally nurturing and raising children—and the experience of having been raised by a mother. The emphasis is on the special abilities that these experiences give a women or the special characteristics that are developed by living through such experiences; this is sometimes labeled "maternal thinking" (Chodorow 1978; Noddings 1984; Ruddick 1980, 1989). Other works have emphasized women's subordination and powerlessness in society and the psychological effects of such societal structures on the traits or characteristics women develop. Women are only able to develop some facets of themselves because they are only allowed to participate in certain aspects of society. Furthermore, some argue that qualities such as submissiveness, dependency, the desire to please, and the inability to act assertively are regarded as signs of good psychological health in women and thus held up as traits for which other women should strive (Miller 1976).[8]

Jean Grimshaw (1986) finds three main themes that seem to recur in one form or another in discussions of a "female ethic." These are

1. A critique of "abstraction," and a belief that female thinking *is* . . . more contextualised, less bound to abstract rules, more 'concrete.'
2. A stress on the values of empathy, nurturance or caring, which, again, are seen as qualities that women both value more and tend more commonly to display.
3. A critique of the idea that notions of *choice* or *will* are central to morality, and of a sharp distinction between fact and value; a stress, instead, on the idea of the *demands* of a situation, which are discovered through a process of *attention* to it and require an appropriate response. (203)

Grimshaw concludes her investigation of these categories and an idea of a female ethic by warning that there is no one view of ethical priorities that can be seen as feminine. It is best to see the differences between men and women not as an idea that women reason differently, but as a view that women have different ethical concerns and priorities. Will Kymlicka (1990) also agrees in that he thinks that the issue of moral concepts—"attending to rights and fairness (justice) versus attending to responsibilities and relationships (care)— is the heart of the debate" (265). Grimshaw (1986) concludes that the different life experiences and activities of women may make it easier for women to question certain dominant social values. This is a result of the private-public distinction and the relegation of women to the private sphere.

Baier (1987), Calhoun (1988), Jaggar (1995), Held (1993,1995), and Okin (1989a, 1989b) argue that an ethic of care and justice are not mutually exclusive. Baier (1987) notes, "It is clear, I think, that the best moral theory has to be a cooperative product of women and men, has to harmonize justice and care" (56). Okin (1989b) states that the best theorizing about justice "has integral to it the notions of care and empathy" and "is not good enough if it does not, or cannot readily be adapted to, include women and their points of view as fully as men and their points of view" (15). I agree with these feminist theorists and support the integration of aspects of care and justice and accomplish this in my framework of gender justice. "(T)here is little disagreement that justice is *a* social value of very great importance" (Baier 1987, 42). There is nothing about the concepts of justice or care that make them mutually exclusive.[9]

Nel Noddings (1990) examines Kant's philosophy—"certainly one of the most influential in all of Western ethics"— and finds that it "is apparently unconsciously genderized. Recognizing this, we might respond in one of several ways when we attempt to construct an ethical system" (162-163). First, we might adopt a deliberately genderized view that extols the virtues of our own sex. Nietzsche is a good example of this, and Kant shows some traces of such an approach. But, she notes, "(t)his way of approaching moral theory is both intellectually dishonest and morally wrong" (165). Secondly, we might avoid genderizing, but this may be impossible in such a genderized society. And if it is desirable, it cannot be accomplished until "we have something like a balanced set of genderized ethics to analyze and then transcend" (163). Third, we might adopt a genderized ethical view on the ground that no other is honestly available; men and women differ in some fundamental ways in their ethical reasoning. Given that the first proposition has no merit, our only present alternative is to adopt a genderized ethic, either on the grounds that it is the only one available (proposition number three) or for critical purposes (proposition number two). She advocates the adoption of a feminine ethic for critical purposes. And, in reply to the anticipated criticism of such an approach, Noddings states, "The introduction of female ethics can hardly be constructed as an attempt to genderize a field that has hitherto been gender-free" (165).

In conclusion, Okin (1990) states

Women and men may well think about moral issues in different ways. The answer is not yet in; further research that overcomes some of the faults of previous methodology needs to be done. . . . It is still not clear what "thinking like a woman" really means. (159)

As articulated by Noddings and Okin, we are left with only one choice once we have found that many political and moral philosophies are founded on gendered terms. We construct an ethical view from the standpoint of women and then see how it matches with the standard moral theories of the present; it is the only way that it can be discovered what "thinking like a woman" really means. We may find new concepts and new ways of thinking that need to be included in moral theories or we may not. But to *assume* that the present standard theories are inclusive of all outlooks and genders when there is some evidence to the contrary is, to use Noddings's words, intellectually dishonest.

Regarding Rawls's original position, impartiality, and the removal of the knowledge of one's sex— the evidence is inconclusive if this can truly be done. There is evidence that women and men do think differently about ethical and moral matters; there is evidence that these studies are flawed (see Okin 1989b, 188, note 26). But most agree that the answer is still to be found, and we cannot say assuredly one way or the other. So with regard to the initial question of "has the removal of the knowledge of one's sex removed sexual bias," my answer is that we do not know if such an intellectual feat is possible. One's sex may possibly have an undue influence over how one reasons or one's orientation, priorities, or concerns when one thinks about moral and ethical matters. The parties in the original position may not, in gendered terms, be able to think from the position of everybody; they may not intellectually be able to think like a member of the opposite sex. Thus, we have received no assurance that the principles of justice and the basic institutions of society will be formed from a condition of (sexual) impartiality.

As noted in the beginning of this section, Rawls calls his theory "justice as fairness" because the principles of justice are arrived at from a situation of equality, freedom, and impartiality. But we have no assurance that the parties include men and women and, even if they do, we have no assurance that the individuals can truly "think from the perspective of *everybody*" (Okin 1989b, 101) and thus have no assurance against one sex deciding on principles of justice that favor one sex over the other. If one believes, for example, that there should be a gendered division of labor, then the veil does not require that one change or give up such a belief. Even if one does not know her or his gender, that person does know what his or her role will be in society if either turns out to be a woman or a man. This reader is not yet convinced that Rawls's justice is truly fair. Even though there are many positive points to be made about Rawls's theory— including positive ideas for women and a truly gender just society— my examination of the original position and veil of ignorance, as articulated by Rawls, leaves me unconvinced.

But what if we make the assumption that people do think in gendered ways? Can the original position still stand as a validation or proof that the principles of justice are truly fair? The original position and veil of ignorance serve to make people free, equal and impartial, and we already have the assumption that people are self-interested. So what if people are free, equal, self-interested, and can only think from their position as a man or a woman? This could mean that the parties may not agree on the specific principles of justice as stated by Rawls, and that they may have different priorities and concerns when thinking about what is most important in designing the basic institutions and rules of society. The argument that the original position serves to ensure that the principles of justice are fair is certainly weakened.

Rawls's conceptions of the original position and veil of ignorance have not proven useful for formulating a theory of gender justice. They do not serve to legitimate the two principles of justice. But leaving this issue aside, I will now turn to an examination of the actual principles themselves. Will these principles bring forth gender justice? Are these principles ones upon which men *and* women would agree?

PRINCIPLES OF JUSTICE

Rawls derives two basic principles of justice that he thinks anyone and everyone in the original position and under the veil would derive. These principles apply to the basic institutions and structure of society and are to govern the assignment of rights and duties and regulate the distribution of social and economic advantages (61).[10]

Rawls's two principles deal with equality and inequalities or differences. As noted in chapter one this is a dilemma in which feminism finds itself. Should women be treated the same—equal—with males or should they be treated differently with their different needs taken into account? On the face of it, Rawls's two principles show some potential for helping us decide how to treat women and men who are unequal and different. And feminists argue that women are disadvantaged in society. The system is set up to disadvantage women so that they can never *really* be equal because the system does not take their needs into account. Rawls specifically speaks to the most disadvantaged group in his second principle of justice.

When all are free and equal, Rawls states, the following are the principles of justice that would be agreed upon:

> First: each person is to have an equal right to the most extensive total system of equal basic liberties compatible with a similar system of liberties for all.
> Second: social and economic inequalities are to be arranged so that they are both (a) to the greatest benefit of the least advantaged, consistent with the just saving principle, and (b) attached to positions and offices open to all under conditions of fair equality of opportunity. (302)[11]

Furthermore, liberties may only be restricted for the sake of liberty; the second principle of justice is prior to efficiency and maximizing the sum of advantages; and fair opportunity is prior to the difference principle. And these specific principles are derived from a general conception of justice that can be stated as follows:

> All social primary goods— liberty and opportunity, income and wealth, and the bases of self-respect—are to be distributed equally unless an unequal distribution of any or all of these goods is to the advantage of the least favored. (303)

First Principle of Justice and Women

The liberties the first principle addresses are the equal liberties of citizenship— the liberties that govern the assignment of rights and duties to individuals in a society. The liberties of citizens are the right to vote and hold office; freedom of speech, thought, the person, and assembly; freedom to hold personal property; and freedom from arrest and seizure (61). The idea of basic liberties that apply to all— basically Rawls's first principle— is commonly accepted. The most popular argument against such a formulation is a libertarian type of argument that would say his formulation is too restrictive; under no circumstances should liberties be curtailed. But the basic idea of granting liberties to all is something to which men and women in the original position, or anywhere else for that matter, would most likely agree. But there are some problems and omissions in Rawls's formulation that are worth addressing.

The individuals in the original position are conceived of as free and equal, and unconstrained in their choice of principles of justice. This is supposed to mirror the equality of humans as rational beings; and as rational men and women, men and women are equal. But men and women are unequal or different, not in terms of intelligence, but in terms of the range of choices available to men and women in a bodily sense. Women, usually at some point in their life, carry a baby for nine months. During this time, a women's choices are either slightly or severely limited, depending on the health of the mother and fetus and the complications of the pregnancy. After the baby is born, the woman usually nurses the infant which also reduces her choices and thus her liberty. And, as has been for hundreds of years and is still prevalent today, women bear more responsibility for the care and raising of children which further reduces their choices and their liberties. The raising of children is, of course, a social practice that can be changed, but the gestation and nursing of children is a biological phenomenon that, for all practical purposes, cannot be changed.[12]

Let us compare the above situation with the situation of men. After impregnating a woman, a man's liberty is not curtailed. His range of choices is not physically impaired nor is his capacity to pursue his life's goals. For example, during the gestation period, a man's liberty is not curtailed except insofar as he *decides* to care for the mother. And though not necessary, it has been the social practice that during childhood the father does not participate as much as the mother in the care and raising of the child, and thus his choices are not as limited as the mother's. Once again, it is a choice that he gets to make about how much to participate in the care of the child.[13] Before birth control, this restriction on women's liberty was severe and involved at least half of women's adult lives. So we are discussing a restriction that involves a significant number of people for a significant period of time—half of the adult lives of half of the population.[14] With birth control and the ability of women to have more, but not total, control over their reproductive functions, this constitutes a less severe restriction on liberties, but a restriction nevertheless. In general, women are not as free as men to pursue their life plans, no matter what basic liberties of speech and thought are granted to all by government, people, a principle, or agreement. Women are naturally and socially unequal in liberty as it is presently defined, until government, people, a principle, or an agreement addresses the issue of child bearing and child rearing.

This argument is very similar to ones made about the public and private spheres. Many argue that no gender equality or justice can be found until the family and the private sphere are included in theories of justice (Okin 1989b; Elshtain 1981). Traditional theorists, with the exception of Plato in *The Republic*, have argued that the private realm is one in which love and familial ties dominate, not ideas of justice. Justice is reserved for the public realm of politics. I argue, along with many others, that child bearing and child rearing are topics that should be addressed by any theory of justice. The inequalities associated with these issues are potentially remediable and against many people's moral standards. The inequalities, as described above, greatly affect one's ability to pursue one's life plan, and such an ability is a common theme in many theories of justice. But, to date, only certain types of constraints are viewed as legitimate topics to be addressed, and these constraints almost always fall into the public realm. I argue that constraints originating from the private realm are also legitimate and necessary topics that any theory of justice should address.

Rawls states:

> The parties qua noumenal selves have complete freedom to choose whatever principles they wish; but they also have a desire to express their nature as rational and equal members of the intelligible realm with precisely this liberty to choose, that is, as beings who can look at the world

in this way and express this perspective in their life as members of society. They must decide, then, which principles when consciously followed and acted upon in everyday life will best manifest this freedom in their community, most fully reveal their independence from natural contingencies and social accident. (255)

In the original position, if women were empowered to consider the natural, and so far social, limitations on their liberty from their reproductive functions, would not one think they would want this problem addressed? Rawls states that the parties in the original position have complete freedom to choose whatever principles they wish. Would not women, and possibly men, want principles of justice to address the aforementioned reproductive and child care issues? Again, Rawls notes that the parties in the original position want to choose principles that when "consciously followed and acted upon in everyday life will best manifest this freedom in their community" and will "most fully reveal their independence from natural contingencies and social accident" (251). The restrictions brought about by child bearing are certainly natural contingencies, as is one's sex. And the social ramifications of one's sex is certainly a social accident.

Rawls states that the family is a basic institution of society, and the principles of justice are *supposed* to govern the basic institutions of society, but it appears that Rawls does not believe the principles of justice apply to it. As Okin (1989b) discusses, the family appears in *A Theory of Justice* in only three contexts: as the link between generations as discussed above; as an obstacle to fair equality of opportunity; and as the first school of moral development (94). And regarding the role of the family in moral development, Rawls views the family as a crucial institution because it is within the family that children develop a sense of justice. But Rawls never discusses or questions the justice of the family itself. He assumes a just family rather than applying his principles of justice to it. As Okin (1989b) notes:

> If gendered family institutions are *not* just, but are, rather, a relic of caste or feudal societies in which responsibilities, roles, and resources are distributed, not in accordance with the principles of justice he arrives at or with any other commonly respected values, but in accordance with innate differences that are imbued with enormous social significance, then

Rawls's theory of moral development would seem to be built on uncertain ground. (22)

So, if we assume that child bearing and rearing occurs within the family—indeed this could be a definition of the family—the principles of justice do not apply. But a point of importance is Rawls's discussion of the division of labor. He says that in a just society, division of labor will not disappear. Each person can be offered a variety of tasks so that they can express different aspects of their personalities. "To be sure, the worst aspects of this division [of labor] can be surmounted: no one need be servilely dependent on others and made to choose between monotonous and routine occupations which are deadening to human thought and sensibility" (529). And the bad aspects are overcome by "willing and meaningful work within a just social union of social unions in which all can freely participate as they so incline" (529). These statements seem to clearly exclude the relegation of child care, and domestic duties in general, to women unless that is their free choice. And it seems to clearly exclude the present problem of women who are full-time mothers being dependent on husbands or partners for food, clothing, and shelter. But, if the principles are not to apply to the family, then the division of labor within the family are not addressed by the principles either.

Once again, the first principle states, "(E)ach person has an equal right to the most extensive total system of equal basic liberties compatible with a similar system of liberty for all" (302). The first principle deals with the aspects of the social system that define and secure the equal liberties of citizenship. These basic liberties are the right to vote, right to run for office, freedom of speech, liberty of conscience, freedom of the person, right to hold personal property, and freedom from arbitrary arrest and seizure (61). As is obvious, there is no reference to the family, child bearing, or related issues. Rawls states that the first principle is necessary for people to secure the human capacity for free choice and to follow their chosen plan of life. This equality of liberty provides an equal respect for all and is the basis of self-esteem (544-45). Rawls strongly states:

(t)he basis for self-esteem in a just society is not then one's income share but the publicly affirmed distribution of fundamental rights and liberties. And this distribution being equal, everyone has a similar and secure status when they meet to conduct the common affairs of the wider society. (544)

Thus, equality of liberty is of prime importance for Rawls. And he believes that equal liberty leads to self-esteem and equal respect.

We could apply Rawls's ideas to the situation of women and child bearing in our present society. Women do not have equal liberty and thus they do not have equal respect. And the very reason why they do not have equal liberty—because of their roles in child bearing and rearing—is the same reason why they do not have equal respect. Traditionally, women are seen as wives and mothers; that is their function, and women are viewed as incompetent to perform tasks outside of domestic duties or to pursue careers other than those of wife and mother. Women cannot follow their rational plan of life. In this example of contemporary society, Rawls's ideas are validated. And it shows the importance of including the limitations that women face in any principle of justice. It is extremely important that equal liberty truly be equal so that women can receive equal respect.

Regarding Rawls's passage quoted above, once the idea that the natural liberty of the two sexes is unequal is included, then the ambiguity becomes apparent. So I will examine some instances in which Rawls discusses unequal liberty to help shed light on this matter.

First, "liberty can be restricted only for the sake of liberty itself. There are two sorts of cases. The basic liberties may either be less extensive though still equal, or they may be unequal" (244). My concern is with the second situation. Regarding this, Rawls continues to state that "if liberty is unequal, the freedom of those with the lesser liberty must be better secured" (244). Rawls is referring to one specific type of liberty (freedom of speech, liberty of conscience, right to vote, etc.) and that it may be lesser or unequal if the whole system of liberty is better secured for the people with less liberty.

Rawls states elsewhere that

> undeserved inequalities call for redress; and since inequalities of birth and natural endowment are undeserved, these inequalities are to be somehow compensated for. Thus the principle holds that in order to treat all persons equally, to provide genuine equality of opportunity, society must give more attention to those with fewer native assets and to those born into the less favorable positions in society. . . . No one deserves his greater natural capacity nor merits a more favorable starting place in society. (100-102)

This passage seems to be supportive of the problems of child bearing and rearing many women face as discussed above. But Rawls also explains that if unequal basic rights are founded on fixed natural characteristics, these inequalities will single out relevant social positions. Distinctions based on sex fall into this category. So, if men, he explains, have more basic rights, then it is justified if it is to the advantage of the women and acceptable from their standpoint (99). But he adds that these inequalities are hardly ever to the advantage of the less favored, which would also be my response. I can envision situations where a division of labor may be to the advantage of all, but I cannot envision any situation where someone having more liberties than another could be to the lower person's advantage.

Another note Rawls makes regarding unequal liberty is that another distinction needs to be made between two circumstances that justify restriction of liberty. "First a restriction can derive from the natural limitations and accidents of human life, or from historical and social contingencies. The question of the justice of these constraints does not arise" (244). What does Rawls mean by these circumstances? It could just be a simple statement to cover the problems of the lesser liberty of children or the requirements that liberty of thought and participation will be restricted in some fashion; the extent of the liberties is not infinite (244). But a much broader implication could be derived from these statements. Pregnancy is a natural limitation and gender is an accident of life. If one is constrained by these factors, is Rawls stating that the justice of such limitations is not a topic that should be covered? Is pregnancy, nursing, and any limitations that follow for a women a "practice of private associations," an informal convention and custom of everyday life, or a voluntary cooperative arrangement to which his principles of justice do not apply? (8) How do we reconcile this with the statement quoted above that inequalities of birth are to be compensated for?

Rawls states that liberty can always be explained by a reference to three items: the people who are free, the limitations which they are free from, and what it is that they are free to do or not do (202). He also discusses liberty in the context of "a certain structure of institutions, a certain system of public rules defining rights and duties" (202). This description of liberty would seem to accommodate and include the limitations of pregnancy, child birth, and child rearing. They are limitations on freedom and affect what one is free or not free to do. But Rawls in no place discusses these. One possible answer to this riddle is his discussion of the "worth of liberty."

The worth of liberty—the value to individuals of the rights that the first principle defines—is different from the liberties granted to everyone. The first principle states that everyone has "a right" to equal liberty, not that everyone "will" have equal liberty. Liberty and the worth of liberty are not the same; some people are better able to take advantage of freedom and "advance their ends within the framework the system defines" (204). Some examples of such people would be those with greater authority or wealth. But, according to Rawls's principle, people with the lesser worth of liberty are compensated "since the capacity of the less fortunate members of society to achieve their aims would be even less were they not to accept the existing inequalities whenever the difference principle is satisfied" (204). But to this reader, this argument seems very weak. I cannot imagine a situation in which limiting my liberties could secure a better system that grants me more capacity than I would have otherwise.

Hart (1977) notes that the distinction between liberty and worth of liberty is arbitrary (259-63). And then Hart asks if the participants in the original position would choose equal liberty without equal worth of liberty, and he reasons they would not. If it is rational to choose equal liberty, it is just as rational to choose equal worth of liberty, he argues (Hart 1977, 269). The inequalities allowed by the second principle inevitably undermine the supposed equality of the first principle. Thus, Rawls's distinction between liberty and worth of liberty cannot be used to reconcile the first and second principles. Unequal worth of liberty cannot be compensated for by meeting the criteria of the difference principle—having more capacity in the unequal system than they would have had under a equal system. I agree with Hart's analysis.

It seems that the limitations many women face could fall under this unequal "worth of liberty" category. Women are just not as able to take advantage of the equal liberties granted to them. The worth of their liberty is not as great as it is for men. It does not seem that this could be the meaning Rawls intended. It contradicts too many of Rawls's other ideas. But just what the implications are of this line of thought are unclear. Another possible interpretation would be that Rawls is describing people who just do not have the mental capacities to excel, even after unfair limitations have been removed. So those with greater wealth or authority will be better able to use their liberty and that is just, Rawls would reason, because the least fortunate are better off than they would be under a strictly equal system.

I immediately think that, overall, men have more wealth and authority in our society and the greater ability that this gives them is *not* just. Certainly there are some wealthy women who have more power and authority than some men, but individual instances should not keep us from discussing the general trend, which is undoubtedly present.[15] To assess Rawls's proposition, I would need to know if the wealth and authority were acquired justly. And an important part of this analysis would be whether or not women's reproductive and child rearing functions were taken into account. But as stated before, Rawls does not appear to include such items in his analysis.

Rawls makes many statements that could be construed to include women's reproductive functions and the unequal liberty this brings them. He also makes many arguments to the contrary. Once again, I am unclear about the actual implications and applications of Rawls's formulation of the first principle. Simply put, does Rawls's idea of "equal basic liberties" address and include limitations brought upon many women from child bearing? In other words, is child bearing a result of the accident of one's own sex at birth and child rearing a result of social accident and thus addressable by the first principle? Or are child bearing and rearing part of natural limitations and accidents of human life, or just part of the unequal worth of liberty, and thus *not* addressable by his theory of justice? The answer is not clear. But it is fairly clear that Rawls does not mean for the principle to apply to the family, which is where most child bearing and rearing takes place.

So, is this really a principle that men *and* women would choose in the original position? *Can* this principle address the female functions of pregnancy and child bearing and the parental functions of child rearing and bring forth justice?

First, it is important to note that child bearing and rearing are important to society and would be something that it would want to promote. The careful raising of children by caring adults is important to society so that there is a competent new generation to take over the running of society. An effective and successful family is something Rawls already recognizes as important (462-67). One of Rawls's goals is to have a society that lasts more than one generation. So it is a topic that those in the original position would want to address and that the principles of justice should include.

Once again, those in the original position do not know their sex. When deciding upon the principles of justice, they do not know if they will be a man or a woman. So, according to Rawls, they would want a society that is the best that it can be for both men and women. I reason that people would see the advantage of having children, and understand that only women become pregnant and give birth. No one chooses if he or she will be a man or a woman, it is an accident of birth. So everyone should want to create a society that does not disadvantage the child bearers, who are women, or the child rearers, who could be anyone but are usually women. But as an individual in the original position (not a family head), you may or may not fill one of these roles and so you would not want to be hurt by such activity.

This could mean many different things depending on what type of economic system was in place. Under an economic system similar to the one in the present U.S., it might mean that for any women that becomes pregnant, her income will not fall below what it was before she became pregnant. Thus, she is not disadvantaged in economic terms by her pregnancy. Furthermore, the society might establish a guaranteed minimum income for anyone with children. Thus, people with children will not be economically disadvantaged because they have to pay for child care or stay home with the children. If this did not occur, the people with children could not pursue their life plan, or at least the part that is outside of having children, they do not have equal liberty, and there is not equal opportunity if they, as very talented individuals, cannot find jobs that do not require them to leave their children. All of these things would be against the principles of justice.

People in the original position would agree upon equal liberty, but not to an unequal worth of liberty. Furthermore, the list of liberties to which this applies would be broadened. Not just equal liberties of citizenship would be granted; equal liberty to pursue one's rational plan of life would be granted. This would need to include and address reproductive issues for women. Society would want children but could not allow women to be disadvantaged by having them.

The idea of the first principle, equal liberties for all, is correct I believe. The particular interpretation Rawls takes regarding this principle is mistaken in some cases. It should clearly encompass the private sphere of the family and issues that are particular to women. The family needs to be just so that children develop a sense of justice, and so that all adult family members are treated according to principles of justice. A "lived out" equality of liberties would need to be granted.

Women need to have equal liberty and be able to follow their rational plan of life. If this means being full-time mothers for some, they should not be disadvantaged and should have equal liberty. If this means having children but also working outside the home, they deserve no fewer or greater advantages or liberties. And if it means not having children, they still deserve equal liberties along with all the other members of society. *Real* equality of liberty is needed, as Rawls rightly points out, so that women are treated with equal respect and so they have an equal and secure status when people meet to conduct the common affairs of the society.

One's sex and thus reproductive capability needs to be viewed as a social accident and a natural contingency. They specifically need to be included in Rawls's idea that no one deserves their greater or lesser natural capacity nor merits a more favorable starting place in society. And since no one in the original position knows his or her sex, all rational women and men would want a principle of justice that includes these issues. No one would want their liberties, respect, or ability to follow their chosen life plan curtailed.

Second Principle of Justice and Women

Again, the second principle of justice is that

> all social and economic inequalities are to be arranged so that they are both (a) to the greatest benefit of the least advantaged, consistent with the just savings principle, and (b) attached to positions and offices open to all under conditions of fair equality of opportunity. (302)

A principle that proposes to regulate social and economic inequalities is particularly important for women. The sexual inequality that exists in society and that manifests itself in economic and social consequences is one of the main problems for women and that feminism addresses. A principle that proposes to have societal structures benefit the least advantaged, which is often women, looks promising. And Rawls addresses a problem discussed in Chapter One herein: when should differences (or inequalities) be addressed? In other words, when are inequalities unjust? Furthermore, a principle that deals with just social and economic inequalities deserves close attention because women have been unequal for many years in exactly these areas. But such a principle also deserves close scrutiny because many liberal theories have served to justify and legitimate these same inequalities.

The second principle is basically a distributive principle. It deals with the distribution of social and economic goods and states when social and economic inequalities are just. So, the first thing we know is that inequalities are allowed. And these inequalities are just when they are to the greatest benefit of the least advantaged and attached to offices and positions open to all under conditions of fair equal opportunity. The first part of the second principle is known as the difference principle, and the second part is the principle of equal opportunity. For Rawls, "(t)he second principle only requires equal life prospects in all sectors of society for those similarly endowed and motivated" (301).

Regarding social and economic inequalities, the subject matter that Rawls is discussing is "the distribution of income and wealth" and "the design of organizations that make use of differences in authority and responsibility, or chains of command" (61). Positions of authority and offices must be open to all, so these categories are the subjects of equal opportunity. He states that we judge social and economic inequalities by levels of income and wealth (97). It seems that these can be adequately described as economic inequalities, but why does Rawls call them social inequalities? Are there not other categories of information that could be defined as social inequalities? As Barry (1973) notes, Rawls never states what is meant by social inequalities (45). Barry notes that Rawls includes power in his list of social primary goods, but in his discussions of social and economic inequalities, Rawls never includes the topic of power.

This is a potentially important point for the application of the principle to women. Inequalities in income and wealth between men and women are, for the most part, seen as unjust. This is why the Equal Pay Act was passed. Talents, abilities, and intelligence should be distributed fairly evenly among the two groups, men and women. If these fairly equal groups do not bring in the same amount of income, it is probably because of other factors, most of which are not right, good, or just. But there are many other ways (besides income and wealth) that women's inequality is manifested. Some of these we might call social inequalities, such as the unequal time spent by men and women doing housework and taking care of children. Another social inequality could be the prejudiced perceptions of the abilities of men and women, and I am sure there are more. Rawls's limitation of inequalities to only differences in income and wealth could contribute to the narrow application and focus of the theory as a whole. In other words, if Rawls had widened the range of inequalities that the difference principle is to address, he might have found a broader application for his theory of justice and included more of the issues that are important for gender justice.

Rawls discusses other goods, such as authority and power, that could be measured. But he argues that these goods are almost always sufficiently correlated with income and wealth, which are much easier to measure (97). But in the case of women, this may not be true. Many people would argue that even if employed women obtained an equal income with employed men, they would still be treated as inferior and discriminated against in other ways. One reason could be because of motherhood. Women who were not employed outside the home, were raising children, and had little or no income of their own, could still be viewed as "lesser beings." Furthermore, the portrayal of women in the media as sexual objects (to use a cliché) to be sexually used by men for their selfish sexual satisfaction would not disappear just because women made the same money as men. Many feminists argue that control of women's sexuality is the core of patriarchy. One can envision a society in which women made the same money as men from jobs in prostitution and pornography. Equality of income does not remove sexual exploitation. Also, if women were still segregated into certain jobs like teaching, nursing, and secretarial work, and even if they made equal money, they could still be viewed as unable to perform "more important" jobs. These are just a few examples. Equality of income does not remove prejudiced perceptions. As Kymlicka (1990) notes, Rawls has nothing "to say about how this systematic devaluation of the roles of women can be removed" (89).

The point to note is that there are many ways women are unequal in society, some more visible than others. Most people already agree that inequality in income between men and women is unjust. The debate arises around the issue of how to solve the problem. A much harder battle is the recognition of the multitude of ways women are unfairly treated since many are invisible to the untrained eye because the treatments are so embedded in our culture or covered up so well. Regarding Rawls's difference principle, if we only measure income and wealth, we might sometimes miss the most disadvantaged group in society.

Kymlicka (1990) suggests that Rawls should have included natural primary goods along with the social goods for examining inequalities. Take the case of a person born with a disability. The difference principle assures that the disabled person is not disadvantaged in the bundle of social goods, but the effects of natural accident are not totally equalized with this. The disabled person needs more medical treatment and has higher living costs. The disabled person has an undeserved burden in their ability to follow their life plan. This problem could be addressed if natural primary goods were included with social goods in defining the principles of justice (Kymlicka 1990, 71-73). This is a good point, but we do not want to distribute natural goods—health, vigor, intelligence, and imagination—even if we could. So the only option is to compensate those with higher costs, for example, by giving them more social goods. This problem seems similar to equal liberty and the equal worth of liberty discussed above. We need to make sure that the advantage or disadvantage is a type of net measurement and not a gross measurement. We need to measure the worth of the social goods, in a way, and not just the amount received. This is something like Norman Daniel's (1983) "effective opportunity" (17).

Rawls uses a troublesome phrase in the second principle. Any inequalities are to be arranged so as to benefit the "least advantaged." He explains that we judge the least advantaged by examining the expectations of a representative individual from the group with the lowest income and wealth (90-98). We could also choose a particular social position, for example an unskilled worker, and then count as the least advantaged all those with the same average income and wealth. Either method would work. And under either method, women could be the least advantaged group or be a large percentage of the least advantaged group. But once again, only income and wealth are counted and these may not always be good indicators of the most disadvantaged in society. But Rawls does state that we could choose a particular social position. The category of women as a gender represents the social manifestations of the female sex. Thus, "women" are a social group because they are socially defined, just as being an unskilled worker is socially defined.

We can view women as the least advantaged in terms of income and wealth. In 1994, for full-time workers, men's median income was $31,612 and women's was $23,265 (U.S. Bureau of the Census 1996a). If we limit our comparison to these two groups, women are, according to Rawls, the least advantaged. Either way, from the criteria of income and wealth or from income, wealth, and other aspects, I can assume that women are the least advantaged group. With this assumption, how can Rawls's principles contribute to a theory of gender justice?

The first situation of when inequalities are just is guided by the difference principle—when they are arranged "to the greatest benefit of the least advantaged." Rawls establishes this principle because allowing distribution based on arbitrary factors is unjust. Factors that are based on pure luck should not influence the distribution of goods and resources. These arbitrary factors include natural talents and social circumstances; these are not by choice and are thus arbitrary. "The naturally advantaged are not to gain merely because they are more gifted. . . . No one deserves his greater natural capacity nor merits a more favorable starting place in society" (102). But it does not follow that we eliminate these factors. We just arrange the system so that the advantages of such factors benefit the least advantaged. The distribution of natural talents is neither just nor unjust—it is a natural fact. But what is just or unjust is the way institutions handle these differences.

Rawls's theory is sounding better and better for women; this is precisely the argument that many feminists make. Being female or male means that the two sexes are different in their biological constitution as a minimum, or that they think, feel, and view the world in very different ways as the other extreme. But these are not problems in and of themselves. The problems arise in how society handles these differences.

It is a matter of pure luck if one is born a woman or a man. So any consequences from such an arbitrary factor should not influence the distribution one receives in society. Again, because many women carry a fetus for nine months and give birth, this should not disadvantage them in the social and economic distributions they receive in society, according to the principle. And because they are the primary caretakers of children (and the same would apply to men if they were the primary caretakers) and this is a social phenomenon associated with the arbitrary factor of them being born female, they should not be disadvantaged in the shares of social and economic resources they receive.[16] And it should not make them unequal unless it is the best off that they could be under any arrangement.

Generally, goods and resources should be distributed equally unless an unequal distribution benefits everyone, or more specifically, the least advantaged. This is an important answer to a common problem in liberal democratic theory, as well as in feminist theory. As discussed in chapter one, feminist theory is at a standstill. Should women and men be treated the same, according to their differences, or somewhere in between? Rawls tells us that men and women should have equal resources unless it benefits the least advantaged, women, for the resources to be distributed unequally.

Janet Radcliffe Richards (1980) slightly reformulates the difference principle and applies it to issues of sexual justice. Richards states that "everyone's well-being is to be considered equally; when social structures are planned no individual or group is to be given more consideration than any other" (93). And her first principle of justice is that "the most important purpose of society is to improve the well-being of sentient things, which should all be as well off as possible" (93). She, like Rawls, uses the level of the worst-off group as the criterion for deciding which state of affairs is just. And Richards states in reply to the anticipated argument that absolute equality is best, that the amount of good to be distributed by society or a theory of justice is not fixed nor finite. How much there is to distribute depends on how much is produced and that depends on social arrangements (95). It is very possible to have complete equality and have everyone worse off than the "worst off" would have been in a system of inequality. This would not be a desirable situation. She thinks that we should all be as well off as possible, even if that entails having some inequality.

Richards uses the term "well-being" instead of primary social goods or specifically income and wealth. But the intention is the same. Both Rawls and Richards want people to live the best lives they can live, and "the best life" has different meanings for different people. Rawls would think the term "well-being" too nebulous, and so he uses something that can be measured and that is a fairly good indicator of how "well-off," in its variety of meanings, a person is. Richards's formulation of the difference principle means that every person's life plan must be given the same consideration. Thus, even the least advantaged would want more rather than less, even it means experiencing some inequality.

Richard's difference principle may not be accepted by everyone. It is feasible to think that some may want a lower level of well-being if it means less inequality.[17] And the same type of argument can be applied to Rawls. Everyone in the original position may not agree to the difference principle. Not everyone would follow the rational choice model and adopt the maximum strategy as Rawls posits.[18] As Barry (1973) notes, "Can it be rational, to espouse a principle which throws away so much *prima facie* relevant information, such as the average *per capita* income, the degree of dispersion round the mean, the distance between top and bottom and so on?" (87) I believe that people would find these other aspects important also.

But, if one believes that strict equality is not best, or believes that strict equality is not achievable, the difference principle may be the next best option. Richards (1980) applies the difference principle to the specific problem of sexual justice. In our present society, women are disadvantaged and feminists make many arguments as to why this is so. Richards (1980) groups these arguments into two categories. First, women have been systematically excluded from nearly all influential, interesting, and money-making activities (the public realm) and left in the private world of home and children. This has resulted from deliberate rules to exclude women. Even though this situation has improved in the last few decades, women are still passed over for many jobs and promotions. There is not equality of opportunity. Richards calls this "selection discrimination" against women. The second category involves the complaint that even if women had equality of opportunity, the system would still be unjust for women. The problem is that the basic social structures and rules under which the competition for the jobs and promotions takes place are designed to favor men. Because women were not included in the design of institutions and rules, their needs were not taken into account, and thus many women do not "qualify" or meet the established criteria. Furthermore, people's prejudices, habits, and expectations would also disadvantage women even if we had a legal system of equal opportunity.

But, as Richards (1980) states, this does not *prove* that the situation is unjust. Inequality does not prove injustice. According to the difference principle, it must be shown that women could be better off in another social organization, that the present scheme is *not* to the benefit of the least advantaged, women. So Richards (1980) shows that selection discrimination, the first category, is always unjust according to the difference principle (99-107). She discusses the situation of not choosing a women for a job that she could do better than a man. The selectors cannot be accused of discrimination, she writes, as long as they chose the best candidate for the purpose in question (99). So, if they do not chose the best person who happens to be a woman, this is unjust.

Richards shows that the difference principle can successfully be used for some issues of sexual inequality. If we view women as the most disadvantaged group, the difference principle only allows inequalities that benefit women. This means that women have more under the unequal scheme than they could have under any other arrangement. The logic behind this principle is that arbitrary factors such as natural talents and social circumstances should not cause someone to have more than their fellow human. Regarding women, the difference principle tells us that men should not have more just because they were born male. But we do not rush to the conclusion that all must be equal. We let the greater talents (of all people) benefit the whole society.

So, how do we handle, according to Richards, a situation of women being less-qualified for the job and if men performed the job, all would be better off? The problem is that it is unfair to systematically disadvantage women—not give them the job—because they are disadvantaged, because they have not been given the job in the past, or because they were not included in designing the structure of the job. But it is not to the benefit of all to let lesser qualified people have jobs. Richards's solution is to compensate women in other ways. We do not have to give them "unmerited advancement" as Richards describes it, but we do have to give them compensation in the form of other primary goods. In particular, we could give women the money the job would pay or we could give women the training the job would provide. Thus, sex has not favored men over women in the distribution of primary goods and we have people performing the jobs for which they are most qualified which is the most beneficial for society.

There are many issues that have not been covered regarding the difference principle. Implicit in the principle is a question regarding motivational factors for those with more talent or intelligence. It is possible to reason that a gifted doctor needs to be paid a large salary or otherwise she would not be a doctor and benefit the rest of us with her care and medical knowledge. Thus, this benefits the least advantaged and justifies the inequality. But, the problem is, it also legitimates the status quo. But these other issues regarding the difference principle are not as important for this project.

In conclusion, the difference principle is beneficial for women if we reformulate it slightly. We need to recognize other inequalities between men and women than just disparities in income or wealth. The worth of goods is important to consider also. Women should not be disadvantaged just because they were born a woman and have the biological capacity to bear children. Goods in society should be distributed equally unless the unequal arrangement benefits women. If women do need to be treated differently in one area because it is the most beneficial for all people, as in the discussed example of men being more qualified for certain higher level, higher-paying jobs, this does not mean that women should be disadvantaged in the distribution of primary goods. Women can be compensated in other forms or ways.

The second part of the principle of justice is "social and economic inequalities are to be . . . attached to positions and offices open to all under conditions of fair equality of opportunity" (Rawls 1971, 302). This is Rawls's equality of opportunity principle. He explains that the basic reason for this principle is not efficiency but justice. "It expresses the conviction that if some places were not open on a basis fair to all, those kept out would be right in feeling unjustly treated even though they benefited from the greater efforts of those who were allowed to hold them" (84). It is a procedural rule to be applied to the distributive shares of society. People have different levels and types of talent because they are raised in different families, Rawls states, and we want their talents to benefit us all. But then we do not institute a system of "careers open to talents" or meritocracy. Rawls's equality of opportunity allows those with similar abilities and skills, similar life chances. This means that all are given equal chances to develop natural abilities, along with selection on the basis of talent (Nelson 1984, 160). As William Nelson (1984) points out, the underlying justification for such a principle is that a person deserves the job in which her or his talents contribute to maximum production (164). According to Rawls, everyone deserves this because it is to everyone's advantage to have maximum production.

But if we really want maximum production, I argue that it might be best to have a central planner figuring what jobs will need to be filled and how to correctly distribute the available talent in order to achieve maximum production. The haphazardly method of equality of opportunity does not guarantee maximum production. Nelson (1984) gives an example of a situation of two persons and two jobs. Person A is better at both jobs and they both want job 1. Job 1 will be awarded to A, and B will have to take job 2. But B would have done well at job 1 but will do poorly at job 2. Since A would do well at either job, a better arrangement would be for B to have job 1 and A to have job 2. But the principle of equality of opportunity does not award the jobs on the basis of the best matched merit for the job and on maximum production.

But Rawls insists on equality of opportunity because some would be excluded from "certain external awards of office such as wealth and privilege" and some would be "debarred from experiencing the realization of self which comes from a skillful and devoted exercise of social duties. They would be deprived of one of the main forms of human good " (84). I contend that neither of these arguments shows that we need his principle of equality of opportunity. Under any system of distribution, some will have better jobs than others and so some will be excluded from awards of office. This is no particular argument for equality of opportunity. Furthermore, why does Rawls believe that only under equality of opportunity one can devote themselves to a job and experience some self-realization, an important human good? This is a topic with which he should be concerned, but there is no reason why it can happen only under his definition of equality of opportunity. Both of Rawls's points could occur under the central planner scenario described above. The rationale for the equality of opportunity principle must be derived from somewhere else.

But there is something positive to be said about equal opportunity regarding women. First, Rawls's formulation says that all are to be given equal chances to develop their natural talents. This would obviously be an improvement from the present situation. And for everyone to *really* be given equal chances, many present biases in education will need to be removed. Studies have shown over and over that boys and girls are treated very differently in school by peers, administrators, and teachers, and this results in an unequal education.[19] A recent report by the American Association of University Women (1993a) has also shown that sexual harassment is pervasive in older elementary grades and in junior high schools. An average of 81 percent of girls and boys report being sexually harassed in some form. Though both sexes experience the harassment, girls are more often the targets of the abuse and the behavior affects them in fundamentally different ways. Girls experience a loss of self-esteem (at least partially from sexual harassment) and girls change their behavior in school as a result; this contributes to their unequal education. In short, in order for all to have equal chances to develop themselves, much of the existing stereotyping of boys and girls will have to be removed. Furthermore, sexual harassment of both sexes will have to end.

Another positive note for women about Rawls's principle is that it states that offices and positions should be open to all. In a world where women have been turned away from jobs simply because they were women, this principle would declare such practices unjust. But despite the passage of the Civil Rights Act in 1964, much sexual discrimination in job hiring and firing still occurs, as well sexual harassment while on the job. Rawls's principle defines this as unjust but offers no help in addressing the present problems and how to end them. The injustice of sexual discrimination is not the present problem; how to end it is.

In conclusion, Rawls's second principle of equal opportunity does not have anything new to offer a theory of gender justice. First, Rawls's arguments for his principle are not persuasive. Furthermore, most people already believe in some form of equal opportunity, including everyone having equal chances to develop their natural talents. This is at the heart of the public education system, desegregation of schools, and the present problems in school funding systems. And we already have many laws that address discrimination. The problem is not that people disagree about the justice of equal opportunity. The problem is how to successfully implement the idea in our educational and business systems. In the end, a principle of equal opportunity is a positive one for women if instituted in a gender just society because it does describe discrimination in employment, and other practices, as unjust. But in an unjust society, such a principle offers little guidance on how to rectify the problems.

CONCLUSION

Rawls proves partially useful for addressing issues of gender justice, even if portions of his theory are flawed or, at least, questionable. Specifically, the veil of ignorance does not stand on a very firm basis. The original position does not serve to legitimize the principles of justice if we consider that men and women, when under the veil and thinking about issues of justice, may very well have different priorities and concerns. The answer is not clear, so the veil of ignorance is certainly not a device upon which one would want to base a theory of justice or a theory of gender justice. It fails to prove the fairness of the principles.

Regarding the principles of justice themselves, Rawls is more helpful. The idea of equal liberties for all is positive, but the scope of liberty needs to be broadened so that all can pursue their life plans. If we consider that men and women are naturally unequal in their liberties, then the design of our social institutions, rules, and principles of justice should be made in recognition of such a fact. Specifically, the first principle needs to include issues of child bearing and rearing. It needs to ensure real equality of liberty so that all are treated with equal respect. The difference principle, if also interpreted in such a broad fashion, proves very useful for thinking about gender and justice. The principle shows that many of the inequalities that women face are unjust. One's sex is an arbitrary factor over which one has no control and so should not advantage or disadvantage anyone. As such, women's reproductive capabilities should not disadvantage or cause them to receive less of society's goods and resources. The equality of opportunity principle is also fairly positive for women, even though it does not contribute anything new to our thinking about justice and gender.

NOTES

*All references to Rawls are to John Rawls's *A Theory of Justice* (1971) unless otherwise noted.

1. We specifically designate "female" head of household when it is a single mother and her children. This implies that when a women is married and a head of household is discussed, it is referring to the man. See also Okin 1989b.

2. And not even every family has a representative. Not every person participates, even in Rawls's own terms—so who does participate? This is a very confusing point. Certainly any theorist would think this an important issue. Who gets to participate? Who is included? Who is excluded? Democratic and liberal theories have wrestled with these issues for hundreds of years. Certainly Rawls would think this important. But we could argue that it does not really matter because the original position is a construct to understand so that anyone could put themselves in such a place at any given time.

3. See Okin (1989b) for other problems that thinking of the parties as heads of families causes for Rawls (94-97).

4. Furthermore, if we examine the theoretical tradition in which Rawls was operating, one would think it incumbent upon Rawls to note his new conception of individuals in the original position, if indeed it was. The social contract theories of Hobbes, Locke, and Rousseau have been criticized for only allowing men to participate in the social compact (Di Stefano 1991; Okin 1979; Pateman 1988). Rousseau explicitly states that women are naturally unequal, that women were made to please men, that women should be weak and passive, and that they are to procreate at the expense of their autonomy (Bien-Aime 1990; Okin 1979). Furthermore, the

Kantian framework on which Rawls so much relies also excludes women from the scope of its conclusions (Elshtain 1986; Okin 1982, 1989b; Pateman 1988). And as Okin (1989b) notes, "(W)hen Rawls refers to the generality and universality of Kant's ethics, and when he compares the principles chosen in his own original position to those regulative of Kant's kingdom of ends," he fails to even briefly mention—even in a footnote—that Kant did not include women but that he does mean to include women in his original position. If Rawls was meaning to differ from his predecessors in his conception of the participants to the initial agreement, why would he not explicitly say so? And why would he continue to use the male terms of reference like "men," "mankind," "he," and "his" if his theory was suppose to differ from his predecessors (who used male terms of reference) and include women?

5. English (1977) makes another good point. In the real world, even when people *do* know that they are part of the present generation, they tend to care about the welfare of future generations. This is regardless of whether they have children or not. For a theory that is to conform to our considered judgments and intuitions, why does Rawls worry about saving in the first place? If he can assume self-interested individuals with no further evidence, why can he not assume saving for future generations, balanced with our present self-interest, since this seems to be what happens in the real world anyway?

6. Rawls says that the original position and the veil of ignorance do not have to ever occur and he is not saying that they occurred in the past. It is a hypothetical place, such that if people were in, they would derive the two principles of justice. The constructs provide a validation and legitimization of the fairness of the principles.

7. Benhabib (1987) argues that the liberal moral self is disembodied and disembedded. It has no bodily existence; the gender-sex system through which one develops a sense of the self is ignored. Furthermore, the social system through which one develops a self is ignored. This conception of the self reflects aspects of male experience. Many communitarians argue that a liberal view of the self, like Rawls's view, ignores the fact that the individual is situated in existing social practices and that one cannot always stand back from or step out of them. (See Kymlicka 1990, 207-215, for a discussion of communitarian ideas on this matter.)

8. And Catharine MacKinnon (1987) and others argue that women might value care because men have valued women according to the care that men have received. This problem of the "chicken or the egg—which came first?" is extremely hard to untangle. The idea of "internalized oppression" is a very difficult one for any political or moral theory. Such theories are not equipped to handle individual, internal barriers to justice or ethical actions. They theorize about external barriers such as institutional and social structures that cause injustice or block just actions and policies. An individual that has adopted the culture's unjust values and then wants to act in accordance with them is very problematical for any theory of justice. Of course, as

noted below, this is not meant to exclude the notion that care and justice are compatible.

9. Calhoun (1988) calls this the logical compatibility thesis and says that it is advanced by Grimshaw (1986), Flanagan and Jackson (1987), Hill (1987), and Sher (1987).

10. I will now examine the principles on their own basis, leaving aside the criticisms of the original position and veil of ignorance noted above.

11. These are stated a little differently in *Political Liberalism* but the rephrasing does not change their meaning for the purposes discussed herein.

12. The point made in this paragraph is from Green (1986).

13. When I state that the father has a choice of how much to participate in the raising of the child, I am discussing a REAL, socially acceptable choice. Before the recent drive to enforce child support orders, a father could not care for the mother or the child and suffer little political or social repercussions. For mothers, who usually have the child physically with them, it is not a REAL choice to not care for the child. For a mother it is thought as something like inhumane, but for a father, it is much more acceptable. Furthermore, because the child is usually physically present with the woman—a circumstance that seems to follow from the gestation and nursing period—if she does not care for the child, she could be criminally charged with child abuse or neglect. But a father, because he is absent, suffers no such threats or consequences. Because of this social reality of the differences between fatherhood and motherhood, I describe the father as having a choice and the women's choice as severely constrained.

14. I emphasize the number of people and amount of time because of the objection to my reasoning that could go something like the following: Everyone has some capacity or incapacity that limits their liberty. Disabled people's liberty is constrained, as is people's with incurable diseases. Furthermore people get sick at different times throughout their lives and have their liberty restricted. All of these things, and more, are by natural causes, just like pregnancy, birth, and nursing. My reply to such an objection is that none of these other things affect half the human population. And even though everyone gets sick at some point in their lives, this is usually for only a brief period of time. Incurable diseases affect only a minority of the population and affect both men and women. I argue that there is nothing as widespread as pregnancy, childbirth, and child rearing that restricts anyone's liberty as much as these do.

15. Furthermore, I am addressing gender injustice in this dissertation. It is unjust that men, as a group when compared to women, have more wealth, income, and power. This is a sex-based injustice, Richards (1980) says, and individual nuances do not make it untrue. "(W)omen suffer from systematic injustices because of their sex" (Richards 1980, 1). Richards also continues, "[Feminism] obviously cannot be one which supports the interests of all women under all circumstances because there must

be many situations where, even now, women treat men unjustly, and a movement concerned with *justice* cannot automatically take the side of any women against any man. . . . Feminism is not concerned with *a group of people it wants to benefit*, but with *a type of injustice it wants to eliminate*" (5). In this same line of reasoning, this dissertation is about gender justice, and particularly the gender injustices that disadvantage women. One facet of this is that women, overall, have less wealth and power in society. This is unjust.

16. Furthermore, women should not be the primary caretakers of children unless that is part of their desired life plan.

17. I think this could very possibly be true after basic necessities are met. As long as the least well-off have food, clothing, shelter, health care, etc.—and not just the bare minimum, but a level that one can live happily and feel satisfied—much of their unhappiness could be derived from the fact that some people have more than they have. The size of the gap is important, I believe, regarding how one views or feels about inequality. And it is especially important in a capitalistic system in which the purchasing and consuming of goods is heavily emphasized and upheld as something for which others should strive. If everyone cannot participate in such activity, it would cease to be held as a value. But when some can participate and other cannot, how do we think that the ones who cannot participate will, nevertheless, be happy because they know that it is *possible* that under a more equal system they *might* be worse off?

18. See·Hare (1977) and Barry (1973) for a discussion of problems with the "maximum" strategy.

19. See, for example, the American Association of University Women's report "How Schools Shortchange Girls" (1992). It documents the inequities that persist in teaching practices, standards for peer interaction, and curriculum design.

CHAPTER 3

Utilitarianism, Gender, and Justice

Rawls was responding to and wanted to replace the dominant theory of justice at the time, utilitarianism (Rawls 1971, vii). In the classical sense, utilitarianism simply claims that a just society is one in which the greatest happiness, satisfaction, welfare, or good for the members of society is produced. Society should be organized or policies should be chosen so that happiness is maximized, with happiness being defined as the maximization of pleasure or the absence of pain. Utilitarianism takes an intuitive way of acting for an individual—people should maximize their pleasure and minimize their pain—and applies it to society. The principle of choice for an individual is the principle of choice for a society.

PROBLEMS OF UTILITARIANISM

One significant problem with utilitarianism is that, as a theory, it is insensitive to distributional issues. Total utility is examined and actual distribution does not matter. For example, if Jane has, let us say, ten units of happiness and Mary has two, this gives a total of twelve; this is more than if Jane and Mary each have five because this only totals ten units. Hence, under a utilitarian paradigm we should choose the first scenario, even though the happiness is distributed very unevenly. Nothing matters but the total for the society.

Utilitarianism's inattention to the distributive aspect is Rawls's major contention with the theory. Why should one individual have less just so another can have more, even if the total for the society is larger? Rawls does not think justice is served by such inattention to inequalities. He derives his two principles of justice, and specifically the difference principle, in order to specify when inequalities are justified in a society. For Rawls, it is necessary to examine individuals and their well-being in order to judge justice.

But despite these problems, utilitarianism still has much persuasive power in the United States. When we look at our society as a whole, who would want less when we could have more? Furthermore, regarding any specific policy, we may not achieve perfection, but we would like to maximize our gains and minimize our losses. As Ely (1978) notes, "(W)e are all, at least as regards the beginnings of our analysis of proposed governmental policy, utilitarians. There may be, indeed there must be, further steps, but the formation of public policy, at least in this country, begins with the questions how many are helped, how many hurt, and by how much?" (407). This, of course, includes health care policy decisions that are made with the intention of helping the most people possible. We see it as problematical that the few with cancer or heart problems receive expensive, elaborate treatment thereby consuming a disproportionate amount of our health care dollar while millions upon millions do not even get basic primary care.

An important and positive aspect of utilitarianism (specifically "act" utilitarianism) is that the rightness of an act is determined by the consequences that flow from it.[1] It requires that we actually check to see whether an identifiable good was created. Morally "bad" acts must also be proven to be so; it is not sufficient to believe that they are so. We do not have to blindly follow rules set by a political leader, religion, or moral principles. Utilitarianism provides a test so that we can straightforwardly resolve moral questions.

Furthermore, utilitarianism does incorporate certain aspects of equality. Each person's utility is counted equally, meaning that just because you are a privileged or important member of society, it does not follow that your utility counts more than anyone else's utility. Jane's one unit is exactly equal to Mary's one unit even though Jane is the president and Mary is unemployed and homeless. Furthermore, no one has a privileged claim to benefit from the calculations. We do not need to make sure that the wealthy or the president are satisfied by the results. Everyone is counted equally and the only judgment about what is just or right rests in the total number of units created by a certain policy or structure of society when compared to the alternatives.

But this also points to a problem with utilitarianism; it excludes the special obligations that we have to particular people. We want to count our spouse, children, family, and friends as more important in some instances. We do not want to treat everyone equally sometimes. And in terms of public policies, sometimes we enact policies to benefit a certain group, even if the utility of the whole is not maximized. Many argue against affirmative action policies on this basis. They argue that we should not target groups to benefit at the expense of other innocent groups; the best talent or person for the job is not found by such a methodology. Another example would be a court ruling that directs a company to pay damages to an individual or employee for some wrong act. This certainly benefits the individual, but it is not maximizing the utility of all. That money could have been spent to produce more goods for all, employ more people, or invest in research that might produce benefits for all. We enact such policies and allow such court awards because of other values that we hold. It seems unjust to not help those that we have hurt, and thus we have affirmative action policies and court awarded damages, but the utilitarian principle is suppose to lead us to justice. As these examples show, utilitarian principles, when applied, leave out some important concerns of justice.

Another problem with utilitarianism is defining welfare or utility. Utility has traditionally been defined in terms of happiness, and happiness is defined as the presence of pleasure and the absence of pain. But other definitions have included utility as anything that is a valuable experience (even if it does not give pleasure), satisfying preferences, or satisfying rational or informed preferences. This last version of informed preferences is a revision of the simple preferences definition; this was needed because a problem exists in that someone may be mistaken about their preferences. But the point here is that there is no agreed upon definition of utility and many utilitarians adhere to many different ones. There is no agreed upon way to measure or define the standard by which we will judge right and wrong actions.

Another question about utilitarianism is the issue of whether or not we should pursue a course of maximizing utility, however we define it. People's desires, preferences, or ends of happiness differ and contradict each other. Utilitarians state that we should satisfy the most—we should maximize—preferences that we can. Does that mean we just take a total for the group or do we look at each person in turn and maximize the number of people who have their preferences satisfied? Furthermore, it seems that we could produce unjust situations with this formulation. Some preferences, desires, or pleasures should count more than others; some are more important and not all units of utility should have the same impact or influence on the course of action we choose. And some preferences—for example the preferences of a white supremacist when looking at racial matters—should not be counted at all because they contradict other values we hold.

Many problems with utilitarianism can be summed up in this statement by Rawls. "The question is whether the imposition on a few can be outweighed by a greater sum of advantages enjoyed by others" (Rawls 1971, 33). Regarding some issues at certain times, this may be considered just; the economic system is somewhat an example of this. We believe that the present economic system gives us the highest level of production or well-being, even though some people benefit more than others.[2] But, with many issues, this affronts our sense of justice. Why should a few or some of the people give up some of their happiness so that others can have their desires satisfied or their happiness fulfilled? This contradicts our values of personal liberty, rights, and self-determination—our individualistic values. This is a problem to which we can view Rawls as providing an answer. "Justice as fairness" lays out principles for when inequalities or "a greater sum of advantages enjoyed by others" is justified. And of course we are really discussing an issue of distribution. Rawls, as well as many others, critiques utilitarianism on the grounds that it does not pay enough attention to distributive aspects. Any theory of justice should pay some, however small, attention to issues of distribution.

The main problem with utilitarianism, many argue, is that "the winds of utilitarian argumentation blow in too many directions" (Sher 1975, 159). Kymlicka (1990) notes that some utilitarians argue for massive redistribution of wealth, due to the declining marginal utility of money, while other utilitarians argue for a laissez-faire capitalistic economic system because it creates more wealth. And both argue that their position would maximize utility, and to some extent both of their positions are correct. But in modern liberal democracies, there are too many other important values that usually preclude us from making strictly utilitarian decisions. For example, in the above scenario, we would also care about the relationship between the economic system and the political and social systems. We would also care about the problems of poverty associated with a pure laissez-faire system, even if the *total* wealth was maximized under such a system. In most instances, we do care how things are distributed.

Kymlicka notes that issues of politics should be debated in the non-utilitarian language of everyday morality. This includes talk of rights, responsibilities, the public interest, and distributive justice (1990, 46). For any theory to be useful, we have to be able to derive answers or solutions from its application. And even if we adhere to the utilitarian doctrine, in a society as complex as the United States, it is extremely difficult, if not impossible, to calculate summations of happiness or satisfaction for the whole society. Even though the theory of utilitarianism fits many of our intuitive notions of justice, and the theory has many positive aspects, utilitarianism is incomplete as a theory of justice.

UTILITARIANISM AND GENDER JUSTICE

So, how can utilitarianism helps us understand gender justice? One affirmative answer has been supplied by Lea Campos Boralevi (1987). She argues that utilitarianism is egalitarian in that it postulates a fundamental equality of the psychological structure of all human beings. Under utilitarianism, arguments such as women are inferior to men or women are less intelligent or rational than men, are no longer relevant; women have interests and can experience pain and pleasure and are to be counted equally in the calculation of utility. She further argues that historical feminism, the movement that fought for women's rights, was derived from the axioms of utilitarianism. She calls Jeremy Bentham the father of historical feminism (165).

One of the most expansive essays on utilitarianism and feminism is John Stuart and Harriet Taylor Mill's "On the Subjection of Women" (1970). They argue that, in the modern world, human beings are no longer born to stay in their lot in life but are free to employ their faculties, and as chances may offer, improve their lot (143). All human beings, of course, except women. The legal subordination of women "is wrong in itself, and now one of the chief hindrances to human improvement" (125), and a principle of equality between men and women will double the mass of mental faculties available for service to humanity and for promotion of the general improvement of society (221).

John Stuart Mill states in *Utilitarianism* that it is crucial to the idea of justice that "all persons are deemed to have a *right* to equality of treatment, except when some recognized social expediency requires the reverse" (cited in Okin 1979, 214). Of course, none exists regarding women. Furthermore, "every restraint on the freedom of conduct of any of their human fellow creatures . . . dries up *pro tanto* the principal foundation of human happiness, and leaves the species less rich, to an inappreciable degree, in all that makes life valuable to the human being" (Mill and Mill 1970, 242). John Stuart and Harriet Taylor Mill argue that women do not have their rational freedom, and after food and clothing, freedom is the greatest of human desires. "[T]he only unfailing and permanent source of improvement is liberty" (Mill 1975, 10). When half the human species is liberated, there will be an "unspeakable gain in private happiness" which is to the direct benefit of all (Mill and Mill 1970, 236). The utilitarian argument is summarized in this passage from *Principles of Economy*: "[t]he ideas and institutions by which the accident of sex is made the groundwork of an inequality of legal rights, and a forced dissimilarity of social functions, must ere long be recognized as the greatest hindrance to moral, social, and even intellectual improvement" (cited in Okin 1979, 210).

The Mills argue that support for the liberation of women is founded on utilitarian arguments, which include arguments about justice and liberty. If women are treated equally with men, the human race will improve because the talent available to improve society will be doubled, and the happiness of society will greatly increase. These arguments seem simple enough now though they were very radical when they were first published. The Mills also argue that any jobs or activities that women cannot do, they will not do! There is no need to have laws barring women from participation in political offices or employment; if they are incapable of performing such jobs, as many argue, it will be proven through their inability to perform.

Even though not specifically stated in "The Subjection," one can draw many more implications from the arguments presented in the essay. The elimination of all sexual roles for men and women are called for by utilitarian principles. To have any arbitrary limitations on what people can do with their lives—and sexually prescribed roles do limit the choices and options available for people—is against utilitarian principles. Such limitations reduce the total utility for a society because the best people are not doing the jobs for which they are best suited, whether by desire or ability. Furthermore, people are not free and this is important for human happiness. The total happiness is reduced if people are not doing the jobs they prefer and the total production is reduced if the best people are not performing the jobs they would do best. Thus, utilitarianism calls for the elimination of forced sex roles, which is a great step forward for women's rights and feminist concerns.

As described above, utilitarianism evaluates consequences. For women, a focus on the consequences of a policy is promising. Equal rights have been granted and anti-discrimination laws have been passed, but the evidence of sexual inequality is startling: the statistics of pay disparity between men and women (U.S. Bureau of the Census 1996a), the "glass ceiling" phenomena (Mahar 1993), the disparity in the amount of housework and child care that men and women perform (Hochschild with Machung 1989), the amount of violence against women in the home as well as in society at large, and so forth. The laws that have been passed have not made men and women equal. New policies need to be instituted that will give the intended effect—some type of equality or equity between men and women. So the fact that utilitarianism examines actual consequences is very positive for women. Laws that grant equal rights, but do not look at outcomes as long as equal rights are not abridged, oftentimes do not produce justice.

But under utilitarian principles, the consequences of an act or a policy are examined by the effects on society as a whole. A theory of gender justice examines the fairness, equality, equity, fulfilled needs, etc. of two groups of people; it compares men and women. Distribution is of great importance. For example, let us hypothesize that men are more materialistic than women and the ownership of property gives them more preference satisfaction and brings them more happiness than it does women. So if only men owned property, this would give us more total utility than men and women owning property together. But, in the United States, we would not think such a situation just. Conversely, one could argue that the happiness of society is, in part, dependent upon some type of gender justice. But we run into the problem described above; do we mean the utility of society as a whole, or the utility of each person in turn and then totaled? The theory of utilitarianism is not clear on such a point, and for comparing men and women, it is very important.

"Utilitarianism, despite its claim to the contrary, needs distributional criteria which it cannot itself provide" (Brittan 1990, 92). This is the main problem for utilitarianism and gender justice. In fact, one could view a theory of gender justice as, at least partially, a theory to outline the correct distribution of societal resources between men and women. This is the most pertinent view for examining gender justice and public policies. Most public policies distribute some resource, and a theory of gender justice should make us consider and help us decide how the resource should be distributed between men and women. Utilitarianism does not address this distributional aspect.

In "The Subjection," the authors state that besides the legal enslavement described above, women experience a psychological enslavement. Unlike any other oppressed group throughout time, women are taught to not only bear their oppression, but also to feel affection for their oppressor. From the earliest of childhood times, women are taught to desire, look forward to, and train themselves for the time when they are an adult and can experience one of the greatest oppressions—marriage. John Stuart and Harriet Taylor Mill argue that every available tool is put forth to enslave women's minds. The oppression of women involves more than just laws; it involves a whole social system that directs the lives of women from the time they are born.

How can a theory of utilitarianism help us with the psychological oppression of women? We can not pass laws prohibiting a psychological mind set. But Mill's version of utilitarianism addresses, at least partially, such problems. He views humans as progressive, morally and intellectually improvable beings. In *On Liberty*, John Stuart Mill states, "Human nature is not a machine to be built after a model . . . but a tree, which requires to grow and develop itself on all sides, according to the tendency of the inward forces which make it a living thing" (56). For John Stuart Mill, the intellectual advancement of the human race will result in greater happiness, and an essential element in achieving the greatest happiness for the human race is moral and intellectual improvement. In fact, John Stuart Mill regards utility as the "ultimate appeal on all ethical questions . . . but it must be utility in the largest sense, grounded on the permanent interest of man as a progressive being" (12). So, with regard to the improvement of women's condition, the intellectual and moral development of society needs to occur along with the legal advances for women. In "The Subjection," the Mills imply that the legal and psychological oppression of women go together, and they need to be lifted together.[3]

But a widely criticized idea that is discussed in "The Subjection" is that women, even though granted freedom, will still want to marry and be a homemaker.[4] The public and private realms, sexual division of labor, and sex roles are assumed. As Elshtain (1981) states

> He grants women full *liberty* in the political realm, thereby freeing them from ignoble private power quests. But he embraces a traditional division of labor *within* the family based on males being actively employed *outside* the home. Women remain private albeit "free" beings and continue to exert their traditional softening effect upon men. . . . (144)

Elshtain concludes that

> Mill was ambivalent about thoroughgoing alterations in private social arrangements between sexes. His way out was a grant of equality of citizenship and civil liberty, together with a formal grant of the *right* to public power to women, knowing full well that the structure of social arrangements forbade the implementation of these rights. (145)

The Mills have left the distinction between the public and private realms intact. So how will women truly have justice, happiness, equality, and freedom? How will the happiness or utility of society be promoted if women are granted equal rights but do not act upon them?

The following is an example of this problem. It is stated in "The Subjection" that in marriage "(t)he rule is simple: whatever would be the husband's or wife's if they were not married, should be under their exclusive control during marriage" (Okin 1979, 228-29). This would not be very beneficial for women because unless much in society had changed, they would not own much property in or out of marriage. In many ways, it seems as if the Mills contradict their own (or at least John Stuart Mill's) principle of utilitarianism and its implications of looking at consequences of actions. One is hard pressed to see how, after examining the consequences of the granting of these equal rights, one could envision much real change for women.

Another contradiction occurs when the Mills state that women should be able to support themselves, but again, think most women will not. Most women will concern themselves with the home and children. How does the granting of equal rights and ability to earn a living, if not actually acted upon, increase the happiness of women and society? We can see some validity in the fact that a certain respect for women is engendered by not having them barred from important societal positions—any women could, supposedly, run for office if she chose—but how this results in widespread improvement for women is hard to envision. And why would women still chose not to support themselves? Is it because of the prevailing social norms or some innate desire of women? This is not made clear in the work.

And this is even more incredible when in *On Liberty* John Stuart Mill notes the tyrannical effect that public opinion can have on people's thoughts and actions. Mill (1975) states that individuals need protection

> against the tyranny of the prevailing opinion and feeling; against the tendency of society to impose, by other means than civil penalties, its own ideas and practices as rules of conduct on those who dissent from them; to fetter the development, and, if possible prevent the formation, of any individuality not in harmony with its ways, and compel all characters to fashion themselves upon the model of its own. (8)

So, John Stuart Mill is certainly aware of the power of public opinion, the problematical effects of it, and how people need to guard against living their lives according to it. Why did he think women would, for the most part, choose not to live independent lives? Is it because that is their nature or because of social conformity? This is not made clear in "The Subjection."

But an important point is that marriage will, under the Mills' formulation, be a marriage of equals. Of course it is difficult to see how the spouses will truly be equal, but the gap would certainly be much smaller. Possibly this is all, or at least the central point, the Mills were hoping to achieve. But when one reads the calls for equality of education, income, career opportunities, political rights, etc., one expects much more from "The Subjection" and is disappointed. Generally, the work has been criticized for leaving the private realm in tact as a place where women work and are not compensated. Men are not encouraged to share this unpaid labor, and thus men and women are left in their respective spheres. But possibly the Mills believe that an equality of rights between the sexes will, psychologically, make men and women equal and the partnership of marriage can be a much more fulfilling relationship for both parties.

"The Subjection," and the theory of utilitarianism in general, argues for the equality of women without telling us how to accomplish such a task. The principles will not give women equal freedom, equal opportunity, equal income, or equal power with men. Utilitarianism, as a theory, can provide us with an argument as to *why* women and men should have equal rights, but it does not give us an adequate description of *how* to accomplish this equality. Though it does have some helpful ideas that can be applied to issues of gender justice, the theory, as a whole, is not very helpful. In the United States, most agree that women should have equal rights with men; this is not the problem. Disagreements arise when we start discussing *how* to accomplish this equality and what equality entails outside of the mere granting of equal rights. The current debate over affirmative action is one case in point. Disagreements arise when we start discussing how to have gender justice and not just an equality of rights as described by the Mills.

Another critique of utilitarianism (made by Rawls) also points out some of the problems with utilitarianism and gender justice. As noted above, utilitarianism extends the principle that an individual uses to make decisions to a whole society. Rawls (1971) views this as problematical because in a society, there are conflicting claims and a plurality of human subjects (4). In any group of people, there are a wide diversity of opinions, ideas, and conceptions of the good, and this is very different from one individual. In fact, this problem of conflicting claims and plurality of people is, as described by Rawls, the basis of justice or the circumstances under which issues of justice arise. Utilitarianism fails to take this into account; utilitarianism conflates diverse systems of justice into a single system of desire, and as such, "many persons are fused into one" (Sandel 1982, 51).[5]

One could restate this critique of utilitarianism and say that utilitarianism does not allow for individual differences. At the risk of over generalizing or essentializing, we can view men and women as being different and having different conceptions of the good. As the psychological studies by Gilligan and others discussed in Chapter Two show, many women might possibly think differently about matters of justice. Furthermore, women have constraints because of reproductive capabilities that men do not have and thus women have different claims to make regarding the division of social resources. Utilitarianism takes none of this into account. I agree with the statement by Rawls (1971): "(p)rinciples of justice deal with conflicting claims upon the advantages won by social co-operation; they apply to the relations among several persons or groups" (16). Utilitarianism does not encompass this facet of relations among different groups that have competing claims on the "appropriate distribution of the benefits and burdens of social co-operation" (Rawls 1971, 4).

So, in conclusion, the positive ideas utilitarianism has to offer a theory of gender justice are the following. Policies should be evaluated by their actual consequences. We do not have to write policies that appear sexually neutral and then just *assume* they are just; utilitarianism directs us to examine the actual effects to see if they are just. This is very positive for women because neutral policies, in their application, can disadvantage women many times. Furthermore, each person or woman should be counted as having equal worth; this is helpful when examining different ethnic and racial groups. White women's needs should not be privileged over African-American or Hispanic women's needs.

Moreover, if we take utilitarian ideas to specific policies, we do not have to worry about the definition of utility which is problematical as discussed earlier. We can just recognize the goals of any specific policy and take utility to be defined as such when analyzing that policy. For example, in medical research, the goal is to obtain information from studies on small groups of people in order to help all people live healthier lives. When we examine that policy, we can use how well medical research is helping all people to live healthier lives as our "utility" of sorts. And since my concern is with gender, the specific goal is to help the most men *and* women live healthier lives. At least part of our concern is to maximize the help that such research provides. We want to maximize health. If "utility" is looked at in such a fashion, as specific to each policy and its goals, it can be helpful for analyzing policies.

NOTES

1. Utilitarianism has been divided into "act" utilitarianism and "rule" utilitarianism. "Act" utilitarianism states that we should apply the standard of utility to acts, whereas "rule" utilitarianism states that we should apply the test of utility to rules, and then perform whichever act is endorsed by the best rules. Under "rule" utilitarianism, we do not have to evaluate each and every act; we just have to follow the rules. In recent years, "rule" utilitarianism has been fairly well discredited, while "act" utilitarianism still has adherents.

2. Of course, most believe that all benefit because everyone or the whole society is better off than if we instituted more economic equality.

3. As a side note, it is problematical that they do not state *how* to accomplish such a task, which is extremely difficult. But this does not diminish the success of the arguments as to *why* such a task should be accomplished.

4. See Okin (1979); Coole (1988); Pateman (1989).

5. Sandel (1982) discusses this problem on pg. 50 forward.

CHAPTER 4

Feminist Theorists and Gender Justice

As discussed in previous chapters, a problematical issue for any theory of justice is how to handle differences among people. From Aristotle we inherited a notion of justice as similar treatment for similar people, and under most theories of justice, similar treatment for similar people results in justice. Different treatment for people that are not similar, the thinking goes, also results in justice many times. But what this different treatment should be, under what conditions it should be called upon, and on what moral principles it should be based are areas of widespread disagreement. Feminist theorists have brought the "women question" into this debate for gender is indeed one particular way that people differ. When, how, and why gender should allow for different treatment by the state and its laws is an area of widespread disagreement though. Many argue that the concept of equality is empty and that a focus on difference poses an intractable dilemma. In this chapter, some explicitly feminist theorists who address the gender question and provide new answers to the question of gender and justice will be explored. I ask, as does Ruth Anna Putnam (19995), "Why Not a Feminist Theory of Justice?"

NEW APPROACHES TO THE EMPTINESS OF EQUALITY AND THE DILEMMA OF DIFFERENCE

Politics of Difference

One contemporary feminist writer who advocates a politics of difference is Iris Young (1990). Her approach is different from the prior difference approaches, even though it still focuses on differences. Young argues that a useful conception of justice should not focus on distribution, even though this is what most contemporary theories do; it should start from concepts of domination and oppression. Where social group differences exist and some groups are privileged while others are oppressed, social justice requires explicitly acknowledging and attending to those group differences in order to undermine oppression (Young 1990, 3).

She looks at the New Left social movements of 1960s and 70s, such as the democratic socialist, environmentalist, Black, Chicano, Puerto Rican, anti-military, anti-interventionist (particularly Third World), gay liberation, feminist, and other movements. They all claim that the U.S. has deep institutional injustices, but they find little theoretical kinship with contemporary philosophical theories of justice. Young argues that the ideal of impartiality, a keystone of most modern moral theories and theories of justice, denies difference. Thus groups who find themselves different from mainstream society and its values and assumptions, find little affinity with these theories.

Young thinks justice requires that the following values be equally available for all: (1) developing and exercising one's capacities and expressing one's experience and (2) participating in determining one's action and the conditions of one's action. These are universalist values, in the sense that they assume the equal moral worth of all persons. Thus justice requires the application of these two principles in order to promote justice for everyone. In conjunction with these two general values are two corresponding social conditions that define injustice: oppression, the institutional constraint on self-development, and domination, the institutional constraint on self-determination.

Young calls the formal equality approach an ideal of assimilation (157). This ideal usually promotes equal treatment as a part of justice, but new social movements of the 1960s and 70s argue that a positive self-definition of group differences is more liberating. This is an egalitarian politics of difference or an emancipatory politics that, as opposed to the assimilationist ideal, affirms group differences and reconceives the meaning of equality. Young states, "In this vision the good society does not eliminate or transcend group difference. Rather, there is equality among socially and culturally differentiated groups, who mutually respect one another in their differences" (163).

This understanding of difference is relational and sees differences as a function of comparisons among groups. No longer are WASPHAMs (white, Anglo-Saxon, Protestant, heterosexual, able-bodied male) the privileged and dominant group, from which the oppressed differ; no longer are groups excluded or essentialized. When we compare men and women, who are different, we have a continuum of difference in which no one group sets the standard. Men are different from women just as much as women are different from men; homosexuals are as different from heterosexuals as heterosexuals are from homosexuals; and so on.

This understanding of difference entails contextualization.[1] Group differences may or may not be important depending on the groups compared, the purposes of the comparison, and the point of view of the comparers. Young gives the example that in the context of athletics, health care, and social support services, wheel-chair bound people are different from others, but they are not different in many other respects. Scott (1990) says that there are times when it makes sense for mothers to demand consideration of their social role, and there are contexts in which motherhood is irrelevant to women's behavior. But to maintain that womanhood is motherhood essentializes women and obscures the choices that are available and the differences among women themselves (145).

Young argues for the justice of group-conscious policies. First, policies that are universally formulated and thus blind to differences of age, race, gender, etc. often perpetuate inequality and oppression rather than eliminate them. Second, group-conscious policies are sometimes necessary in order to affirm groups and to allow them to affirm their own affinities without suffering disadvantage in society. Groups cannot be socially equal unless their experience, culture, and contributions are affirmed and recognized in the wider social context. This democratic cultural pluralism requires a dual system of rights: a general system of rights which are the same for all, and a more specific system of group-conscious policies and rights.

So what are some implications of this theory of differences for public policy? Young gives a few examples for women. With regards to pregnancy and childbirth, she is against the inclusion of maternity leaves under gender-neutral leave and benefit policies that apply to any physical condition not allowing a person to work. She argues that this views pregnancy and childbirth as a disability rather than a natural, socially necessary, and positive process. It implies that women do not have a right to benefits and job security when having children. This is based on a male-model of uninterrupted work; if you have to be off the job, it is because there is something wrong with you.

She does support gender-neutral parental leave from jobs in order to care for children, so as not to perpetuate the association of the care of children solely with women and so men who choose to care for children will not be penalized. But these are the only concrete examples (with respect to gender) that she gives. She admits that by only looking at childbirth, she avoids some of the hardest questions. There are myriad ways that women are disadvantaged in the workplace: women are socialized to pursue certain types of occupations, women experience sexual harassment, unequal pay, and male-dominated environments where masculine norms and styles predominate, to name only a few. But Young does not specifically address the issue of what types of policies should be pursued to end the disadvantages that women encounter in the workplace.

Young's work makes many contributions to the area of justice and gender justice in particular, but the implications for policy are not clear. She avoids the argument of sameness and difference—she discards such a paradigm—and addresses groups who have been oppressed for whatever reasons. She starts with real people speaking about real injustices that do not match up with the theories. Are the theories wrong or are the groups wrong? Have they really not experienced injustices because the injustices have not been defined by the theories as such? She suggests that theories of justice may need to start with the wrongs that people in the world experience. Finally, she does not try to arrive at an universal theory of justice; her ideas are more situational and contextual.

Gender as Dominance

Another alternative framework is offered by Catharine MacKinnon (1987, 1989). MacKinnon notes that the reason why sex equality laws have been so ineffective at getting women what they need is that they have been stuck in questions of sameness and difference. She believes that equality is an equivalence, not a distinction, and sex is a distinction. The two sexes are defined by their unlikeness, but the legal mandate of equal treatment is a matter of treating likes alike and unlikes unlike. A built-in tension exists between this concept of equality, which presupposes sameness, and the concept of sex, which presupposes difference (1987, 32-33).

MacKinnon's point is this: to treat issues of sex equality as issues of sameness and difference is to take a particular approach. This approach is grounded in sex difference. One sex, men, have become the measure of all things. This approach—"we're as good as you"—has gotten women access to many things like employment anti-discrimination and educational anti-discrimination laws. But its successes are limited because it ignores the gender inequalities that are built into the very definition of societal positions. This approach views sex equality in terms of the ability of women to compete under seemingly gender-neutral rules for roles that are in fact grounded in a male-dominated society. This is similar to many critiques discussed in Chapter One.

MacKinnon argues that before we decide whether gender should be taken into account, we need to know how it has been taken into account in the past. Her conclusion is that one will probably find that most important social positions and roles have been structured in gender-biased ways. MacKinnon (1987) writes that

> virtually every quality that distinguishes men from women is already affirmatively compensated in this society. Men physiology defines most sports, their needs define auto and health insurance coverage, their socially designed biographies define workplace expectations and successful career patterns, their perspectives and concerns define quality in scholarship, their experiences and possessions define merit, their military service defines citizenship, their presence defines family, their inability to get along with each other their war and rulership—defines history, their image defines god, and their genitals defines sex. For each of their differences from women, what amounts to an affirmative action plan is in effect, otherwise known as the structure and values of American society. (36)

There are many differences between men and women. What the formal equality standard fails to recognize is that men's differences from women are equal to women's differences from men (MacKinnon 1987, 37). This is the same point that Young made above. The difference is in the relationship between the two; the two are different from each other.[2] The present status quo, where the male sets the standard by which women are judged as not just being different, but being inferior, is wrong and unjust.

MacKinnon is critical of emphasizing differences. For example, she thinks women also created art and have a history and it is good to affirm them, but she states, I am critical of affirming what we have been, which necessarily is what we have been permitted, as if it is women's, ours possessive (MacKinnon 1987, 39). To take another example, Gilligan (1982) found that women value care. Well, MacKinnon replies, maybe women value care because men have valued women according to the care they have given them. Maybe women think in relational terms because their existence is defined in relation to men. The damage of sexism is real, and reifying that into differences is an insult to women's possibilities (MacKinnon 1987, 39).

MacKinnon proposes an alternative approach that "provides a second answer, a dissident answer in law and philosophy, to both the equality question and the gender question. In this approach, an equality question is a question of the distribution of power. Gender is also a question of power, specifically of male supremacy and female subordination" (40). Her dominance approach centers on the most sex-differential abuses of women as a gender, abuses that sex equality law in its formal equality/difference approach can not confront. This includes not only the connection of sex segregation and poverty but the range of issues termed violence against women. It combines women's material desperation with rape, sexual assault of children, wife battering, prostitution, and pornography. MacKinnon (1987) states, "These experiences have been silenced out of the sameness/difference definition of sex equality largely because they happen almost exclusively to women for this reason, they are considered not to raise sex equality issues" (41).

MacKinnon's dominance approach is not an abstract approach; it is grounded in social reality. This type of approach became the implicit model for race in the 1960s when race relations came to be viewed as a matter of white supremacy and not just a matter of black/white difference. To consider gender in this way—observe again that men are as different from women as women are from men, but socially the sexes are not equally powerful. To be on the top of a hierarchy is certainly different from being on the bottom. If gender were merely a question of difference, sex equality would be a problem of mere sexism, of mistaken differentiation, of inaccurate categorization of individuals. This is what supporters of the formal equality/difference approach think sex inequality is and to which the approach is sensitive. "But if gender is an inequality first, constructed as socially relevant differentiation in order to keep that inequality in place, then sex inequality questions are questions of systematic dominance, of male supremacy, which is not at all abstract and is anything but a mistake" (MacKinnon 1987, 42).

In moving from gender as difference to gender as dominance, gender changes from a distinction that is presumptively valid to a detriment that is presumptively suspect. Sex discrimination stops being a question of morality and starts being a question of politics. Once sex is defined into bipolarity in society, to require that one be the same as those who set the standard—those which one is already socially defined as different from—simply means that sex equality is conceptually designed never to be achieved (MacKinnon 1987, 44).

Equality as Acceptance

Another model that has been proposed by law professor Christine Littleton to address the formal equality/difference problem is "equality as acceptance." The foundation of this approach is that "(t)he difference between human beings, whether perceived or real, and whether biologically or socially based, should not be permitted to make a difference in the lived-out equality of those persons" (Littleton 1987a, 1234-35). She says that to achieve this type of sexual equality, male and female differences must be costless relative to each other. Women, or the rare men, who engage in culturally female behavior, such as child rearing, should not be forced to individually bear the costs of such actions. Equality as acceptance cannot be achieved if women performing traditionally female jobs or filling feminine roles of caretaker and child rearer are penalized and men and the growing population of women performing traditionally masculine jobs of wage-earner—in professions and trades that earn higher salaries than feminine jobs—are highly rewarded in comparison.

Equality as acceptance recognizes that it is not the differences between men and women that are the problem; it is the way that these differences are permitted to justify inequality that is the problem. "It asserts that eliminating the unequal consequences of sex difference is more important than debating whether such differences are 'real,' or even trying to eliminate them altogether" (Littleton 1987a, 1296). What is important are the consequences of gendered difference, not its sources, and these are what equality as acceptance addresses.

Littleton chooses to keep the word equality but transform its meaning. Equality as acceptance specifically addresses the criticisms noted in Chapter One about formal equality. First, it calls for "equalization across only those differences that the culture has encoded as gendered complements" (1312). A good example of this is the issue of comparable worth. The model would not call for equal pay for *all* jobs; it would call for equal pay for similar jobs that are not paid equally because some have been defined as women's work and some as men's work. This same way of thinking could be applied in a more general way to all kinds of forms and behaviors that are labeled masculine and feminine; this is what her equality as acceptance calls for.

Furthermore, when a real difference between men and women is found, Littleton says that we need to assess the cultural meaning of the difference; differences are located in relationships among things and persons, not in objects or people themselves. Under equality as acceptance, neither male, female, nor androgynous characteristics are held as superior, but the equal validity of men's and women's experiences is held as a value. And regarding the third critique noted above, the new model recognizes that women and men stand in different positions in relation to social institutions sometimes. It recognizes that neutral does not always mean equal, fair, or just.

Equality as acceptance would challenge male norms in job descriptions, even if they are necessary to the business or to perform the job. The problem is in how the job or business is structured; many times the job, its definition, the physical surrounding in which the job will be performed, and tools with which to perform the job were all designed with males in mind. Since many females cannot meet the height, weight, or strength requirements, or cannot work 10 or 12 hour shifts, stay late on short notice, or work night shifts because they have children at home means they are not "qualified" for the job. Under traditional equality doctrine, it is not discriminatory because if a woman was qualified—was tall or strong, for example—she could have the job. Equality as acceptance would advocate redefining the job, restructuring the physical surroundings, making new tools that are smaller or do not require as much strength to operate, shorten the number of hours a shift lasts, etc. An effort should make the job, business, and the public world in general receptive to men and women and their abilities and needs. This is true whether these abilities or needs are biologically or socially derived.

In conclusion, equality as acceptance provides a framework for assuring that sexual differences do not turn into sexual inequalities. Presently, society devalues women because they differ from the male norm. It is always necessary to ask, "What difference do the differences make?" There is a need to examine differences in the context of arising out of a relationship of among two things and not give preference to one over the other. This means there is a need to reduce inequality, not so much the differences, and give equal value to traditionally female occupations and lifestyles. Differences between men and women, whether they be cultural or biological, need to be made costless when compared to each other.

The Engendered Body

Zillah Eisenstein argues in *The Female Body and the Law* (1988) that sex equality is

> an elusive phrase. Depending on context, it can be vitally significant or virtually meaningless. It categorizes women according to both difference and sameness—indicating that women are either completely determined by their biological sex or entirely free of it—but in both cases men set the standard. (1)

She argues that the male body is privileged and that we need to refocus the discussion of sexual equality to include the female body. In particular, she focuses on the pregnant body to decenter the privileged male body (1). Eisenstein uses the pregnant body to remind us of the potential difference between males and females that makes the formal equality model inadequate and to remind us of diversity (1-2). Her ultimate purpose is to deny that we can have any one homogeneous standard for sexual equality. "I mean to argue that the concept of equality is best reconstructed through a completely pluralized notion of difference(s), one that rejects a politics of inequality and demands a radical egalitarianism" (5).

Eisenstein believes that a concept of sexual equality that recognizes the female body as a potentially pregnant one, is a theory that forces us to recognize the importance of abortion, reproductive choices, maternity and paternity leaves, child-care needs, parental sick-leave, and other related issues (191). But we have to be careful in these policy distinctions. Policies regarding child bearing affect only females, but policies regarding child rearing affect both males and females. But to date, most policies do not focus on these aspects of men's and women's lives.

But even when a policy aimed at childrearing appears to be sex-neutral, such as the Family Leave Act of 1993, we should examine it closer to see what are the actual implications. Eisenstein argues that policies like the Family Leave Act are not sex-neutral. As long as women make less money than men and as long as women are segregated into lower-status and lower-paying positions, it will be women who will be expected to take unpaid leaves to care for children or sick relatives. Single parents, and most single parents are women, will most likely be excluded from unpaid leaves; they simply could not afford it. So, this policy that appears to be sex-neutral is, in reality, restrictive for women and only reinforces and exacerbates present inequalities (Eisenstein 1988, 215-216).

A commitment to equality cannot deny sex and gender differences, but it should require that these differences not unduly restrict men and women. In this line of thought, sex/gender-specific policies are not, at face value, problematical or helpful. The context, the individual's circumstances, and the consequences of such policies need to be examined in order to make such judgments. This involves interpretation, and this is problematical. But, Eisenstein argues, it is no less or no more problematical in the new conception than it is under the formal equality or difference paradigms.

In closing, Eisenstein states:

> I argue that equality must encompass generalization, abstraction, and homogeneity as well as individuality, specificity, and heterogeneity. The homogeneity of woman's difference from man is displaced by her plural specificities similarities. Sex discrimination is redefined to mean the treatment of an individual woman as a member of a sex class that restricts her freedom of choice and self-determination while ignoring both her individual differences from members of her sex class and her similarities with men. Sameness is no longer equated with equality nor is specific legislation equated with discrimination. Once the oppositional differentiation of woman from man is replaced by a notion of sexual heterogeneity, equality cannot mean sameness. Difference is no longer oppositional. . . . A person can be different and (not un)equal. (221-22)

Gender as a Disadvantage

Another alternative paradigm has been put forth by Deborah Rhode (1989). Rhode also thinks we need to move away from sex-based difference (as do Young and MacKinnon) and toward a concern with sex-based disadvantage. She also thinks we need to move away from a focus on abstract, individual rights (as do Young and MacKinnon) and move toward a concern with the social context that constrains such rights.

Rhode says that the difference-oriented approach is inadequate in theory and practice. It draws heavily from Aristotelian traditions, which views equality as similar treatment for those similarly situated. Theoretically, it permits different treatment for legitimate purposes, but provides no criteria for knowing what is legitimate and what is not. Practically, the approach has both over- and under-valued gender differences. Sometimes, biology has determined destiny, as when occupational restrictions for women were upheld by the courts. And other times women's needs have gone unaddressed, as with pregnancy discrimination when the courts said it was not a question of gender but a question of "pregnant and non-pregnant persons" (Rhode 1989). "Reliance on 'real difference' has deflected attention from the process by which differences have been attributed and from the groups that are underrepresented in that process. Such an approach has often done more to reflect sex-based inequalities than to challenge them" (3).

We also need to move away from a focus on abstract, individual rights. The formal equality approach has not been very successful in getting institutions to change to accommodate women's interests, values, and concerns. Similar treatment for those similarly situated fails to address the social forces underlying women's dissimilar and disadvantaged status. The "just add women and stir" approach does not transform the existing social order.

But Rhode is concerned about the implications of a dominance framework such as MacKinnon's, even though MacKinnon and others like her have made many positive contributions to feminism. First, an approach that only views women as oppressed and men as dominators presents a limited view of relations between gender groups. It does not account for the varying experiences of women. It does not account for the effects of race, age, class, religion, etc. Secondly, it also presents a limited view of the relations between women and men. Furthermore, as a legal and practical strategy, it is weak. Most people do not see themselves as oppressors and oppressed and would be reluctant to embrace such a theory. A theory of gender disadvantage is easier to fit within our traditional legal and political systems.

First, there is a need to recognize that the sexes are not similarly situated. Then follows the need to analyze whether recognition of sex-based differences is more likely to reduce or reinforce sex-based disparities in political power, social status, and economic diversity (3). This approach requires a substantial commitment to creating a society in which women as a group are not disadvantaged in controlling their own life choices. It goes beyond discussing the rationality of means, the legitimacy of ends, and the guarantee of rights. The critical issue in the gender disadvantage framework is not differences, but the difference that differences make; it is concerned with the consequences of the differences. This framework demands close attention to context and the complexity of sex-based classifications and women's interests. Sometimes, a policy may help one set of women but hurt another. Rhode says we cannot formulate abstract rules; we can only analyze what particular situations would need. We should ask of any policy: which women benefit, by how much, and at what cost. "We must insist not just on equal treatment, but on women's treatment as an equal" (83).

A gender disadvantage framework involves a refocusing of the inquiry. Our goal will be to reach a society in which sexual identity does not correlate with social inequality (Rhode 1989, 318), and this involves a reconceptualization of the public and private. The mythical boundary between the two needs to be broken and the mutually reinforcing patterns of subordination in the home and in the workplace need to be made explicit and addressed. We need to reassess our ends as well as means. The goal is not only to ensure women's participation in social, economic, and political power; we also want to change the institutions and the way power is distributed and exercised. We need to focus on women as a group and how they are disadvantaged, as well as the consequences of various policies for various groups of women.

Rhode is a legal scholar a provides an excellent historical and contemporary analysis of case law as it relates to gender. But what might be some implications of this framework for public policy? Using a gender-disadvantage approach, how might one reform existing policies or what new policies should be implemented? She offers little insight into such questions.

The Dilemma of Difference

Martha Minow (1990) defines the "dilemma of difference" in her book *Making All the Difference: Inclusion, Exclusion, and American Law* as "the conundrum of equality in a legal and social world that has made certain traits signify important differences in people's statuses and entitlement" (12). She specifically addresses the formal equality/difference debate described in Chapter One herein, even though her work is in no way limited to women. The beauty of the work is the broad application to the general issue of how everyone, but especially lawyers and the law, classify, analyze, simplify, categorize, and label people, events, and the world. "It sounds familiar. It also sounds harmless. I do not think it is. . . . Sometimes, classifications express and implement prejudice, racism, sexism, anti-Semitism, intolerance for difference" (3). She, like others, refuses to accept a dichotomy between difference and formal equality but instead refocuses the discussion to how differences are defined and the consequences of those definitions for people in the legal system. She describes three contrasting approaches to difference that currently appear in legal thought: the abnormal-persons approach, rights-analysis approach, and the social-relations approach. She asks, "Why does difference seem to pose choices each of which undesirably revives difference or the stigma or disadvantage associated with it?" (49) She, in the end, advocates an approach that combines caretaking, mutual obligations, rights, individual boundaries, and restraints in public and private power.

Minow identifies five related and unstated assumptions that underlie difference dilemmas. First, we assume that differences are intrinsic to specific individuals instead of as expressions of comparisons of people regarding specific traits. Everyone is different and similar to others in innumerable ways. An analysis of difference selects some traits and makes them more important than other traits. The second assumption is that we adopt an unstated place of reference by which we determine who is the same and who is different. And many times the point of reference is the majority view or the view of those who have access to power. The unstated reference point promotes the interests of some people or groups at the expense of others (Minow 1990, 50-51). And the reference point is important for issues of equality. Who is equal with whom and on what basis?

The third assumption is that the judger or seer is without a perspective, prejudices, or biases. The judge or jury in a court case is presumed to be neutral and able to objectively apply the legal tests to the facts at hand. But, Minow and many others argue that no one is without a perspective (52). A fourth assumption is that the perspective of the judged is irrelevant or already taken into account by the judger. Since it is supposed that one can be neutral and a sort of blank slate, other views can be ignored because if they were not taken into account by the neutral person, it must be because they were not important. Once the truth is found, all other perspectives, and especially the judged's perspective, are nontruths. And the fifth assumption is that existing societal arrangements are natural, neutral, uncoerced, and good. Thus the status quo is hard to change and changes are viewed as against neutrality, the natural, and the good. Society is viewed as a place where all are free to make their choices about how to live their lives in this neutral environment. But when much of society is designed according to unstated norms, and then is presumed to be neutral, many person's views or needs are labeled as different and abnormal. And when society is neutral and natural, the actions a person takes are seen as choices a completely free person would make and thus the individual is held 100 percent responsible and accountable. The effect of these five unstated assumptions is that they make the difference dilemma seem intractable.

Three different approaches have been used in legal analysis regarding how to define and treat those who are different. The abnormal-persons approach assumes that difference is inherent in some people. People are either normal or abnormal and a different set of rights is assigned to each group. Normal people are rational and reasoning beings and can be held responsible for their acts. Abnormal people are incompetent and incapacitated in their reasoning faculties in some fashion and are subjected to legal restraints and denied rights. This incompetence is part of their nature and personhood, not a function of social circumstances, and is unchangeable. This approach views all other similarities or differences between people as unimportant. Mental competence is the only important characteristic of a person and is the dividing line between two very differently treated groups.

The rights-analysis approach grants equal rights to all equal persons but equality is taken to mean sameness. When "real" differences are found, unequal rights may be granted. These may be in the form of special treatment or as with the abnormal-persons approach, it may mean a loss of rights. This rights approach is the same as the formal equality approach discussed in Chapter One.

Minow (1990) states that these two approaches maintain an unstated norm that is based on one group of people. People who diverge from the one group are counted as different and lesser people (108). Both approaches treat similar persons alike, and differently situated people differently. Equal treatment depends on similarity of particular characteristics that the dominant group deems important.

But the rights approach acknowledges that many times social groups are defined as different when they are really not different in any ways that matter. We only need to think of the civil rights claims of African-Americans and women to see how progressive a rights approach can be. Thus, the rights-analysis can be a more inclusive approach than the abnormal persons framework. But it still does not find an answer to the problem of when are attributes of difference acceptable and when are they false. Furthermore, it does not tell us what attributes count to label a person as different or when they should be addressed. Also, it only focuses on individuals and not on groups of people or relations among them.

The rights approach is philosophically derived from the social contract and natural rights traditions. And both "the historical and heuristic versions of social contract theory claim to be inclusive, participatory, and egalitarian, yet both replicate the process of exclusion and subordination that preserves the two track legal system" (Minow 1990, 149). The United States Constitution is one example of a document that was produced through an exclusionary process. The rational consensus idea in social contract theory excludes those who do not manifest the rational elements as defined by the theorists (150). At different times throughout our history, women, the sick, the disabled, children, and elders have been defined as mentally incapacitated or lacking reasoning capabilities as defined by some other group. And once the initial contract creates the rules and institutions for society, the exclusiveness of them manifests itself over and over throughout the life of the society. How does such a society grant freedom and equality for all?

The social contract tradition, Minow asserts, also employs a concept of the abstract autonomous individual who can separate himself or herself from others and their particular surroundings. First, this excludes those who do not have the time or ability to undertake such an enterprise. Second, it excludes those who view themselves as member of groups and not as autonomous individuals. Also, as discussed in Chapter Two herein, many wonder if the type of separation from oneself, others, and their historical circumstances called for by social contract frameworks can even be achieved. This autonomous individual claims to have universal values but actually has only particular views. These views get counted as the norm and those who disagree are different and their rights are limited.

The third approach used in legal analysis regarding difference is the social-relations approach. This approach conceives of difference as a function of social relationships and acknowledges that the burden of difference, that is actually a measure of the distance or gap between two people or two groups of people, is assigned to only some individuals or certain groups. Minow most often discusses cases involving mentally retarded people as examples of how marginalized people are labeled and treated. With regard to the social-relations approach, litigators developed arguments that mental retardation is a stigma that deprives some individuals of their liberty and rights. The focus is on how certain people came to be labeled retarded and thus different from "normal" people. Basically, this approach sees differences among people as socially constructed and changeable. Also in the social-relations framework, emphasis is placed on relationships. This includes relationships between people, concepts, and between the observer and the observed (Minow 1990, 174). In this approach, difference is viewed in a relational context, not as an inherent trait of some particular individuals in society. In political theory, a growing emphasis on community is one manifestation of this approach. Feminist scholarship has also emphasized this perspective and Minow discusses Carol Gilligan's work at length, as well as feminist psychological, moral, and legal theorists.

Minow advocates a new approach to difference that combines the social-relations and rights approaches. Whereas the abnormal persons and rights approaches are unable to move out of the either/or problem—either you are the same or you are different—the social relations approach moves past this dichotomy. A decision-maker should be aware of the power of categorizing people or problems. The social relations approach invites one to examine the context in which events occur and to focus on particularity;

one should beware of "solution by category" and abstraction (215). This approach assumes that people live in networks of relationships—that people are fundamentally connected rather than autonomous. And it assumes that everyone has their own perspective, their own truth, and that a certain person's or group's truth should not be privileged.

But relational approaches are risky; a better approach incorporates rights also. The best approach, Minow states, remakes "rights so that so that they do not recreate the differences etched by prejudice and misunderstanding into the structures and crevices of inherited institutions" (228). We need to develop a method of attending to relationships without losing sight of the larger patterns of power. Many times the characterization and description of problems, people, and their needs should be altered. Furthermore, the process for change should be a highly participatory one, especially including the people who are supposedly going to be helped. As Minow characterizes the Progressive reforms, "these public assistance and social work interventions too often in effect controlled and restricted those people and subjected them to governmental regulation without protection against power imbalances" (267). Minow also states

> Is there no way to rescue what seemed valuable in a world of mutual obligation while still pursuing the protection of rights against coercive power? Especially from the vantage point of different people—disabled persons, children, women, and members of historically disfavored minorities—danger comes from either a system of hierarchical status relations or a system of autonomous individualism that leave each person free to protect himself or herself in an indifferent or hostile world. (268)

Minow concludes that a focus on rights, along with the social-relations approach, is the best way to achieve our goals.

Rights and rules of law are only applicable in a communal, social setting of people where some system of relationships and interdependence already exist. When rights are or are not assigned to certain people and groups, patterns of relationships are formed. Every granted right or freedom redefines everyone's rights and freedoms. In the traditional conception of rights, rights grant and legitimate spheres of authorized individual action. But in Minow's conception, rights are the legal manifestations or consequences of particular patterns of human and institutionalized relationships. She gives some examples. Property rights, rather than expressing some intrinsic autonomy of persons in a "free" market, express the complex and overlapping relationships of individuals and the larger community to limited resources (278). Tort law defines the relationships among strangers. Contract rights govern the formation and dissolution of commercial relationships. And in family law, certain rights are granted or not granted to persons involved in intimate and familial relationships. In these various areas, certain rights are granted or not granted to specific categories of people because of the relationships they have, and then the law institutionalizes or perpetuates these relationships.

"Rights provide a language that depends upon and expresses human interconnection at the very moment when individuals ask others to recognize their separate interests" (296). Particular rights depend upon a continuing, communal process of communication. Rights are contingent upon the community's willingness to signal their meaning to the community through the threat of force. Rights set boundaries and articulate connections regrading the relationships among various people. "The language of rights thus draws each claimant into the community and grants each a basic opportunity to participate in the process of communal debate. The discourse of rights registers commitment to a basic equality among the participants as participants" (Minow 1990, 296). But there is a difference between this form of equality that creates a type of community and the ways in which inequality of power and status can remain within a community under the disguise of rights. Minow quotes Carol Gilligan, "If you have power, you can opt not to listen. And you do so with impunity" (Minow 1990, 297).

The equality of rights in Minow's approach is an equality of attention. Rights, even under the traditional conception, structure a system in which even the less powerful are supposed to be heard.

> Rights—as words and forms—structure attention even for the claimant who is much less powerful than the authorities, and even for individuals and groups treated throughout the community as less than equal. Unstated here are assumptions about the presumed standard for comparison: equal to whom? An adult, white, competent male citizen is the likely reference. But by including any who can speak the language of rights and by signaling deserved attention, rights enable a challenge to unstated norms, to exclusion, and to exclusive perspectives. Rights discourse implicates its users in a form of life, a pattern of social and political commitment. (297-98)

In the end, rights discourse draws people into the community and asks the community to pay attention to those asking for rights, but it also underscores the power of the established order to respond or not respond to the requests. Furthermore, a request for the recognition of rights of another group or individual may be made that jeopardizes the claims already made. So how do we decide and know which claims will be recognized by and persuade the community and what the consequences will be for prior and subsequent claims and past and future relationships? We do not know and there is a risk that views silenced in the past will continue to be silenced. Claims for rights are issues of struggle. But nevertheless, an interpretive conception of rights as a method for expressing and strengthening communal relationships entails many possibilities for change, and is a way of doing so that relies on inherited traditions. The comparison of rights to language and conversation fosters an idea of community created through an exchange of words in a struggle for meaning. This affirms the idea of community, but only a particular type of community:

> a community dedicated to invigorating words with power to restrain, so that even the powerless can appeal to those words. It is a community that acknowledges and admits the historical use of power to exclude, deny, and silence—and commits itself to enabling suppressed points of view to be heard, to making covert conflict overt. Committed to making available a rhetoric of rights where it has not been heard before, this community uses rights language to make a conflict audible and unavoidable, even if it is limited to words, and certain forms of expression. If the very introduction of rights rhetoric to a new area triggers conflict, it is over this issue: should the normative commitment to restrain power with communal dedication reach this new area? The power in question may be public or private. (299)

Minow also defends her choice of rights rhetoric against a "needs" framework. First she notes that she shares some of the same criticisms of a rights framework that those who advocate needs do. Mainly this involves the false idea of autonomy that is so much a part of traditional rights discourse. As a scholar, she has the luxury to make such criticisms. She interestingly states that in the real world, it is helpful, useful, and maybe even essential to frame ideas within the discourse of rights. She believes that this is the way to bring about change in our world. The idea of rights is too valuable to give up, and the idea of need too neglectful of power to use. Rights rhetoric is remarkably well suited for challenging structures of power and for giving voice to previously silenced claims.

In conclusion, Minow's rights approach analogizes rights to language as a vocabulary for defining roles an relationships within communities. Meanings of words are determined by their use, and if we can put rights rhetoric to new uses, we can change the meaning of it. Rights are not neutral, fixed concepts. Rights can and should be renegotiated within a community, and this should be with a focus on relationships and that all members have claims. No one can speak for another and any community is an interdependent web of relationships of which all are a part. Again, no one is autonomous with inherent, separate characteristics. All persons are born into, grow, live, and are thus defined by their community and their relations within them.

A Humanist Justice

Susan Moller Okin (1989b) defines gender as "the deeply entrenched institutionalization of sexual difference" and calls for a humanist justice where "one's sex would have no more relevance than one's eye color or the length of one's toes" (6; 171). All sex and gender roles would be eliminated. Paid and unpaid work, productive and reproductive labor, would be equally shared by men and women. Men and women would participate in all spheres of life in more or less equal numbers. This especially includes institutions of decision-making so that important social issues like abortion, rape, sexual harassment, and divorce settlement will no longer be made by institutions composed primarily of men whose power is in large part due to their advantaged position in the gender structure (171-72). Even though Okin is not very theoretical and does not incorporate other feminist scholarship in her ideas, she has some important proposals nevertheless.

On a side note, Okin could be interpreted as supporting the formal equality position described in Chapter One with her call for gender neutrality. Jean Bethke Elshtain (1992) states that "Okin endorses analyses that see in any articulation of difference a peril, a trap, and an inequality" and she "sees in difference the reprise of arguments that wind up 'confining women' " (47). But Okin is not asking for women to be treated the same as men in the present state of affairs. She calls for the present problems of gender differences to be addressed and rectified so that women and men can be treated as if their gender does not matter. One may disagree as to whether that could be possible, but most would agree that the present injustices that women face *because they are women* need to be addressed.

Okin's main point in *Justice, Gender, and the Family* is that the private sphere of women, children, and the family needs to be addressed by and included in theories of justice. This is the best road to a genderless society. Justice should be applied to the family because if not (1) gender inequality and gender injustice for women will persist, (2) equal opportunity for both sexes will be thwarted because of gender roles and stereotyping, and (3) children will not learn justice when their primary source of learning about themselves and the world—the family—is unjust. Okin tries to establish which standards of justice are appropriate to the family and supports a modified Rawlsian framework of "justice as fairness."

Okin bemoans the fact that much of recent feminist theorizing has claimed that justice and rights are masculine ways of thinking and should be discarded. Even if women and men think in different ways, both ways and ideas need to be included in any thinking about justice. And for Okin, a focus on freedom and different people's values and life choices about marriage, family, and gender are important to include. Public policies must respect different people's choices.

Regardless of people's choices, policies or the lack of policies cannot result in the vulnerability of women and children. The division of labor between the sexes should not result in injustice. Okin asks what kind of arrangements would someone in a Rawlsian original position agree to regarding marriage, parental and other domestic duties, divorce, the workplace, and the schools (174). After the veil is lifted, we have to remember that we may be feminists or traditionalists that want to keep a gender-structured society. Various views need to be accounted for. Okin thinks that the model one would arrive at under the veil would be one in which gender is absolutely minimized, with special protection built in for those who wish to follow gender-structured lives.

It is not useful to detail all the policy changes that Okin discusses, but a few examples will be noted. Okin states that shared parenting and child care would be assumed and facilitated. This means substantial changes in the workplace would need to be made. Employers would be required by law to end sexual discrimination, including sexual harassment, and provide leave for pregnancy and childbirth for women and to care for ill family members for both men and women. Large businesses should provide high-quality on-site day care and the government should give direct subsidies to parents whose income is not high enough to pay for good quality day care. In marriages in which one spouse does not work outside the home, the earnings of the employed spouse should be considered the earnings of both. But we would not do this by assuming this is this case since they are married; this is what happens presently and leaves women very vulnerable to poverty. It would be done by having the paycheck made out to both the husband and the wife. Furthermore, schools should teach students the politics of gender and students should be discouraged from following sexual stereotypes.

Okin addresses some of the pervasive present problems in our society for many women. She does not say that men and women should be treated equally and leave it there. She notes specific policies that should be implemented that will address the present problems women face. Once these are successfully implemented, women and men will have equal chances to do as they wish with their lives, once freed from stereotypes and assigned roles in the division of labor. Her ideas are a combination of treating men and women the same and differently. The present ways that men and women are treated differently need to be addressed first. Men and women need to be treated differently so that they can be treated the same, and so there can be a true system of gender neutrality, and not a false one as has been under most past and present formal equality arguments.

Unfortunately, Okin's discussion ideas for a genderless society are not very theoretical. This makes it difficult to understand the usefulness of her approach. She offers some concrete policy proposals that she thinks anyone under Rawls's veil of ignorance would choose. Everyone's point of view needs to be taken into account. The basis for her proposals is that people should strive for a society in which gender does not matter. This is accomplished by addressing the issue of justice within the family and the division of labor for women and men. A genderless family is more just because it is more just for women, it is more conducive to real equality of opportunity for women and all children, and it enables children to learn principles of justice in the earliest and most important social institution, the family. If the family is not just, how can we ever expect children and thus adults to learn, know, and implement justice in their lives?

Okin is criticized for not moving beyond liberal individualism and for not addressing the vast feminist literature on issues of gender and justice

(Held 1991;Young 1992). Okin does stay in the genre of liberalism which is still a valid form of feminism. Her work would have been richer if she had addressed other feminist literature on the subject, but this was not the intention of the book. The main aspect of her work that troubles me is that the present power structures are left intact. There are no policy proposals to change the hierarchal relations embedded in our society. Okin could believe that injecting women into the present societal institution of government and business will make them just, as her proposals for injecting men into the family structure will make it just, but I am not so convinced. Since she invokes the Rawlsian original position and veil of ignorance to address issues of justice within the family, why does she not address questions about the larger societal institutions and structures of power? Why does she not ask what type of societal structures people under the veil would choose, instead of assuming, as she critiques other theorists for doing so with the family, the present institutions? If she had done so, she may have arrived at different answers and policy proposals.

COMMON THEMES OF FEMINIST NOTIONS OF GENDER JUSTICE

As noted at the beginning of this chapter, the feminist theorists discussed herein reject the formal equality/difference framework as discussed in Chapter One. Okin (1989b) comes closest to the formal equality approach in her "humanist justice." But all agree that, presently, men and women are treated differently in society and this results in injustice and disadvantages for women much of the time. At the present time, this different treatment needs to be analyzed and the injustices need to be addressed.

So the first important matter is the issue of difference. As MacKinnon (1987) notes, the formal equality/difference framework is obsessed with sexual difference, and the difference is framed in the context of women's difference from the norm, the male. This notion of difference needs to be redefined. Difference needs to be viewed as a facet of relationships, of a comparison of two things; difference is not inherent in any one thing, person, or group. Regarding gender, women are different from men just as much as men are different from women. We should not privilege either sex and make one the definition of "normal" and the other the definition of "different." We need equal validity of men's and women's bodies, needs, and experiences.

Furthermore, it is a very tricky thing to designate the cause of difference. For gender differences, some might say that they are biological and an inherent, natural part of being female and male. Others would say that they are socially defined—a result of socialization—and still others would say that we have no idea. But if we stay away from defining the cause of difference, and view it as a facet of a comparison of two things, then we are freer to redefine and relocate difference and thus enact change.

Power and difference is also a common theme. Those with power can define difference, and thus who deserves to be counted as the same and equal and who is different and unequal. Those with power can also choose the particular traits of individuals or groups that are deemed important enough to be considered in the definition. Gender is certainly a characteristic that has been deemed important enough to define difference and sameness, and thus inequality and equality. MacKinnon (1987) notes that gender is a question or a relation of power. So if we view gender as a relevant differentiation that systematizes and institutionalizes inequality, then we can view sexual inequality as a question of dominance and oppression as Young (1990) notes. So unless we change the current conceptions of equality, difference, and gender, justice between women and men may never be achieved.

Another common theme is that difference, whatever it is and however it is defined, should not disadvantage some in the actual lived out equality of persons. The consequences of difference are important—the difference that difference makes—not so much the cause or if the differences are real or not. Just because a policy treats all equally or the same does not mean that it is neutral or that it institutes equality, equity, or justice. Therefore, we should look at results or consequences of policies many times, not just the policy itself, when analyzing a policy. A common problem is that the society in which we live has often been defined by males and with masculine needs in mind. Thus a policy that seems neutral or is supposed to treat all equally and the same can disadvantage women because the neutral policy is implemented in a biased world. One needs to examine how the policy interacts with other facets, and particularly other gendered facets, of men's and women's lives and the society at large. We do not want sexual differences to turn into inequalities, injustices, or disadvantages.

Regarding this same idea, the place to start in designing policy is to have the following goal: certain values, options, access, or distributions should be equally available to all. And because people are different in many ways, people will chose different values or options, but men's and women's choices should not be limited just because they are a man or a woman. Our goal is to have, in the end, a type of equity, equality, fairness, or justice among men and women. This means that the actual consequences of policies have to be examined to see if the policy actually makes its goods equally available to all, as discussed above. Again, just because a policy appears neutral and does not differentiate by sex does not mean that it makes its goods equally available to all.

The examination of whether women are being disadvantaged by certain policies brings me to the next point: context is very important. MacKinnon (1987) notes that before we can decide if gender should be taken into account or is important regarding a certain issue in the present, we need to know how gender has been taken into account in the past. We cannot issue a single proclamation of how to institute gender justice. In some cases, gender is important and in others it is not. We cannot arrive at *one* principle that will work in all cases. Rhode (1989) says that for any given situation, we need to analyze whether the recognition of sex-based differences is more likely to reduce or reinforce sex-based disparities in power and status. Context is also important in that a policy may help one set of women but hurt another. Thus, the recognition of the diversity of women is extremely important. Rhode states that we must ask which women benefit, by how much, and at what cost.

One issue that is very important and agreed upon by all is that the distinction between public and private needs to be reconceived or abolished. The fact that the private realm has traditionally been associated with females and has been neglected by the law has meant that many problems of women's lives have not been addressed. If important issues for women fall within the context of the family, then such problems should be potentially addressable by public policies just like any other societal problem. The private realm of the family and the home needs to be a moral and legal concern just like any other area of life. This means that issues of reproduction, child bearing, child rearing, child care, as examples, should be addressed by theories of justice and public policies.

Another important issue is that women should participate in the social institutions of power; women should participate fully with men in the making of the rules, and hence policies, by which all live. This is related to the point that everyone's perspective, views, and values should be taken into account.

No person's perspective should be privileged just because they occupy powerful positions, are wealthy, or are of a certain sex. Because many past and present policies have been made by males and have been biased, it has been shown that one group may not be able to design policies that treat all people's needs as equally valid and equally in need of being addressed. Policies, rules, and the institutions of society should be designed by people of both sexes from a variety of racial, ethnic, age, and "sexually-oriented" groups.

NOTES

1. Also see Scott (1990).

2. See Minow (1990) for a discussion of how, in many different fields of study, the "social relations" approach is being used that stresses the relationships between things rather that on the discrete things themselves.

CHAPTER 5

A New Framework for Gender Justice

In Chapters Two, Three, and Four, Rawls's theory of justice, utilitarianism, and many feminist theorists' ideas were examined. The purpose of such an analysis was to derive ideas for what a more inclusive and effective theory of gender justice might encompass. As discussed, each of the theories have some merit and address some of the needs of women. Conversely, many of the theories contain limitations or flaws. In this chapter, the various important components of gender justice that arise from an understanding of the differential effects and impacts of public policies on men and women will be discussed. A framework of gender justice will be developed that recognizes the complexity of issues surrounding the meeting of women's needs. This framework offers no simplistic solution—no universal, totalizing principle—to the problem of gender and justice. Rather, the framework of gender justice is composed of various principals and questions that we should ask of policies. It gives explicit criteria upon which to judge policies in effort to ensure that critical issues for women are not overlooked. The three principles of gender justice are self-determination, equality and gendered consequences, and diversity. Each of these are discussed below.

IMPORTANT ASPECTS OF GENDER JUSTICE

Self-Determination

Typically, contemporary theories of justice focus on the distribution of benefits and burdens, or goods, in society. This is one important aspect of justice and is useful when discussing some gender problems such as inequality of income, unequal distribution of high-status and high-paying jobs, or hours spent doing housework and taking care of children. Though a distributive focus works well for material goods or clearly identifiable items, it works less well for non-material items such as power, freedom, respect, opportunity, and participation in decision-making structures, and such issues are important for women (Young 1990). For example, domestic violence and rape are important topics in which distributive issues are not primary concerns but issues of autonomy, freedom, power, respect, and a right to live free of violence and coercion, to name a few, are.

A focus on distribution also masks the institutional context in which distributions occur, gives primacy to "having" as opposed to "doing," and makes social groups invisible. I find Iris Marion Young's (1990) example useful; she argues that when thinking about justice, one should start by thinking about injustice, and she then describes injustice as the existence of oppression and domination. Oppression is defined as the institutional constraint on self-development and domination as the institutional constraint on self-determination (37). These concepts are useful for thinking about gender justice because oppression and domination are proclamations that feminists have used for many years to describe women's situation in society and the state from which they want relief.

We can formulate corresponding components of justice to these ideas of injustice. First, justice should be concerned with the degree to which a society's institutions and policies support the structural conditions necessary for developing and exercising one's capacities; in short, supporting self-development (Young 1990). Rawls focuses on this same issue in his notion of people being free to develop rational plans of life or pursue their life plans.

A related aspect of self-development is the ability to express one's self and to have others listen and legitimate one's experience, needs, values, view of the world, and so forth. With such recognition and legitimation, one is valued or respected and can go forth in the world with some measure of self-worth and confidence that they can make a contribution. Thus, justice should also be concerned with the degree to which societal institutions and policies support the expression and recognition of people's experiences.

Third, justice should be concerned with the degree to which a society supports individuals determining or at least participating in the determination of their actions (Young 1990, 37). I label this notion democratic freedom. These three criteria will be discussed more below, but to review, the first principle of gender justice is self-determination and is composed of three criteria: self-development, recognition, and democratic freedom.

Self-Development

Developing one's abilities involves becoming the type of person one chooses and doing with one's life what one desires, and people should be given the right to do these things to some degree.[1] This is an important concept of gender justice because women have been hindered in this fashion by gender socialization, cultural constraints, reproductive concerns, educational limitations, business practices, and outright discrimination to name a few. All of these have limited what women can do with and in their lives; they have constrained women's choices. I agree with Martha Nussbaum (1995), as she quotes Aristotle, "[A] good political arrangement is one 'in accordance with which anyone whatsoever might do well and live a flourishing life' " (81).

Therefore, we should judge public policies on their ability to help women develop their capacities and abilities. Policies may need to address past constraints on women's ability to develop themselves, if appropriate, and remove past hindrances if possible. We can ask: "Does the policy contribute to the ability of women to develop their capacities and abilities?"

Recognition

The next criterion of the principle of self-determination involves women being able to express themselves or have a voice, and others recognizing and respecting that voice. Respect is an important facet of gender justice. For Rawls, self-respect is one of the most important primary goods. Without it, nothing may seem worth doing, our plans may seem of little value, one might have little will to accomplish things, and one might have no desire to pursue their life plan (Rawls 1971, 440). And our self-respect depends, at least partially, on the respect of others.

This suggests that people should pay attention to women and their needs. Martha Minow, among others, discusses the need to recognize that everyone has their own perspective and no certain person or group's perspective should dominate. Much of our present society and our governmental policies have been critiqued as privileging the male perspective. Recognition of women's experience is very important because many of women's concerns and needs have historically fallen on deaf ears. For example, the public system of unemployment compensation in the U.S. mainly benefits men when they are out of work but there is no public system of child care so that women can work in the first place; we have a public system of worker's compensation for men when they are hurt but no payment system whatsoever for traditional "women's work" of housework, child rearing, and care of other family members. Furthermore, rape has been used as a tool of terror in war for many years but only in 1996 was it recognized as a war crime—a crime against humanity—by the United Nations Court (Simons 1996). Previously, the crime of rape was not addressed and, of course, it is a crime that primarily affects women. Previously, women's experience remained invisible and "crimes against humanity" did not include women much of the time.

Public polices will never address women's concerns if policy makers do not first recognize women, their life experiences, and their needs, and then treat them as legitimate considerations. Basically, policy makers need to respect women. As Young (1990) notes, "To treat people with respect is to be prepared to listen to what they have to say or to do what they request" (57).[2] In short, if women's needs are recognized and treated as legitimate needs, they are more likely to be addressed by public policies. If women's needs remain invisible and characterized as needs that are undesirable for government to address, then their disadvantaged status may never change. So a criterion of recognition needs to be part of a framework of gender justice. Thus, we can ask of public policies: "Does the policy contribute to the ability of women to express their experiences and have them recognized and legitimated?

Democratic Freedom

The ability of women to participate in determining their actions is another important aspect of self-determination and thus of gender justice. People should be able to decide where and how they would like to live their lives and what, where, how, and under what circumstances they will act and behave; control over one's life and choices about what and how to pursue one's goals and fulfill one's desires is very important. People should experience some set of liberties or freedoms, and thus I call this criterion "democratic freedom." Individuals should be free to do as they wish, within limitations, and thus the democratic part is the insistence that people be able to participate in the defining of such limitations or restrictions. Rawls addresses this idea in his concept of the original position and all people participating in the definition of liberties for the society. This principle also recognizes the community in which we all live and should be able to participate in, as well as the power that can easily become entrenched in social relations as Minow and MacKinnon remind us.

As such, public policies should be evaluated according to their ability to help women determine their own actions. We need a governmental commitment "to a society in which women as a group are not disadvantaged in controlling their own destiny" (Rhode 1989, 4). This is important for women because part of the injustice or inequality they have historically experienced involves being controlled by others—husbands, fathers, male legislators, etc. A related aspect is that policies may need to address the specific past hindrances on women's ability to determine their own actions; policies may need to specifically address past problems and eradicate them.

Another important aspect of women determining their own actions is women's participation in the policy- and rule-making institutions of society. One reason why women's needs have been overlooked in the policy-making process is that men have filled the rule-making institutions that define what needs to address. Historically, women have had little voice in such matters. But under a framework of gender justice, women's perspectives need to be taken into account, their experiences recognized, and their concerns legitimated so that their needs can be addressed by public policies. One very important step in this direction is to have women in the rule-making institutions of society so that their needs can receive careful attention, and so women can participate in creating policies and defining the issues that policies need to address. In summary, the institution of gender justice in society requires that women gain more control over the determination of their actions and an important aspect of this is to increase the participation of women in the powerful policy-making structures. So, we should ask: "Does the policy further the ability of women to participate in determining their actions?"

Equality of Gendered Consequences

Another important principle of gender justice involves examining the actual consequences or effects of policies. We should not presume that policies produce sex-neutral outcomes just because they use sex-neutral terms; many policies have gendered consequences. Examination of the actual consequences of policies has been part of utilitarian theories for some time, and feminists have applied this idea to gender issues. Policies that treat everyone the same or equally, when instituted in an unequal world, all too often cause or reinforce existing inequalities and injustices. One example is employment practices and child care problems. Employers can and are even encouraged to hire women. All people, women and men, are (supposedly) treated the same in terms of hiring practices. But the world into which these sex-neutral hiring policies are instituted is gendered in terms of child rearing practices in that women are more often responsible for the care of young children. If a condition of employment is to be free from child care duties from nine to five, then many more women than men will not be able to fit the "sex-neutral" requirement. The supposedly sex neutral policy or the policy treating all the same really has gendered consequences when we examine its actual effect. As Rhodes (1989) states, "[W]e need not simply mandates of equal treatment for women; we need strategies to secure women's treatment as equals" (319). This involves moving toward a framework that examines the results of—the actual applications of—policies and asks if women are disadvantaged in the outcomes.[3]

As Okin reminds us, the private realm and the family need to be included when thinking about justice. Because the family has been left out of most contemporary theories of justice, it is an important missing piece that needs to be considered when thinking about gender justice. Private realm issues, including issues of reproduction, child rearing, and the importance of children learning about injustice and internalizing unjust values as a result of growing up in an unjust family, cannot be exempted. The gendered consequences of policies may quite often involve such issues.

In practice, this treatment as equals or women not being disadvantaged can suggest different things. Sometimes an unequal distribution of a policy benefit to women would be justified if it was to secure women's treatment as equals. The idea is not so much to give women more because they are disadvantaged—a sort of compensation—even though this may be the case sometimes; the idea behind this application of the principle is to give women more so as *to keep them from* being disadvantaged. In the example described above about child care and employment, the women (and men) with young children would need to be provided with child care so they are not disadvantaged in terms of employment. Then the consequences of the hiring practices would not be gendered. Some might argue that women are getting *more* in such situations, but since the goal is to have women treated as equals and not be disadvantaged in policy outcomes, the different distribution would be justified.

So we want to ask of public policies: "In the actual consequences of outcomes, do women achieve a lived-out equality or parity with men with respect to the policy's goals?

Diversity

An issue that is closely related to all of the above discussed principles is diversity. For example, an examination of whether a policy helps or hinders the recognition of women's experiences should also pay close attention to the many differences among women. It is minority women's experiences that are more likely to be discounted than white women's experiences. Also, an analysis of the actual application and outcome of a policy forces us to recognize the diversity of people and the varieties of contexts to which the policy may be applied. Almost any policy will not have the same effect on all women or all men; class, race, ethnicity, sexual orientation, disability status, religion, and so forth, are very important items to consider along with gender.

Furthermore, in recognizing the diversity of people and varieties of circumstances, we are forced to realize that one monolithic standard or guiding principle will not provide the solution to our gender justice problems. Claims of universalistic paradigms do not usually serve women's and society's diverse needs, and feminist theorists have been particularly successful in moving this point to the forefront. "Contemporary feminist theory offers no single view of our appropriate destination, but it does suggest certain preferred means of travel" (Rhode 1989, 317). A gender justice framework needs to acknowledge the diversity of women and make sure that policies address their assorted needs—hence the need for the principle of diversity. Thus, the question to ask becomes: "Does the policy recognize the diversity of women—age, class, race, ethnicity, sexual orientation, disability status, etc.—and address their differing needs?"

CONCLUSION

To summarize, the framework of gender justice includes the principles of self-determination, which is composed of the criteria of self-development, recognition, and democratic freedom; equality and gendered consequences; and diversity. This framework moves away from a focus on equality or a focus on difference. It incorporates these issues into meaningful and useful criteria that focus on what women need and how they have been hindered historically. The framework moves toward a focus on women being empowered to live their lives in the manner they see fit without losing sight of the community, responsibilities people have toward one another, and the social-relations within those communities.

The goal is to reach a society in which sexual identity does not correlate with sexual inequality. If we view gender as a relation of power, gender as a differentiation that systematizes and institutionalizes inequality, then policy questions involving gender become questions of power. Women should not be disadvantaged by the consequences or results of any given policy.

Furthermore, the framework of gender justice has not tried to derive one dominating principle; such an approach would be unrealistic and misguided. Instead, the framework has specified a few important principles that any policy will need to meet in order to be considered just. The principles start us on a new path of thinking about what a gender just society should be and what it should incorporate for women.

NOTES

1. The concepts of development, human functioning, and capabilities, as well as the implications of these criteria of justice in a world setting, are discussed in Martha Nussbaum and Jonathan Glovers' *Women, Culture, and Development* (1995).

2. Young (1990) advances the idea of recognition and respect of group differences in *Justice and the Politics of Difference*.

3. Rhode (1989) advocates the use of a principle of gender disadvantage.

PART TWO

Gender Justice and the Health Care System

Gender Justice and the Health Care System

In Part One, how many policies in the United States have been based on the male model and how most approaches to issues of gender and justice focus on formal equality or women's differences was discussed. A new framework is needed and various ideas of justice were examined for their contributions to the idea of gender justice. Important criteria that a theory of gender justice should include were outlined and questions were derived out of the principles. The importance of such a task is to have criteria by which to judge public policies—to judge how well they institute gender justice.

In Part Two, the framework is applied to health care. I evaluate two issues that are of great importance for women: one, medical research and funding for research and two, access to health care. These are two significant areas for women that have recently been acknowledged and policy proposals have been put forth to address the problems. Recent changes in the research policies of the NIH and the FDA, and President Clinton's Health Security Act have both been introduced in effort to address some of the inequities and injustices within the health care system. Though the Health Security Act was not implemented, managed care organizations have revolutionized our system of health care finance and delivery . Thus, managed care's effect on health care for women will be examined.

Health care offers a unique opportunity for the application of a theory of gender justice for many reasons. Regarding many social issues, it is sometimes difficult to discern if men and women have different needs, but regarding many health care issues, men and women clearly have different biologically-based needs: females live longer and thus need not only *different* health care but also *more* health care. It is estimated that one in nine women will develop breast cancer. But there are also many illnesses that affect men *and* women; for example, heart disease is the number one killer of all adults. Such health care issues offer excellent opportunities for analysis since there are some clear differences between men's and women's needs. In those areas in which it is clear that women and men need different care, are women having their needs met? Or are they receiving the care that a man would receive?

Moreover, medical research is a particularly potent issue to analyze because, until recently, women were systematically excluded from much research. Some of the reasons for exclusion were related to women's reproductive functions, so this topic encompasses issues of women being viewed as reproducers and women as an human beings with their own health care needs. Furthermore, medical research is important to analyze because recent policy changes have been made in an effort to implement a more just system; these can be analyzed according to the criteria of gender justice. Additionally, the health care system is in crisis and many policy proposals have been put forth to address the problems. Managed care has revolutionized how health care is delivered and an analysis of its implications for women needs to be accomplished.

CHAPTER 6

The NIH and the FDA:
Medical Research Policies and
Gender Justice

Historically, women have been excluded from and underrepresented in medical research. Medical research policy has been guided by male-centered paradigms: the assumption that women are different from men and thus need protection from the harms of research, and secondly, that the female body is similar enough to the male body that results obtained from studying men can easily be applied to women. Unfortunately, neither of these is true and so not only has there been unfairness, injustice, and inequality, there has also been disease, death, and despair for women.

In this chapter, the issue of medical research, gender, and justice will be explored. First, the history and problems of exclusion of women in medical research will be investigated. Next, an exploration of the faulty reasoning behind such policies will be undertaken. Then, newly enacted policies governing medical research will be analyzed according to the gender justice framework. The changes that managed care is bringing to the health care system will also be analyzed, as well as ideas of universal coverage and a standard benefits package.

HISTORY OF WOMEN AND MEDICAL RESEARCH

Women have been excluded from medical research since the late 1960s and early '70s. As Johnson and Fee (1994) point out, this exclusion arose from a variety of political, social, and legal forces. Emphasis on the need to protect all subjects arose in the 1950s and '60s in response to revelations of abuse of research participants by medical personnel. But particularly for women, cases of deformed infants resulting from drugs taken during pregnancy raised concerns about the inclusion of women in drug trials. In the 1960s, many women took thalidomide, a drug used to prevent early miscarriages, and the drug caused over 1,000 birth-related defects. Inadequate research standards and failure of the manufacturer to acknowledge early evidence of side effects were blamed. Also, in the 1960s and early '70s, problems from the drug DES came to light. DES is a drug that women took in the 1940s and '50s to prevent miscarriages; about 20 years later, many daughters of women who had taken the drug developed reproductive anomalies and had an increased risk of developing cancer of the vagina. From litigation brought by these daughters, the pharmaceutical companies incurred, and are still incurring, substantial costs. So in the 1960s, companies became more concerned about the liability issues surrounding the testing of drugs on women.

Furthermore, women's rights were sometimes abused and ignored. For example, in a study of the side effects of oral contraceptives, dummy pills were given to women who sought treatment to prevent further pregnancies (Goldzieher et al. 1971a and b). None of the women were told they were participating in the study, none gave their consent, and none were told they were given placebos; significantly, most of these women were poor Mexican-Americans. There are also ethical questions about the initial testing of the oral contraceptive pill that was carried out on poor Puerto Rican women (Zimmerman 1980).

People belonging to minority groups have been viewed as more expendable and used in dangerous and unhealthy research. One famous example is the Tuskegee Syphilis experiment of 400 African-American males. From 1932 to 1972, the Public Health Service (PHS) conducted a study of the effects of untreated syphilis. Poor, illiterate, Southern black men were watched for 40 years to obtain data on the progression of syphilis, and as many as 100 men died as a result of the disease (Jones 1981).[1] Most of the men were never told they had syphilis, no drugs or treatments were given or tested in this experiment, and, in fact, most of the subjects did not even know they were participating in the experiment.

In 1974, the National Research Act was passed that called for the establishment of a National Commission to Protect Human Subjects to "identify ethical principles" and "to develop guidelines" for research. Political debates over abortion, artificial reproductive technologies, and fetal tissue research also raged at the time (Johnson and Fee 1994). With the legalization of abortion in *Roe v. Wade* in 1973, the anti-abortion movement, with its emphasis on fetal rights, grew. Whether written policy or not, excluding women from most medical research became the established norm in the medical community.

In 1981, women's underrepresentation in drug trials and the problems associated with such exclusion were documented (Kinney 1981). The article noted how the Food and Drug Administration's (FDA) policies of excluding women "of childbearing potential" in early drug trial testing also led to their exclusion in later testing phases. The article received little attention and reflected the consensus of the time about the need for women, or their potential fetuses, to be "protected" from the harms of research.

In 1981, an article was published that documented women's underrepresentation in drug trials and the problems associated with such exclusion (Kinney 1981). The article noted how the Food and Drug Administration's (FDA) policies of excluding women "of childbearing potential" in early drug trial testing also led to their exclusion in later testing phases. The article received little attention and reflected the consensus of the time about the need for women to be "protected" from the harms of research.

Two years later in 1983, a PHS Task Force on Women's Health Issues held hearings across the U.S. to identify regional perspectives on women's health.[2] The task force also sponsored a symposium at the National Institutes of Health that included PHS personnel, task force members, and representatives of various national organizations with specific concerns regarding women's health. "The theme that seemed to dominate all of the regional sessions was that women's health is directly related to their access to sound information and quality medical care" (U.S. DHHS, PHS 1985, vol. II, 2). Attention was also drawn to the problems of economically disadvantaged women being medically underserved. With regard to medical research, interest was expressed for studies to include women and that there be increased attention on research and health issues that apply specifically to women's health. Furthermore, the report noted that research should be undertaken to better understand those cultural and socialization practices that affect women's health differently from that of men and that a systematic effort must be made to address gender bias issues.

WOMEN, MEDICAL RESEARCH, AND THE MALE-CENTERED PARADIGM

The past policies that have governed medical research and women were derived from a focus on women's differences from or similarities to men. Such a focus is incorrect and unjustified, and commonly leads to policies that disadvantage, or are at least not beneficial for, women.

Women as Reproducers: Damage to the Fetus

The reasoning behind precluding women from participating in medical research is that research would harm women. Women, but not men, need to be protected from the possible harmful effects of participating in clinical studies. More specifically, women have been excluded because of potential harm to a fetus that a woman might be carrying. Thus, it is not concern for women that drives this policy; it is concern for the fetus. And it is not even a *real* fetus; it is not that pregnant women are excluded. All women of childbearing potential are usually excluded. They are excluded because they *might* be pregnant and the drug or therapy *might* harm the fetus that *might* be there. And this is regardless of any woman's use of contraception or abstention from sexual activity or any specific evidence that the treatment *would* damage a fetus. The reasoning seems to be as follows: women are different from men because they can become impregnated and thus they should not participate in medical research, but it is okay for men to participate and possibly be harmed and/or damage their reproductive organs or sperm.

This raises many issues. For example, concern for a fetus and the harm that might be caused to it is a legitimate concern. In performing medical studies, we should be concerned about causing harm to any living being—any woman, man, child, or fetus. But to reduce women solely to "fetus carrying beings" and to exclude women of "fetus carrying potential" is not legitimate. Concern about the possible harmful effects of research on women should be no greater or no lesser than for any other group and should always be weighed against the potential benefits of the research.

Another issue is that women of childbearing age are treated as continually "potentially pregnant." They are a carrier or a vessel for fetuses and are not treated as human beings in their own right—as women. Because they cannot be included in activities that might harm a fetus, they also cannot be included in activities that might help them as women. Specifically, women do not get the direct benefits of participating in studies particular to them as a class. Also, all women do not get the benefit of the medical knowledge that could be obtained from women participating in studies.

A third point is that women cannot be trusted, it seems, to use contraception or to abstain from sexual activity. Most contraception is fairly effective, and abstention is 100 percent effective. Why is this not protection enough to alleviate concerns about possible damage to fetuses? Harm-free research cannot be guaranteed to any subject, man or woman, so why cannot women be informed about the risks and then take all precautions to prevent harm to the women or any potential fetus? If any particular problems do arise, they can be handled on an individual basis. Perhaps a woman may choose to have an abortion if she accidentally becomes pregnant and there is a high chance that the fetus has been damaged. Why are women not offered the same or similar treatment men are given as research subjects?

Men participate in the reproductive process, but their roles as such are not emphasized. Potentially dangerous treatments and drugs are given to men that may harm their reproductive organs. In some cases, even if a drug has shown to cause reproductive harm in male animals, it can still be tested on males if the men are informed of the risks and advised not to conceive while participating in the trial (Institute of Medicine 1994, vol. 1, 138). Studies show that various substances from occupational and pharmaceutical sources such as lead, morphine, thalidomide, caffeine, ethanol, and anesthetic gases affect the male reproductive system (Moreno 1994, 30). But never has the class of men of "reproductive potential" been excluded from studies. In fact, in one drug trial, Proscar was found to cause defects in the offspring of male laboratory animals. The male human subjects were only asked to pledge that they would use "mechanical contraception" (Moreno 1994, 32).

The desire to exclude women rests on her reproductive capability. As in many other cases throughout history, women are conveniently viewed as needing protection. This "protection" also means, for women, being precluded from exercising their full liberties and exercising freedom of choice. And women's reproductive function is used as the excuse; women's life activities need to be restricted so that women are available for reproduction. In the past, this protection has meant restricting the type and amount of work women could perform; restricting women's access to education; restricting women's ownership of property; and restricting women's access to the ballot box. Women were protected from the "strain" and damage that participating in these activities might have on their reproductive functions and any potential or actual fetus. Because women were precluded from participating in these activities, women were also denied the benefits that come from such participation: money, autonomy, influence, knowledge, and the power that flows from having these things.

More recently, women's access to family planning and abortion services has been restricted under Presidents Reagan and Bush, but somewhat restored by Clinton. In the case of abortion, women were and are restricted from controlling their own reproduction. These restrictions cause, reinforce, and/or reflect the traditional view that a woman's role is to have children, and other activities that may impinge on this function are secondary, at best.

The same reasoning is at least partially behind excluding women from medical research. Women, because of their reproductive role, need to be protected from any potential harm that participation in a medical trial might cause. Thus, women are denied the medical knowledge that could be obtained for women from participation in studies. Once again, women are precluded from participation and denied the benefits—medical knowledge and better health care for women—that could come from such participation. And, the reasoning goes, men are immune, or able to withstand such potential harm, or such harm is somehow acceptable when incurred by men. Men are able to experience the benefits, knowledge and power, that come from such participation.

Women as Deviant: The Gender-neutral Subject

Another reason researchers give for excluding women is that their monthly hormonal cycles make them more difficult to study. Clean, simple data is needed and the more alike the subjects are, the more any variation can be attributed to the treatment at hand (Dresser 1992). Even in animal testing researchers have failed to include female subjects unless the research focused on reproductive issues (Rosser 1992). Research is "complicated" by the inclusion of women; more variables and factors have to be taken into account.

Thus women are viewed as different from men and do not fit the "gender-neutral" model of the medical subject. But the neutral subject means the male subject. The clinical trial process has been modeled on males who do not become pregnant and who do not menstruate. Pregnancy and menstruation raise different concerns that are specific to women. Of course, there is no scientific reason why the model of the medical subject could not be a woman and thus have the inclusion of males be a "complication." But presently, women are labeled as different, deviant, or abnormal and thus are excluded because they do not fit the model of the clinical subject.

This is a specific case of the more general problem of men being the norm and women being the other. This is a case of false universalism and is a particular aspect of oppression (DeBruin 1994, 132). Men are not conceived of as gendered beings; they are human beings, persons, and their identity and experiences are conceived of as the standard. This makes women appear as a deviant form of human beings. Societal structures have to change—have to make special accommodations for—these individuals who do not fit the norm. There is usually resistance to such change and a common response is that if women cannot "make the grade" or "do the job," then they do not deserve to participate. If they do not have the skills, ability, or training, then they do not supposedly deserve, based on merit, the award. And, the reasoning goes, there is nothing discriminatory about this. It does not matter if you are a man or a woman; what matters is that you meet the set qualifications.

This scenario occurs frequently in the area of employment. Employment structures are designed with a conception of males as the standard. In particular, these are people who are not the primary caretakers of children, as well as people who do not conceive, carry a fetus for nine months, give birth, and breast feed. When women apply for jobs, they do not fit the model of the supposed gender-neutral employee. If one has children to care for, then she does not fit the assumed job description of being free of such duties.

Pregnancy, maternity leave, and the workplace have been fiercely debated in this country as described in Chapter One. The employment structure is not accommodating to women who need time off to give birth and care for an infant. The employment structure is not accommodating and rarely tries to meet women's child care needs. And, if a child becomes sick, most employers begrudgingly "let women off" work to care for a child. Again the test is, in the end, whether one is male or female and is free from child care duties. In medical research, the test is whether one is free from pregnancy and menstrual cycles.

Another problem is that using the male as the test subject may lead to less accurate models, not just for women but even for men. It has been found that males also have cyclical or episodic changes in virtually all hormones. Females may actually be better research subjects on two levels: first, because they have steady or rhythmic hormone cycles and thus could serve as a more predictable model for both sexes (Hoffman 1982 as cited in Rosser 1992, 131), and secondly, studying both women and men would allow researchers to compare and contrast the differences in the cyclical natures of the two and derive the benefits which often come from such analyses.

Medical studies are performed to increase our knowledge about certain diseases and conditions so people can live healthier, happier, and more productive lives. A study's potential benefit to society is supposed to be a criteria upon which governmental funding is dependent. Even if using only one homogeneous group of people (but there is no reason why this one group should always be white males) created a cleaner and easier study, findings from such studies may not be medically relevant. People come in all colors, sizes, genders, and with a variety of other biological manifestations. So studies about widespread conditions such as heart disease that use only white males do not show much promise for advancing our knowledge and benefiting society overall. Data from such studies mainly help only one group of people: white males. And even though such narrowly focused studies may sometimes be useful, such as in preliminary investigations, why are they usually performed on only white males?

If medical research is to benefit society, we need studies on women of "childbearing potential" and pregnant women. If we do not, we will never know what drugs and treatments are safe for pregnant women to undertake. For example, as of 1987, fewer than 12 drugs were specifically approved for use during pregnancy (Berlin 1987, 53). Altered physiological states such as pregnancy and breast feeding do change drug absorption, distribution, kinetics, metabolism, and excretion. There is also some concern that they may also change the mode of drug action.

Concern for testing on pregnant women is warranted; outright exclusion is not. Medical knowledge needs to be obtained so that women can get as high a quality of health care as men. This means that studies need to be performed on menstruating, pregnant, and menopausal women. The idea of the male as the gender-neutral subject needs to be replaced with a conceptualization of the subject as a gendered being. Studies should be performed on all types of people so that they can receive quality health care. The application of a gender just theory would create the kind of decision-making that would be more inclusive of women's needs.

Women are the Same As Men:
Misguided Applications of Research Results

Ironically, women are treated as being different as described above and, at the same time, treated as if they are just the same as men. Results from medical studies using only men are commonly put forth to the medical community and public as findings applicable to both men *and* women. But if women have not been included, we have no idea if the findings from such studies *are* or *are not* applicable to women. In such cases, women become the unsuspecting subjects of widespread, uncontrolled medical studies. And their health may not be helped at all; some treatments or drugs could actually harm them. For example, male-only studies of heart disease and cholesterol led the American Heart Association to recommend a diet that could actually increase the risk of heart disease for women. Furthermore, oral contraceptives can cause higher cholesterol levels, and it has *not* been proven that the cholesterol-lowering medication proven effective in men works for women when taken at the same time as oral contraceptives (Dresser 1992).

This is particularly a large problem regarding prescription and over-the-counter drugs. More than a billion prescriptions are written every year and there is unlimited self-administration of non-prescription drugs. Furthermore, one study reported that 40 percent of pregnant women use some form of legal drugs in the first semester of pregnancy (Steinbock 1994, 23), but as stated before, very few drugs are approved for use during pregnancy. How will we ever know if drugs are safe for women when researchers follow the FDA guidelines that allow them to exclude women of "childbearing potential?" If we are truly concerned about damage to fetuses, why would drugs not *fully* be tested so women could be assured of their safety?

Research performed on men and then applied to women neither minimizes risks to women nor to any potential fetus. It does not minimize risks or maximize the benefits of medical research. Treating women as if they are the same as men is unjustifiable. Treating women differently, as deviants that do not fit the ideal medical model, and which results in the practice of protection by exclusion, is also unjustifiable. Women deserve to participate in medical studies so that knowledge can be obtained to help all women.

Women As Non-participants: The Biases of Recruitment

A third set of reasons for the exclusion of women are one, the availability of women to participate in medical studies and, two, if researchers do include them, the reliability of women to correctly self-report. For example, in a study of the effects of aspirin on the occurrence of heart disease, the researchers said they wanted to include women but could not find enough to do so. Their choice of a study population was physicians over the age of forty. Also, a NIH official said that a sufficient number of women would not be "interested in participating and be content to go through the hassle of taking a placebo" (Cotton 1990).

A 1988 study of 6,000 women, the Women's Health Trial, was denied continued funding because of the methodology of the study which, after teaching the women new ways to cook and eat, relied on them to report their eating habits. Many think that the ability of the women to accurately state what they ate was questioned (Berney 1990, 24). But there are large studies of men who were taught to cut down on saturated fats and the integrity of their self-reports were not questioned. Why were men presumed to have greater integrity than women?

The first situation, the availability of women to participate, is an example of the past discrimination of women resulting in and being used to justify present discrimination. Regarding the study discussed above on the effects of aspirin using physicians over the age of forty, the researchers stated that while they wanted to include women, they were unable to find enough potential subjects to do so (Dresser 1992). Of course it is probably true that there were not as many female doctors over the age of forty, given past discriminatory practices, as there are male doctors over forty. The researchers may have needed to broaden the geographical area from which they drew participants so they could find more female doctors. But why could they not also include nurses, which are predominantly women, in their study? Why did the researchers want to include only medical personnel in the first place? It is difficult to believe that a valid justification existed for such a choice.

Though not usually cited by the medical community as a reason for excluding women, one can imagine that child care may be a problem for many women. Researchers may need to have quality child care available for women when they come to the research facilities. And if such care is not provided, past discrimination is, once again, justifying present discrimination. Women have been given the role of child rearing and have had their freedom, wealth, influence, and power in society reduced, at least partially, as a result. Because they now have children to care for and have to endure the injustices that result from this fact, researchers should not be allowed to compound the problem. Researchers should not be allowed to exclude women who have children to care for by not offering child care services for them.

The second argument that women may not correctly self-report is, at face value, nonsensical. Why should men be trusted to give true answers and women mistrusted? There are certainly problems with any questionnaire or measures that require people to give honest answers, but there is no reason why such problems would be more applicable to women than to men.

Policies have excluded women from medical research because they are primarily viewed as reproducers, as deviant from the "gender-neutral" male subject, and as unwilling or unavailable to participate. But when it comes the application of research results—namely, medical and pharmaceutical knowledge—women are viewed as being no different from men and diagnosis and treatment is made accordingly. These policies and practices result in unjust treatment for women.

INADEQUATE ATTENTION TO WOMEN'S HEALTH ISSUES

In 1987, only 13.5 percent of the NIH budget was devoted to the broadly defined area of women's health issues. And this was up eight percent from the year before (Berney 1990). Many claim that medical research and the NIH budget favors male diseases over female diseases. Furthermore, many diseases that occur in men and women are presented as male diseases. Heart disease is the best example of such a case. Of course, the lack of research on women may cause or contribute to this problem because there may be no diagnostic criteria for women. Some diseases may occur in men and women but manifest themselves differently and thus women show different symptoms that the medical professional does not recognize.

Breast cancer has doubled in incidence since the 1960s. Presently, a woman has a one in nine chance of developing the disease. The disease strikes 180,000 people a year and kills 46,000, almost all women. In 1988, the NIH stopped a major study on breast cancer and low-fat diets because of cost considerations. In 1989, $16 million was devoted to basic research on breast cancer at the National Cancer Institute. In 1990, $18 million was spent on basic research (Auerbach 1992). After hard lobbying efforts by women's rights and women's health advocates, in 1994 the National Cancer Institute planned to spend $263 million studying breast cancer. The breast cancer research budget has almost tripled since 1991 (Lauver 1994). Today, breast cancer is receiving widespread attention and study, unlike many years before.

Of course there are many problems still with breast cancer research, but funding for and study of it has increased and it has received widespread attention. Other important women's health issues have not been so lucky. Some other issues regrading women's health concerns where women's needs have not been adequately addressed are discussed below.

Women as Reproducers: Responsible for the Difference

When women's health issues are pursued, Sherwin (1992) notes, it is usually concentrated on reproductive matters. This reinforces a view of women as principally defined in terms of their childbearing function. In fact, this is one area in which women have received a disproportionately large share of research attention. Examples of this type of research are studies of in-vitro fertilization, artificial insemination, and amniocentesis; such clinical research has resulted in the increasing medicalization and control of women's pregnancy, labor, and childbirth (Rosser 1992). Furthermore, almost all contraceptive research has explored means of controlling female fertility and ways to control male fertility are rarely investigated. Similarly, efforts to treat infertility have focused on procedures that can be done to women, even when the fertility problem is associated with such male conditions as low sperm count (Klein 1989).

A disproportionate share of the burden, risks, expenses, and responsibility for managing fertility now belongs to women, in part because this is where the knowledge base lies. This is unjust in that it disadvantages women. Women are defined by their main difference from men—their biological capability of conceiving and giving birth. It perpetuates the view of women as reproducers and discounting the role of men. Once again, policy is being driven by women's difference from men.

Sherwin (1994) notes that this problem specifically, and women's oppressed status in general, is inseparable from their traditionally assigned roles in the spheres of sexuality and reproduction. The concentration of medical research on women's reproductive role not only assumes the conventional view that women are continually available and responsible for reproduction, it also legitimizes, reinforces, and further entrenches such views and attitudes that accompany them, such as employment and child care issues and sexual harassment. Furthermore, sometimes the knowledge is used by those in power to regulate and control women's reproduction and fertility through population control programs and sterilization of women who are deemed unsuitable mothers (Sherwin 1994, 14). And all women are not affected equally by the knowledge produced from studies of women's reproduction. Those who are poor, belong to minority groups, or mentally disabled are at a far higher risk of imposed contraception or sterilization than are privileged white women. Furthermore, reproductive technologies aimed at facilitating conception are usually only available to the most affluent and advantaged women in society.

Women and Inadequate Testing: Women are Lesser Beings

Past cases have shown that prior adequate testing of some contraceptive devices or drugs have not been performed. The Dalkon Shield and early doses of birth control pills are two such examples. DES and thalidomide, drugs prescribed during pregnancies, are also examples of treatments offered to women without adequate prior medical research to study their effectiveness and safety.

Breast implants are another example. In use since the 1960s, breast implants were exempted from pre-market testing by a "grandfather clause" in the Medical Device Amendments of 1976. After many problems, in April 1992, the FDA banned the use of silicone implants except to women who are participating in clinical trials. This was after the FDA requested silicone implant manufacturers to provide evidence that the implants were safe and effective. Now the implants are finally being tested for their safety.

Oppression involves a society devaluing the interests of those who are oppressed. There is significant danger that victims of oppression may face higher risk of harm when they are singled out for new, unproven treatments. When dealing with treatments specifically for historically oppressed groups, it is especially important to ensure that the patient's interests are protected. Regulations demanding testing and monitoring before therapies are mass marketed to oppressed groups may be necessary to improve safety standards.

Women in Relation to "The Privileged Diseases"

A justice model that concerns itself with oppression also allows us to object to the fact that most health research is aimed at conditions that affect the most privileged. For example, there is little research done on lupus, a disease that is found three times as often in African-American women than in the general population (Jones 1990). Also, even though AIDS has received funding, little research has been done regarding women and AIDS, despite the fact that women are the fastest growing group with AIDS, and African-American women face a risk 12 times higher than the general population. Hypertension afflicts one out of three African-Americans and the American Heart Association says that African-Americans have a 60 percent greater chance of dying from stroke and coronary heart disease than whites because of high blood pressure (Sherrod 1990). But little research is performed on this disease in comparison to the number of people it afflicts.

Furthermore, the bulk of research is performed around a model of crisis intervention rather than prevention. Thus, even though the links between poverty and illnesses are well known, efforts are concentrated on developing ways to respond to illnesses rather than preventing them in the first place. Too many studies explore expensive, highly technological solutions which, even if successful, will be accessible to only a small proportion of the population (Sherwin 1994). In general, research agendas usually reflect the interests, power, and privilege of those who set them; they are seldom defined by the health needs or interests of those most marginalized in society.

So most clinical studies tend to produce knowledge that strengthens the health and opportunity of those who are well placed in society. This is why one of ORWH's goals is to bring more women into biomedical careers.

A gender just system will challenge the process by which research agendas are set and research programs are carried out. As Sherwin (1994) notes, we may need to rethink current views of research as an objective, technical activity in which investigators belong to an elite group of knowledgeable scientists and subjects are regarded as their passive research tools. As Sandra Harding (1991) notes, we may need to think of research as a collegial activity in which subjects and researchers negotiate the terms of participation to achieve a shared commitment to the success of the activity. Possibly models of participatory democracy in which those who have a stake in the research help to formulate priorities could be adopted. Women not only need to be included as subjects, they also need to be included as investigators and active participants in setting the research agenda.

The So-called "Male" Diseases

Heart Disease

Heart disease is the number one killer of men *and* women and has been since 1908. Every year, 2.5 million American women are hospitalized for heart disease and about 250,000 die from it. But despite these statistics, the common conception is that mostly men have heart attacks, women do not contract heart disease as often, and it is not as serious (Institute of Medicine 1994, vol. 1, 64). Some might have the impression that breast cancer is the major killer of women because it is a female disease and has recently been widely publicized. Yet, only 46,000 women die each year from breast cancer, compared to 250,000 from heart disease.[5] Nevertheless, medical research on heart disease has predominantly been done on male subjects.

Heart disease strikes women later in life and half of all women, but only 31 percent of men, die within one year of having a heart attack (U.S. DHHS 1992, 9). It predominantly strikes postmenopausal women. It is thought that the loss of estrogen, which seems to have a protective effect, is the cause. The rates of death are higher for African-American women up until age 75, but higher among white women thereafter. Furthermore, heart problems are found more often in African-American women who have had several children. Hispanic and Native American women have remarkably less cardiovascular disease than white and black women.

There is much evidence that men and women differ in terms of risk factors, risk modifications, diagnosis, and treatment of heart disease (U.S. DHHS, ORWH 1992, 176). Most importantly, men and women differ in their initial manifestation of the disease, thus showing different symptoms. Blood cholesterol levels seem to play a different role in female patients. Recently, Estrogen Replacement Therapy has received attention for its possible effects of reducing heart disease in women. Much more research needs to be done in this area; the results are not conclusive at this point in time. And the safety of Estrogen Replacement Therapy on a long-term basis has not been proven. Recent research has shown that it may increase one's chances of having breast cancer.

Studies have shown that women are less likely to be referred for bypass surgery and cardiac catheterization and are more likely to have their symptoms dismissed as non-cardiac or just in their heads. Male patients are ten times more likely to be referred for further testing.[6]

Heart disease has been perceived as a male disease. This is a cause and an effect of the fact that women have been excluded from most major studies of the disease. Insufficient attention is given to the subject of women and heart disease with the result that more women suffer and die.

AIDS

AIDS is another area in which critics claim that women have been ignored. When AIDS was first discovered in 1981, it was primarily found in homosexual men, even though the first reported case of AIDS in a woman also occurred in 1981. Even though many more men have AIDS than women, presently women are the fastest growing group of people infected with the virus. This rapid growth started in 1986. From October 1992 to September 1993, according to the Centers for Disease Control, the number of reported AIDS cases in women more than doubled. Women also die faster than men after being diagnosed as having AIDS (Auerbach 1992). Furthermore, in 1992, heterosexual contact surpassed intravenous drug use as the primary mode of transmission for women and young women are more susceptible to infection during heterosexual contact than men. A United Nations report stated, "Suddenly we see young women emerging as the next leading edge of the epidemic" ("U.N. Finds Teen-Age Girls at High Risk of

AIDS" 1993). Moreover, the disease more often afflicts minority women. In the United States, about 20 percent of women with the disease are Hispanic, 25 percent are white, and most of the remaining—over 50 percent—are African-American women.

The response of research on AIDS has not kept pace with the spread of the disease among women. This delay in examining how AIDS manifests itself in women has caused women's conditions to be excluded from the list of conditions defined by the Centers for Disease Control (Institute of Medicine 1994, vol. 1, 66). This exclusion has resulted in denial of benefits and treatment programs for women. AIDS affects women differently than it does men and thus they have been left out of research, treatments, and possible benefits available for people with AIDS. Women have been defined as not having AIDS because they did not fit the male model of an AIDS patient.

And when women have been studied, it has usually been with a focus on how women transmit the virus to a fetus. Furthermore, until recently, hardly any research was done on what women can do to reduce their chances of contracting AIDS through heterosexual contact and how the disease progresses and manifests itself in women.

In 1993, a new definition of AIDS was given by the Centers for Disease Control after much criticism that the old definition was ignoring symptoms peculiar to women. The new definition added symptoms that included tuberculosis of the lungs, recurrent pneumonia, invasive cervical cancer, and a dip in the body's immune cells (CD4s) to 200. These diseases are more common to women and IV drug users; the old list of symptoms from 1987 was more applicable to homosexual men. In the first quarter of 1993, 60 percent of the new AIDS cases fell under the new definition, and reported cases was up 204 percent from the same quarter of the previous year.

In July 1993, the government relaxed the Social Security rules defining who is disabled and thus qualified to receive benefits. These new regulations recognize many infections from AIDS that are specific to women, like pelvic inflammatory disease and cervical cancer. The new rules state that officials must carefully examine medical evidence and be aware of the variety of medical conditions specific to or common in women with HIV.

In 1994, the first major federal study of AIDS and women began. Some research has recently begun on finding a substance that women could insert into their vagina that would kill HIV or prevent it from infecting cells.

Finally, women are starting to be recognized as victims of the disease. Finally, HIV infected women, because they are different from HIV infected males, are no longer invisible.

The Female Diseases

Osteoporosis

Many criticize the NIH and other research agencies for not focusing enough attention on osteoporosis which is primarily a woman's disease, even though 20 percent of osteoporosis sufferers are men. About 66 percent of women aged 60-64 have osteoporosis, rising continually with age until nearly 90 percent of women aged 75 and over have osteoporosis. Bone fractures are the most common consequence of osteoporosis, which occur at the rate of 1.3 million per year (U.S. Congress, House 1990). And even though the fractures are not a major cause of death, women who are hospitalized for fractures have a mortality rate as high as 30 percent from complications.

Osteoporosis is preventable and more research is needed on preventive measures. In 1985, only $5 million was spent on the disease, increasing to around $20 million in 1990. But it costs the nation $10 billion a year and 200,000 people are hospitalized with the disease per year (U.S. Congress, House 1990).

It is thought that Estrogen Replacement Therapy (ERT) may help stop the loss of bone mass, but the effectiveness has not been adequately tested. There is also concern that ERT increases a woman's risk of developing endometrial and breast cancer. Since ERT might also reduce a woman's chance of developing heart disease, this is something that deserves much study. The Women's Health Initiative will study diet, calcium supplementation, ERT, the loss of bone mass, and the development of heart disease.

There are many other diseases that are more prevalent in women, such as Alzheimer's disease, depression, diabetes, and arthritis. The above cited diseases are examples of the insufficient attention given to women's health issues. Once again, women are not the same as men and thus need to have diseases that affect both men and women studied in both men and women. Also, diseases that occur primarily in women deserve adequate attention, study, and funding. The Women's Health Initiative is one recent effort aimed at eradicating this injustice. But other initiatives have also improved medical research for women.

THE NATIONAL INSTITUTES OF HEALTH (NIH)

Even though the 1985 PHS report discussed earlier received little attention and most of the recommendations were never addressed, in 1986, an NIH Advisory Committee on Women's Health Issues was established and announced a policy that "*urged* grant applicants to consider the inclusion of women in the study populations of all clinical research efforts" (U.S. GAO 1990; emphasis mine). It also stated that if women were not to be included, a clear rational for their exclusion needed to be made, and that researchers should evaluate gender differences in their studies. But despite these directives, little changed within NIH or the research proposals it funded.

The real catalyst of the current surge in attention to women's health research was a 1990 General Accounting Office (GAO) report on the progress of the 1986-87 NIH policy (Auerbach 1992). By this time, the women's health movement had gained force and was pressuring Congress for changes in many aspects of health care policy; the Congressional Caucus for Women's Issues was a strong force in this campaign and requested the GAO report. The 1990 report noted that little progress had been made in carrying out the 1986-87 policy: the new directive had not been well communicated nor understood within the NIH and the scientific community, the directive had been applied inconsistently, and NIH had been very slow to implement it. In fact, the application booklet used by most NIH grant applicants was not even updated to include the new information regarding gender until April 1991, over four years after the policy was first developed. Furthermore, the GAO report stated that the component of gender analysis—the evaluation of gender differences in a study—had not been implemented, and it was impossible to determine the impact of the policy as a whole because implementation began so late and no data had been kept on the gender composition of funded studies.

Throughout the early 1990s at the urging of women's health advocates, legislative packages were introduced in Congress that addressed women's health concerns regarding research, care, and prevention issues. In 1990, the Office of Research on Women's Health (ORWH) was established within the NIH and was given the mandate to ensure that research supported by NIH includes important issues that pertain to women's health, to ensure appropriate participation of women in clinical research that is supported by the NIH,[3] and to increase the participation of women in biomedical careers.

In 1991, the NIH also established the Women's Health Initiative (WHI), a 14-year, $625 million effort to study approximately 150,000 women at 45 clinical centers across the United States. The WHI is the largest research study ever funded by the NIH. Furthermore, in 1993 the NIH Revitalization Act was signed into law that, among other things, authorized additional funding for breast, ovarian, and other reproductive cancers, and osteoporosis.

As part of this 1993 NIH Act and internal NIH policy changes, medical research policies regarding women and minorities were drastically revamped in the early 1990s. Now all applications, both for intramural and extramural research, are *required* to include women and minorities as research subjects.[4] "In conducting or supporting clinical research for purposes of this title . . . the Director of NIH shall . . . ensure that—(A) women are included as subjects in each project of such research; and (B) members of minority groups are included as subjects is such research" (NIH Revitalization Act of 1993). The Act also requires that a valid analysis be carried out to show whether the variables being studied affect the various subpopulations in different ways. Exemptions are allowed in cases where the research is inappropriate with respect to the health of the subjects, the purpose of the research, or other circumstances determined by NIH (NIH Revitalization Act of 1993). The 1993 Act also requires that a "data system for the collection, storage, analysis, retrieval, and dissemination of information regarding research on women's health that is conducted or supported by the national research institutes" be established (Institute of Medicine 1994, vol. 1, 68). In 1994, the NIH issued new guidelines for the inclusion of women in medical research in accordance with the 1993 Act (U.S. DHHS, NIH 1994a).

NIH also published an "Outreach Notebook." The Notebook is not law but was published in effort to help researchers understand and implement the new guidelines. It offers suggestions for deciding how to include women and minorities and recruitment strategies for obtaining such subjects. The ORWH held conferences with Institutional Review Board (IRB) chairs in 1994 and again in 1996 to discuss and assess the progress of the implementation of the guidelines.[5] Also, as of February 1996, the ORWH has 5,000 clinical studies in its database and has issued preliminary results about the implementation and success regarding the inclusion of women and minorities in clinical research supported by NIH.

Presently, NIH will not fund "any grant, cooperative agreement, or contract or support any intramural project to be conducted or funded in Fiscal Year 1995 and thereafter which does not comply" with the new policy regarding the inclusion of women and minorities. Furthermore, researchers must report annually on the gender and ethnicity of the enrolled research participants (U.S. DHHS, NIH 1994a, 14509).

THE FOOD AND DRUG ADMINISTRATION (FDA)

Before reviewing the FDA policies regarding gender and research, it is important to note the differences between the NIH and FDA. The NIH funds medical research; as with any grant process, researchers submit detailed proposals that are reviewed and deemed fundable or not fundable, as judged by various criteria. The FDA does not fund research. It issues guidelines as an aid to organizations, typically pharmaceutical companies, involved in the evaluation of new drugs and medical devices for FDA approval. FDA guidelines specify information they expect new applications to include.[6] In addition, the NIH conducts its own research—intramural research; the FDA does not. The FDA is only a regulatory agency with a mission of ensuring that drugs and medical devices are safe and effective. The agency sets parameters for the studies it reviews as part of the approval process for a new drug, but it does not usually ask that studies on certain drugs or devices be performed.

The FDA's 1977 guidelines stated that pregnant women and "women who are at risk for becoming pregnant" should be excluded from Phase I studies. They further recommended that women of "childbearing potential" be excluded from large-scale clinical trials, which includes Phase III studies, until the FDA Animal Reproduction tests have been performed (Institute of Medicine 1994, vol. 1, 137). Then, "if adequate information of efficacy and relative safety has been amassed during Phase II, women of childbearing potential *may* be included in further studies" (U.S. DHEW 1977; emphasis mine). "Childbearing potential" is broadly defined as a "premenopausal female capable of becoming pregnant." Included in this category are women who are using contraception, celibate, lesbian, and women whose male partners have been vasectomized.

In 1992, at the urging of women's health advocates, Congress asked the GAO to investigate the FDA and the inclusion of women in drug and medical device research. The GAO report noted that women were underrepresented in drug trials and recommended that the FDA revise its policy to ensure the appropriate participation of women and to ensure that gender analyses are performed.

In 1993, as a result of this report and public criticism, the FDA issued new guidelines (U.S. DHHS, FDA 1993). The guidelines state that subjects in a given clinical study should reflect the population that will receive the drug when it is marketed, and *suggest* that subjects include both genders in the same trial so that direct comparisons can be made. The FDA expects there to be an analysis of gender differences in terms of effectiveness and adverse effects of the drug. Though the 1977 guideline about excluding women of "childbearing potential" is lifted, the new guidelines do not *require* that women be included in the early phases of drug trials.

The new FDA guidelines specify precautions that are to be taken in clinical trials that include women of childbearing potential. Investigators should obtain the informed consent of the women, and the investigator should advise participants to take precautions to prevent the exposure of a fetus to potentially toxic drugs. Information should be provided about the risk of fetal toxicity and should recommend the use of contraception or abstinence. But the guidelines still recommend that large-scale exposure of women of childbearing potential should not take place until after the results of animal toxicity tests are analyzed.

The guidelines also contain exceptions and other provisions that weaken their ability to affect change in how drug research is actually performed. For example, the guidelines state that the FDA does not perceive a need "for requiring that women in general or women of childbearing potential be included in particular trials" (39408; also see Rothenberg 1996, note 262). Also the guidelines do not have the force of law; they are only recommended procedures to be followed and may or may not affect the approval of the drug. The FDA recognizes this drawback and states, "[T]he change in FDA's policy will not, by itself, cause drug companies or IRB's to alter restrictions they might impose on the participation of women of childbearing potential" (39408; see also Rothenberg 1996, 1241). It further states that it is "confident that the interplay of ethical, social, medical, legal, and political forces will allow greater participation of women in the early stages of clinical trials" (39408-09). The FDA is only "determined to remove the unnecessary Federal impediment to inclusion of women. . . ." (39409). Moreover, no FDA policy mentions or addresses the need for more research on drugs and devices that could particularly benefit women, such as breast cancer drugs or more reproductive control devices.

In conclusion, by 1993 the NIH and FDA had revised their policies regarding the inclusion of women in clinical trials, though the NIH has enacted more radical alterations; most importantly, the NIH regulations are written into law and no research will be funded that does not adhere to them. We have no similar guarantee with the FDA policy changes and do not know if the FDA will continue to approve drugs that have been tested in trials that exclude or underrepresent women. As one author noted, the NIH has moved from "encouragement to requirement" and the FDA has moved from "exclusion to encouragement" (Rothenberg 1996, 1230 and 1236).

GENDER JUSTICE AND MEDICAL RESEARCH: RECENT CHANGES IN POLICIES REGARDING WOMAN AND MEDICAL RESEARCH

The recent laws and guidelines that compose the new policy regarding the inclusion of women in medical research will be examined according to the criteria of the new gender justice paradigm developed in Part One. Have the new policies rectified the gender injustices? Do the new policies meet the criteria laid out in Chapter Five for a gender just policy?

A few general comments are in order before examining the specific questions. The policy states that women are to be included in research. NIH must "(e)nsure that women and members of minorities and their subpopulations are included in all human subject research" (U.S. DHHS, NIH, 1994a, 14508). This is a first large and necessary step. No longer are women to be excluded simply because they are women. The issue of addressing women's needs is more complex. Treating health concerns, or any other policy issue for that matter, like a recipe—"just add women and stir"—and health policy will improve is much too simplistic. The solution does not become one of simply including women, nor is the answer to just treat women differently from men. Neither approach will result in policy that really meets women's needs.

ARE THE NIH AND FDA MEDICAL RESEARCH POLICIES GENDER JUST?

Principle of Self-Determination

Self-Development

The question to ask about self-development is "does the policy contribute to the ability of women to develop their capacities and abilities?" So what might this mean with regards to medical research policy? First, the purpose of medical research is to provide information to help all humans live healthier lives. The information obtained from small groups of subjects (trial participants) provides knowledge about diseases and treatments that can potentially help all of us. Also, clinical trials offer the potential benefit of new treatments or drugs to the actual participants in the research. Therefore, research helps people live healthier lives and healthier people are better able to develop their capacities and abilities. Health is a first-order need like food and shelter, that needs to be addressed so that humans can satisfy higher-order needs.[7] So medical research on some women provides information to help all women live healthier lives. And women need information from studies done *on women* to know how diseases progress and manifest themselves within the female body. This, of course, contributes to their ability to develop their capacities and abilities. The healthier one is, both mentally and physically, the better situated one is to develop one's self.

We should also be concerned with the specific topics that are being studied. Women want and need information about diseases and conditions that affect women. Some of these diseases may also affect men—perhaps in similar ways or perhaps in different ways—and some of the female problems may not occur, or only rarely occur, in men. Any research that utilizes women as subjects needs to be part of a valid and scientific project that will yield useful results for women. Precaution is needed so that women are not used as guinea pigs for illegitimate experiments or for legitimate experiments on subjects that are not useful for women. Furthermore, even if it is a valid, scientific project on matters that are beneficial for women and includes female subjects, the data must also be collected and analyzed in a way that takes into account gender differences. In other words, gender must be a variable by which the data are analyzed so we can know if differences exist between men and women regarding the disease, treatment, drug, therapy, etc. In addition, women need information from different races and ages of women to know how race or age may affect the presence or progression of a disease or the treatment of it with a drug. Just as medical knowledge needs to encompass both sexes as not to be biased, it also needs to encompass different ethnic and age groups so that we do not only obtain information about, for example, middle-class, middle-aged white women.

Only if research is performed in this fashion will it provide useful results for women that will contribute to their ability to develop themselves. So, much of the analysis of the new policies and gender justice turns on whether or not these precautions are being taken and extra efforts are being made. First the NIH policy will be evaluated according to the criteria of development and secondly the FDA policy will be analyzed.

NIH

The 1994 NIH guidelines state that one of the major purposes of the new regulations is, for Phase III clinical trials, to "ensure that women and minorities and their subpopulations" are included "such that valid analyses of differences in intervention effect can be accomplished" (U.S. DHHS, NIH 1994a, 14508). They go on to state that "it is imperative to determine whether the intervention or therapy being studied affects women or men or members of minority groups and their subpopulations differently" (14508). These guidelines are "intended to ensure that all future NIH-supported biomedical and behavioral research involving human subjects will be carried out in a manner sufficient to elicit information about individuals of both genders and the diverse racial and ethnic groups and, in the case of clinical trials, to examine differential effects on such groups" (14508). The requirement of participation of different gender and race/ethnicity groups is with the goal of "detecting major qualitative differences (if they exist) among gender and racial/ethnic subgroups. . . . Other interpretations may not serve as well the health of women" (14512). So the guidelines are implementing policies to ensure that women are included and that studies contain an analysis of the gender differences.

The NIH guidelines also explain that the term "valid analysis" of gender and minority differences means an "unbiased assessment," an assessment that "will, on average, yield the correct estimate of the difference in outcomes between the two groups of subjects," and it "does not need to have a high statistical power for detecting a stated effect" (14511). The principal requirements for a valid analysis are:

- Allocation of the study participants of both genders and from different racial/ethnic groups to the intervention and control groups by an unbiased process such as randomization
- Unbiased evaluation of the outcome(s) of study participants, and
- Use of unbiased statistical analyses and proper methods of the inference to estimate and compare the intervention to estimate and compare the intervention effects among the gender and racial/ethnic groups. (14511)

Thus, the guidelines require that women be included and that gender and racial differences be detected if they do indeed exist. These detailed instructions prevent any misinterpretation of the policy and help assure that researchers adhere to it.

The NIH guidelines also address the issue of when women and minorities can and cannot be excluded. Cost is not an acceptable reason. Women and minorities must be included "unless a clear and compelling rationale and justification establishes to the satisfaction of the relevant Institute/Center Director that inclusion is *inappropriate* with respect to the health of the subjects or the purpose of the research" (14509, emphasis added); furthermore, if inclusion would duplicate data from other sources, certain groups may be excluded. These reasons appear to be "catch all" categories for various issues that may arise that would deem inclusion of women and minorities inappropriate and unless abused, are not problematical. But a trial may also include "only one gender where the disease, disorders, or conditions are gender specific. In all other cases, there should be approximately equal numbers of both sexes in studies of populations and subpopulations at risk, unless different proportions are appropriate because of the known prevalence, incidence, morbidity, mortality rates, or expected intervention effect" (14512). This allows for only women or only men to be included in a study if the condition only affects one group, and it also allows for more women to be included if the condition affects more women. Equality when appropriate, and "inequality," to phrase it in one way, when appropriate allows men's and women's various health needs to be met. This will provide medical knowledge that will truly be beneficial for women, help them live healthier lives, and help them develop their capacities and abilities. Yes, this is gender justice.

FDA

With regards to the FDA policy, the language used regarding the inclusion women is much weaker. The FDA guidelines request that women, even those with childbearing capabilities, be included and state that men and women should be included in drug studies if both sexes would receive the drug when marketed. In fact, the population of a clinical study should reflect the population that will receive the drug when it is marketed. Furthermore, the FDA uses the weaker language of *expecting* that an analysis of gender differences be included as opposed to *requiring* it. Unfortunately, this is only a reiteration of a 1988 guideline,[8] and in 1992 the GAO found that in clinical trials (for new drugs), more than one-half of the studies did not analyze the results for gender-related effects. The GAO recommended that the FDA *require* drug manufacturers to analyze trial data by gender (13; emphasis added). As already noted, the FDA did not change its policy and only *expects* that such analyses be included.

The GAO also found that women were included in most drug trials but were underrepresented; women were not represented in the trial in the same proportion to the women in the general population that experience the disease or condition. The 1993 FDA guidelines do provide more explicit information regarding FDA's expectations about the inclusion of both genders and the basis for the expectations so as to help drug researchers attain a better understanding. But it never states that new drug applications will be rejected if this information is lacking. Furthermore, the 1993 guidelines do not provide any information as to what constitutes an adequate representation of women in trials, despite the fact that the 1992 GAO report found that drug researchers were unclear about this and recommended that the FDA "tell drug manufacturers how to determine when enough women are included in drug trials. . . ." (13) In general, the new FDA research policy is an improvement over prior policy but is fairly weak. The policy purports to have women included but it is difficult to make such a judgement since the policy offers no assurance of this or that gender differences will be analyzed. The recommendation or expectation is not absolute. Overall, the FDA has made some progress toward a gender just policy but the improvements only slightly further the self-development of women.

Recognition

The question to ask regarding the principle of recognition is "does the policy contribute to the ability of women to express their experiences and have them recognized and legitimated? So how would medical research policies fulfill the criterion of recognition? One important issue is the recognition of the past problems of women and medical research. As discussed previously, women and minorities have been used in abusive research which, in part, led to the later exclusion of women. Because of this past exclusion and abuse, women, and especially minority women, may be hesitant to participate, so researchers will need to make extra efforts to recruit and retain them.

Women may also not want to participate because medical research involves doctors—typically white, male doctors—and many women have not had successful experiences with regard to doctors listening to their problems and treating them as legitimate issues.[9] For example, a Commonwealth Fund survey found that one in four women reported they had been "talked down to" or treated like a child by a physician, one in five had been told a medical condition was "all in your head," and 41 percent of the women had changed their physician because of dissatisfaction as compared to only 27 percent of men (Commonwealth Fund 1993). Women may fear coercion or belittlement and may not want to willingly subject themselves to a potentially oppressive situation. In addition, women may find participation difficult because of child care and family duties, as well as job commitments. Women's life experience regarding these matters needs to be recognized and addressed by the NIH and FDA policies if medical research is to be truly inclusive.

NIH

In noting important factors for the successful recruitment and retention of women, the NIH Outreach Notebook suggests that researchers recruit female, minority investigators and staff for the project. It is thought that having more women researchers will help increase the attention given to women's issues and needs, as well as make female subjects feel more at ease and thus join and stay with the project.

The NIH guidelines state that with regard to recruitment strategies, "the purpose should be to establish a relationship between the investigator(s) and staff(s) and populations and communities of interest such that mutual benefit is derived for participants in the study" (U.S. DHHS, NIH 1994a, 14510). The outreach efforts should represent a thoughtful and culturally sensitive plan of outreach and generally include involvement of other individuals and organization relevant to the populations and communities of interest, e.g. family, religious organizations, community leaders and informal gatekeepers, and public and private institutions and organizations. The objective is to establish appropriate lines of communication and cooperation to build mutual trust and cooperation such that both the study and the participants benefit from such collaboration. (14511-512)

Furthermore, the Outreach Notebook specifically notes that many people of color remember the Tuskegee Experiment and will be skeptical about participating; past abuses are well known in these communities. The Notebook suggests gaining the trust of opinion leaders and then they may serve as a link to many people of color.

The use of terms such as "mutual benefit," "culturally sensitive plan," and "cooperation to build mutual trust" show respect for the trial participants and recognition of possible gender or culture problems for the investigator. The mention of the Tuskegee Experiment shows an important recognition of people of color's experience and legitimates the skepticism that many may feel about participation. If these suggestions are followed, such efforts should ease some women's hesitation.

The NIH Outreach Notebook also notes that "[i]n some instances, women may wish to share their decision to participate with family members or others in the community" (U.S. DHHS, NIH 1994b, 9). Furthermore, the Notebook states that other factors may affect the ability of differing aged women and family statuses to participate, such as child care, location of research site and ease of access and transportation, and time off work. These factors should be weighed when designing recruitment and retention strategies (9).

Recognition of the above-described issues is a very positive step for women and contributes to the recognition and legitimation of women's experiences. Of particular importance is the recognition of child care issues.

Again, since costs can not be considered a reason for exclusion, the non-provision of child care for study participants should not be an excuse either. And because women are more likely than men to have lower-status and lower-paying jobs that make taking time off more difficult, the Outreach Notebook states that researchers should consider such issues when designing recruitment plans.

Overall, women's needs that previously were invisible, unaddressed, and partially formed the basis of their exclusion from research, are now recognized and legitimated. Investigators are now instructed to address these areas and they are directed that such reasons cannot form the basis for women's exclusion. In terms of gender justice and the criterion of recognition, this is a great improvement over prior guidelines, prior medical research practices, and many other public policies; overall the NIH has made substantial progress.

FDA

Unfortunately, the FDA offers no such counterpart regarding the recognition of women's experiences. The FDA does not address issues of attracting minorities and women to research; does not offer outreach programs to help drug researchers include such people; and has no examination or analysis of the relationship between the research project and the female subject. Again, the FDA only lifted its prior ban on the inclusion of women of childbearing potential and says that it expects women to be included and a gender analysis to be performed. It offers no assistance or guidelines as to how drug researchers may accomplish this. Therefore, the FDA barely heeds the criterion of recognition.

Democratic Freedom

Does the policy further the ability of women to participate in determining their actions? With regard to medical research, the issue of democratic freedom raises the matter of informed consent. Women must be fully informed of the risks and benefits of participation in any clinical trial and must be allowed to make their own decision about participation. Furthermore, it is important that all participants be provided with full information and that no coercion occurs. This has particular implications for minority women.

Also, the representation of women in higher-level policy-making boards such as the NIH, FDA, Institutional Review Boards (IRBs). The inclusion of women on IRBs is important so that a female voice can be heard and be part of the evaluation of informed consent procedures.[10] Responsibilities given to IRBs include the review of risk-benefit ratios, confidentiality protections, informed consent processes and documents, and procedures for selection of subjects (Institute of Medicine 1994, vol 1, 40). Consequently, IRBs become important elements in the analysis of democratic freedom and informed consent procedures.

NIH

The NIH policy notes that as IRBs implement the new guidelines and include women and minorities, they must also continue to regulate for the protection of human subjects. Such regulations require that before awardee institutions are permitted to carry out research involving human subjects, the awardee's informed consent procedures must, before work is begun and at intervals of no more than one year, be reviewed and approved by an IRB (Institute of Medicine 1994, vol. 1, 130). The NIH Outreach Notebook explicitly states that it should be assumed that all Office for Protection from Research Risks' (OPRR) regulations concerning ethical considerations in clinical and community trials apply to *all* individuals regardless of gender, race, or ethnicity. "However, successful implementation of these regulations depends on the ability of the research team to understand implications of conducting research in particular populations, settings, and trials" (21). The NIH explains that different people may comprehend the purpose and benefits of participation in different ways; in fact, for some potential subjects, it may be harder to understand. But issues of autonomy are "paramount in the decision to participate" and, as such, more time may be needed, multiple sessions may be required, and translators my need to be sought to further the potential participant's understanding so they can make an informed choice. Importantly, the NIH is recognizing that the burden of informed consent rests with head investigators, as well as themselves, to do whatever is needed to ensure that women fully understand the benefits and risks of participation.

The Outreach Notebook states that "women of childbearing potential must understand the requirements of the study and decide whether it is appropriate for them to participate (e.g., do the benefits outweigh the risks?)" (9). So women must be fully informed and decide whether to participate, not the investigator, NIH, or the FDA. Women are being empowered to make their own decisions and it is recognized that each individual woman should have control over her body and her actions. Also the Notebook notes that, even with IRB approval, researchers should make special efforts to ensure that women fully understand the demands of the study and what they will be asked to do. "Informed consent is essential" (9). The NIH, with its focus on the provision of information and consent of the woman, is adhering to the criteria of democratic freedom and clearly addresses the past problems of excluding women in studies.

Regarding the possibility of coercion, the guidelines state that ethical concerns should be clearly noted so there is minimal possibility of coercion or undue influence in the incentives or rewards offered for participation. IRBs should also address these concerns. The Outreach Notebook explicitly states that issues of coercion or undue influence are of particular importance for women, and especially minority women and women of lower economic resources. It goes on to note that incentives to participate should not be of the sort to seem coercive and what "coercive" entails may change from group to group or community to community. Once again, gender, cultural, and class differences are being acknowledged in a positive manner that helps women, and especially minority women, to determine their own actions and have greater control over their lives.

With regard to the representation of women in policy making positions, Bernadine Healy was appointed Director of the NIH in 1991 and it is thought that her leadership brought many of the policy changes discussed herein. Again, the ORWH was established with one of its goals being to increase the number of female researchers; furthermore, a woman, Vivian Pinn, was given leadership of the ORWH.

FDA

In its 1993 guidelines, the FDA is not as specific as the NIH guidelines detailed here. But the FDA does revise the prior policy of excluding women of childbearing potential and states that one reason for the revision is the initial determination of risk of fetal damage is "properly left to patients, physicians, local IRBs, and sponsors, with appropriate review and guidance by FDA, as are all other aspects of the safety of proposed investigations"

(U.S. DHHS 1993, 39408). This is an important advancement in terms of women determining their own actions regarding participation. The FDA guidelines discuss informed consent and state that all available information about the potential risk of fetal toxicity should be given to women. If no relevant information is available, the informed consent document should reflect this. Furthermore, the guidelines state that a reliable form of contraception may be provided, or abstinence, for the duration of drug exposure so that fetal exposure is limited. The FDA also developed an information document for IRBs that outlines the change in policy. It adds that women should be counseled about pregnancy testing and contraception but the type of contraception is not specified because this decision is best left to a woman and her health care provider. Again, even though not as explicit, detailed, or advanced as the NIH's guidelines, the new FDA guidelines are certainly an advancement over the prior policy of exclusion of women of childbearing potential. Though a critique could be made regarding the continued focus on the fetus, this new FDA policy greatly increases the ability of women to determine their own participation in drug trials and thus adheres much more closely to the notion of democratic freedom.

In conclusion, regarding the principle of self-determination, the NIH has made great advancements toward this component of gender justice. Women's ability to develop themselves is enhanced by the new policy, a recognition of their concerns is articulated and many issues are addressed in the assistance documentation, and the ability of women to determine their own actions regarding participation in clinical trials is greatly increased. The FDA has made some tentative advancements; the policy changes *may* help women be healthier and thus develop themselves, and it greatly increases women's ability to determine their actions but offers little recognition of women's experience.

Principle of Equality of Gendered Consequences

In the actual consequences of outcomes, do women achieve a lived-out equality or parity with men with respect to the policy's goals? This suggests many things with regard to medical research policies. First, the goal of the policy is to have women included in clinical trials, and the underlying goal is to have somewhat equal amounts of medical knowledge about men and women. No longer can women be considered abnormal patients or their bodies assumed to be just like male bodies. So the desired outcome of the policy is to have equitable amounts of men and women in studies that are on topics that apply to men and women. But, as stated before, some illnesses are more prevalent in women and some diseases are exclusive to women. So we also want an equitable number of studies done on diseases that are unique to women and diseases that are unique to men. Thus, another important facet is whether women's specific diseases receive adequate funding when compared to funding of male diseases.

NIH

With regard to the inclusion of equal amounts of men and women, few data are available to analyze, but the ORWH has put forth some preliminary results. For Phase III trials awarded in 1994, and only considering trials that include both men and women, 57 percent of the subjects were men and 42 percent were women. Only about seven percent of the applications were rejected for not including minorities and women (Hayunga, et al. 1996). The NIH is establishing a data base so that such information can easily be obtained and analyzed. NIH does require that researchers make annual progress reports; the following year's funding is dependent on sufficient progress being made. This has been standard NIH practice for many years, but now, additionally, researchers have to provide information on the gender and racial composition of the study group. Once this information is computerized, more analyses can be performed on the effectiveness of the new policy.

I am hopeful with regard to the outcome of this process for several reasons. If the data gathered over time indicate that progress has indeed been made, then this principle is being adhered to. But the fact that the NIH is gathering this kind of data will place pressure on researchers to be sure that compliant, positive answers are given; the threat of the loss of funding for research projects is a formidable incentive. But even if the data show inequality, NIH personnel will know what the problems are and where the problems lie, such that a positive plan can be implemented to see that the required changes are made.

The other important issue is whether women's specific diseases are receiving adequate funding. The ORWH was established to address this need and has begun the Women's Health Initiative (WHI) to study more than 150,000 women on a variety of issues important for women. This is one positive step. As stated before, the NIH has been criticized for only devoting 13 percent of its budget, or about $1 billion in 1988, for the study of health issues of specific concern to women. As reported by the Congressional Budget Office, this had increased to only 14.2 percent of the total budget or $1.56 billion and this number includes the WHI (Society for the Advancement of Women's Health Research 1995, personal conversation). The 60 percent increase in the money devoted to women's research is to be applauded, but the fact that NIH only spends 14.2 percent of its funds on women's specific health issues is to be questioned.[11,12] The reasons for the continuation of this problem at NIH are unclear, especially when such great policy advancements have been made regarding the inclusion of women and minorities in research.[13] But, overall the NIH has moved closer toward the implementation of equality of consequences but is still lacking in areas as noted.

FDA

The FDA lifted its ban on the exclusion of women of childbearing potential. This is certainly a positive step and stops their total disregard for the principle of equality of gendered consequences. But by not *requiring* their inclusion, women may still be excluded and hence disadvantaged. The FDA's use of words such as "should" and "expect" as opposed to "require," weaken the policy's potential impact. For example, the FDA guidelines state that subjects in a clinical study should reflect the population that will receive the drug when it is marketed. If the FDA does not require that researchers provide information as to the gender and racial composition of the study group, as well as the gender and racial composition of the group to which the drug would be marketed, how will the FDA know if the guideline is being followed?

With regard to the actual effect of the 1993 FDA guidelines, unfortunately neither the FDA nor any other agency has yet studied the effects of the changes. No data has been gathered or studies implemented to evaluate the consequences. This is a tremendous shortcoming of the implementation (or lack of implementation) process of the guideline and particularly in light of the 1992 GAO findings noting the many problems.

I am not hopeful about the actual changes and consequences of the 1993 policy. The FDA has made little progress toward the principle of equality of gendered consequences.

Principle of Diversity

Does the policy recognize the diversity of women—age, class, race, ethnicity, sexual orientation, disability status, etc.—and address their differing needs? One application of this principle with regard to medical research concerns the topics that are studied. For example, many studies about the prevention of AIDS focus on heterosexual relations. This is not very helpful for lesbian women who need information about how to stop the transmission of the virus in lesbian sexual encounters. Also important is the idea that women of various races and ages participate in studies, so investigators should develop appropriate and culturally sensitive outreach programs and activities for such people. Thus, language issues are also important.

NIH

As discussed before, the 1994 NIH Act directly and explicitly addresses many important issues regarding the diversity of women. Women and members of minority groups and their subpopulations are to be included in research; investigators should develop appropriate and culturally sensitive outreach programs and activities for such people. The objective is to recruit the most diverse study population consistent with the goals of the research (U.S. DHHS, NIH, 1994a, 14510). And, of course, a valid gender and racial analysis needs to be carried out so that differences in intervention can be detected. The NIH will not award any grant, beginning with fiscal year 1995 that does not comply with the new policy.

Regarding recruitment strategies, language issues are also addressed by the NIH in the Outreach Notebook, reminding researchers that they may not be familiar with a community's language, meaning of expressions, or colloquial phrasing. The literacy level of the individual in her first language and in English should be ascertained and special efforts may be needed to develop and translate informational materials so that they are sensitive to the "linguistic and cultural differences among genders and subpopulations" (11) because "(o)utreach strategies that are productive in one population or setting may be counterproductive in another" (12). This is, once again, recognizing the diversity of women's needs and addressing and thus legitimating them. Overall, the NIH policy does a very good job in explicitly recognizing and addressing the needs of a great diversity of women—in short, the policy institutes gender justice in this regard.

FDA

Once again, the FDA is not very explicit on diversity issues. The FDA states that "drugs should be studied prior to approval in subjects representing the full range of patients likely to receive the drug once it is marketed (U.S. DHHS, FDA 1993, 39409). It goes on to state that "analyses of effectiveness, adverse effects, dose-response, and, if available, blood concentration-response, to look for the influence of: (1) Demographic features, such as age, gender, and race" (39410). So gender, race, and age are at least being mentioned in the policy and this is a positive step. But overall the FDA is fairly vague about the diverse women that need to be served. Just stating that studies should include the range of patients that will take the drug after approval is not particularly helpful. As noted already, the 1992 GAO report recommended that the FDA more clearly specify what constitutes an appropriate inclusion of women. The FDA did not do so.

CONCLUSION

The three principles of gender justice used to analyze the NIH and FDA policies are self-determination, equality of gendered consequences, and diversity. Overall, the NIH has greatly improved its medical research policies and has made great strides toward having gender just policies. The NIH guidelines contribute to the self-development of women, pay attention to women's experiences, and further the ability of women to enjoy democratic freedom. The initial information about the actual consequences of the policy show that it has been successful with regard to the inclusion of women, but not so successful with regard to the funding of studies on diseases that are specific to women. Furthermore, the diversity of women is recognized. The NIH still has considerable room for improvement but overall, the NIH has moved significantly towards gender justice—its policies and the enforcement of its policies have considerably improved justice for women as it relates to medical research supported by NIH.

So, what does this mean for women? It means that a growing body of knowledge about diseases, conditions, and treatments will be amassed that will benefit women. No longer will women be treated as abnormal "human" bodies. Of course, such knowledge will need to be dispersed to the medical community and, most importantly, medical school educators. But gradually, women will receive health care that is fit for women; thus, justice lies within their reach.

Overall, the FDA has made slight improvements, though it lags quite far behind the NIH in comparison. The FDA has taken small steps toward improving justice for women with regard to its policies for drug development, but it needs to do much more. They have improved their policies, but not very substantially and certainly to a much lesser degree than the NIH.

But why has the FDA lagged so far behind the NIH? Why the vast difference in policy? One could argue that the NIH has more control over its research because it funds and closely monitors its research projects. If one does not follow NIH rules, their project does not get funded. The FDA only reviews and accepts or rejects research on drugs; it only regulates and does not fund research and thus has less control and less power to implement rules. This is not persuasive though because the FDA could, conceivably, require that drug applications contain certain pieces information and reject them outright if they did not. The FDA could adopt a more regulatory approach, as opposed to its more voluntary strategy, as did the NIH. The FDA chose not to do this. In fact, the FDA states in its 1993 guidelines:

> The agency recognizes that this change in FDA's policy will not, by itself, cause drug companies or IRBs to alter restrictions they might impose on the participation of women of childbearing potential. *We do not at this time perceive a regulatory basis for requiring routinely that women in general or women of childbearing potential be included in particular trials, such as phase 1 studies.* However, as this guideline delineates, careful characterization of drug effects by gender is expected by the agency, and FDA is determined to remove unnecessary Federal impediment to inclusion of women in the earliest stages of drug development. The agency is confident that the interplay of ethical, social, medical, legal and political forces will allow greater participation of women in the early stages of clinical trials. (39408-409; emphasis added)

Thus, the FDA makes no guarantee that women will be included and does not feel it necessary to mandate the inclusion.

NOTES

1. And as Karen Rothenberg (1996) notes, despite all the attention given to the Tuskegee experiment since the 1970s, little concern has been noted about the women who were the sexual partners of the men exposed to syphilis.

2. The Public Health Service (PHS) is part of the Department of Health and Human Services. The National Institutes of Health; the Alcohol, Drug Abuse, and Mental Health Administration; and the Food and Drug Administration are all housed under the Public Health Service.

3. There are two important issues regarding women and medical research. One is the exclusion or underrepresentation of women in all medical studies of diseases common to women and men and drugs or treatment for such diseases. The other issue is the study of diseases or conditions that only occur or more commonly occur in women, such as breast cancer and osteoporosis. In 1987, only 13.5 percent of the NIH budget was devoted to the broadly defined category of women's health issues (Berney 1990), but this number is contested by some as constituting *more* than what men's issues receive (Kadar 1994).

4. Extramural research is research performed outside of the NIH at other institutions, usually universities. Intramural research is performed in-house at NIH facilities in Bethesda, Maryland.

5. Institutional Review Boards (IRBs) are local administrative bodies established to protect the rights and welfare of human research subjects participating in studies at the institutions under the IRB's jurisdiction. All research involving human subjects must be approved by an IRB and the IRB has the authority to approve, require modifications, or disapprove research activities (Institute of Medicine, vol. 1, 1994, 131). IRBs are composed of local scientists, ethicists, and non-scientists.

6. Approval for a new drug with the FDA is a long involved process. After preclinical testing (testing in laboratory and in animals), sponsors submit an Investigational New Drug (IND) application to the FDA. This application includes the plan for Phase 1 studies on humans. If approved by the FDA and a local Institutional Review Board, clinical trials begin. Phase I involves 20 to 80 healthy individuals to determine safety and dosage of the drug. Phase II involves 100 to 300 subjects to evaluate effectiveness and to look for any side effects. Phase III uses 1,000 to 3,000 subjects to verify effectiveness and to monitor adverse reactions from long-term use. Each phase lasts one, two, and three years respectively. After this, a new drug application is filed with the FDA and the review/approval process begins. If the drug

is approved, Phase IV studies begin which are post-marketing testing studies (Wierga and Eaton 1993).

7. Nussbaum (1995) divides her conception of the human being into two levels of capabilities. The first level includes needs of the human body, and the second and higher-order level includes items that if a person or society was to do without, we would not think they lived a *good* life. Incorporated into the second level are "[b]eing able to use the senses; being able to imagine, to think, and to reason—and to do these things in a way informed and cultivated by an adequate education. . . . Being able to form a conception of the good and to engage in critical reflection about the planning of one's own life" (84). Justice is determined by a society's ability to further the quality of life as defined by these levels of needs. These items are very similar to what I am describing herein about self-development.

8. The FDA issued "Guideline for the Format and Content of the Clinical and Statistical Sections of New Drug Applications" in 1988 in which it stated that the FDA expects new drug applications to contain an analysis of gender differences.

9. See Sherwin (1992), Smith (1992), and Todd (1989) for some recent works on the problems of powerful, male doctors and female, powerless patients.

10. Of course, women should be adequately represented and at all levels—as principal investigators, at the NIH and FDA, and in Congress—but I have chosen to focus on IRBs because they actually evaluate the informed consent procedures of specific research projects. Moreover, a discussion of women as investigators, in high-ranking positions at the NIH, FDA, and in Congress is too large to be included here.

11. These numbers have been criticized by NIH officials as well as others because the numbers do not include overhead expenditures. Furthermore, the numbers may be misleading because they do not include monies spent in other projects that study issues the occur in men *and* women. Moreover, others argue that about 80 percent of the budget is devoted to health issues that affect men and women, and thus only about 6 percent is devoted to afflictions unique to men (Kadar 1994). More analysis needs to be done because it is possible that though 80 percent is devoted to issues that affect men and women, if many of the diseases occur more predominantly in men, it could still be a source of inequality. It is not sufficient to say that the majority of the budget is devoted to men *and* women; more details need to be uncovered.

12. But, on a very positive note, funding for breast cancer research has increased dramatically over the last few years as a result of women's health advocates efforts. For example, breast cancer research funding at the National Cancer Institute (NCI) totaled $77 million in 1990. In 1995, NCI funding, along with Department of Defense (DOD) spending for breast cancer research, totaled $465.

13. One factor could be time lag in that research projects last for many years so, at any given point in time, the percentage of all NIH projects that are new studies is very low. Another possible problem is the process through which any new proposal has to go through in order to get funded. Only about one-third of all proposals get funded, so the competition is keen, but the battle for studies on women's health issues is even greater. Proposals have to pass through many peer reviews and committees and these have been described as "good old boy networks" (Nechas and Foley 1994, 33). Moreover, one has to be adept at writing grant proposals and senior, experienced researchers are more likely to have such skills, and senior researchers are more likely to be male. Furthermore, fewer women apply for the grants: in 1989, 12,545 men sought funding and only 2,929 women (Nechas and Foley 1994, 32). But that is a ratio of nearly 1 to 4, whereas women's issues are funded on a 1 to 7 ratio. Of course, not all women who submit a grant application to NIH want specifically to study women's health issues. Given these facts, change is likely to be slow.

CHAPTER 7

Health Care Insurance: Access for Women and Gender Justice

In the United States, unlike nearly all other western industrialized nations, we allocate and ration health care by the ability to pay for it, whether indirectly through health insurance or directly by paying for the medical care itself. Health insurance can be private or public. Private insurance is primarily obtained through one's employment, even though a significant portion of the population purchases a personal policy because their employer does not offer one; others just live without any coverage. Public programs are available for the poor, disabled, and nearly all of those over the age of 65.[1] Thus insurance is an important part of the health care system in that it greatly influences how and what type of, if any, health care one receives.

Women are *more* likely to be insured than men because women compose more of the population on Medicaid and Medicare; because women are poorer, they are more likely to be enrolled in Medicaid and because they live longer, they compose a larger portion of Medicare recipients. Thus these programs are very important for women in that without them, many more women would be uninsured.

But the fact that more women are insured does not mean that they are better off. Women are less likely than men to receive insurance through an employer, make less money so are less able to buy insurance on their own, spend more of their income meeting health care needs, and are more likely than men to receive insurance indirectly as a dependent. Therefore, women are more dependent on their spouse and the government for insurance and so their independence is compromised. Furthermore, women—whether

161

insured or uninsured—are more likely not to get the health care that they need (Commonwealth Fund, 1993).[2]

The issue of employment and insurance raises issues of inequality in pay, job status, labor force participation, and marital status. Lower-paid and lower-status jobs are less likely to carry health insurance as a benefit, and women fill these type positions disproportionately to men. Furthermore, the marital status of an individual becomes important regarding insurance; if one does not have insurance, one may be classified as a "dependent" and obtain insurance through a spouse's plan.

Women live longer, suffer more chronic conditions, visit hospitals and doctors more often, have more disabilities, and provide care to other family members in much greater proportion than men. Thus, how well health insurance covers or helps with such issues is very important for women. In the words of Senator Edward Kennedy, "[O]ne of the most serious aspects of the Nation's health care crisis [is] the unequal access available to the majority of our people, who are women. It is clear that women are second class citizens in the current system" (U.S. Congress, Senate 1994, 5).

In this chapter, issues surrounding access to quality health care for women will be examined. Health care is a complex area to cover because it is so inter-connected with nearly every other aspect of a woman's life. Employment, poverty, insurance, marital status, income, job status, children, and age all affect a woman's ability to access the health care system. The picture is further complicated by issues of financing and coverage.

In the first section, the relationship between employment, insurance, and the private health care system and how that relationship affects women's health care needs will be discussed. Next, the public forms of health care insurance, Medicaid and Medicare, will be addressed. The issues of uninsured women, basic benefits, long-term care, and other areas of concern will also be reviewed.

Next will follow an analysis of how male-centered paradigms underlie many existing policies of our current system of health care. The unfair consequences for women—the unfair consequences of a system based on a simplistic and paternalistic paradigm—will be exposed by showing the many ways in which women are disadvantaged.

In the next section, recent changes in the health care system will be discussed. These include the growth of managed care and reforms in Medicaid. Also two proposed reform measures will be presented: universal coverage and a basic benefits package. These changes—both implemented and proposed—will be examined with regard to how well women will fare under them. They will be judged according to the framework of gender justice to see if these changes will institute justice for women in the health care system.

INSURANCE, ACCESS, BENEFITS, AND WOMEN

Private Insurance and Employment

Since the 1950s, health insurance has been obtained mainly through and paid for by one's employer. But even though women's employment rates have grown tremendously, they are less likely to obtain insurance through their employer. Women have traditionally obtained insurance through their spouse's employment; women comprise nearly three-quarters of those who receive employer-based coverage as dependents. And unfortunately, employers have greatly cut back this type of benefit in the last few years as health care costs have risen (U.S. Congress, House 1993b; GAO 1997). The Institute for Women's Policy Research (IWPR 1994) notes that 28 percent of non-aged adult women obtain their insurance indirectly through an employer (generally through their spouse), but only 10 percent of men obtain their insurance in this fashion.

Married men have employer-based coverage at a rate 19 percent higher than married women (Perman and Stevens 1989), and married individuals are more likely to have coverage than single individuals and single-parent families (U.S. Congress, House 1993b). Moreover, divorce affects women's coverage differently depending on her employment status. After divorce, only 32 percent of nonemployed divorced women have private health insurance, as compared to 77 percent of employed divorced women. The Consolidated Omnibus Budget Reconciliation Act of 1985 ("COBRA") forces employers to continue coverage for a former spouse after divorce, but the former spouse has to pay the employer's as well as the employee's share. With the rising costs of insurance and the lower income of divorced women, this proves impossible much of the time.

Whereas the most important determinant of insurance is employment (in 1995, more than 90 percent of people under the age of 65 with private insurance were insured through an employment-based plan), coverage differs by industry and full- or part-time work status, as well as temporary or permanent working condition. The majority of uninsured workers are employed in retail trade, service, manufacturing, and agricultural sectors of the economy, and women disproportionately work in retail trade and service sectors (U.S. Congress, House 1993b; GAO 1997). Insurance companies also "redline" certain industries and occupations such as florists and hair stylists with the belief that such workers are more likely to include HIV-positive men, but these workers also include many women (Starr 1994). Also, part-time workers and individuals in families headed by a part-time worker are less likely to have insurance than full-time workers (U.S. Congress, House 1993b; GAO 1997), and women constitute two-thirds of part-time workers. Moreover, women are more likely to be temporary workers and not receive any benefits, and the hiring of temporary workers is a growing trend among employers. Furthermore, women quite often have gaps in their employment, usually because of child bearing and rearing concerns, and when not working experience gaps in their health care coverage.

Regarding direct and indirect employer coverage, nearly one-half of women in two-parent families have indirect coverage and 30 percent have direct employer coverage (IWPR 1994). If we look at married women who are not parents, only 23 percent receive indirect employer coverage as compared to 41 percent who receive direct coverage. And among single women, 1 percent receive indirect coverage as compared to 36 percent who receive direct employer coverage (IWPR 1994). Thus, married women with children are most likely to be dependent on their spouse for insurance coverage. This also explains why separated women are the highest uninsured group; when the couple separates the woman loses her health insurance that was provided through her spouse. In short, being married and a mother makes a woman dependent on her spouse for health insurance and separating makes her the most vulnerable.

Race is also an important factor. About the same amount of African-American and white women receive insurance directly through their employers (39 and 40 percent respectively), but only 28 percent of Hispanic women do. And 31 percent of white, but only 19 percent of Hispanic and 10 percent of African-American, women obtain insurance indirectly through a spouse's employment (IWPR 1994). But when only employed women are considered and the types of jobs held and personal characteristics of the workers are statistically controlled for, African-American as well as other minority women are less likely to have direct employer insurance; these findings also hold for African-American men so it appears that race exerts an independent effect on the obtainment of employer-based insurance (IWPR 1994, 32).

Access to health insurance through employment has been falling (IWPR 1994; GAO 1997). In 1995, 64 percent of the nonelderly population was covered by an employment-based health insurance plan, compared with 69 percent in 1987 (EBRI 1997c). And as men's access to insurance through employment falls, women's indirect access also decreases. Still, even with declining coverage offered by employers, about 56 percent of employed men have health insurance coverage through their work, while only 37 percent of employed women have such coverage (U.S. Congress, House 1993a).

This decline in employer coverage has primarily affected low- and moderate-wage earners who already have less access to insurance. Women disproportionately compose the lower-income groups of the United States. In 1994, for people above the poverty level, 75 percent had employer-based insurance, and for people below the poverty level, 19 percent had employer-based insurance (GAO 1997).

In summary, health care insurance for men has traditionally been obtained through their employment, but for women it has traditionally been obtained through their spouse's employment. Married women with children are the most dependent upon a spouse for insurance. But even employed women have employment-based insurance at a lower rate than employed men. Employed African-American and other minority women are even less likely than white women to have employment-based insurance. Factors that help explain this lower employment-based coverage for women are their greater part-time work, temporary work, employment in industries or sectors that have lower coverage rates, and intermittent employment.

Public Insurance and Women: Medicaid

The two public insurance programs in the United States are Medicaid and Medicare. In 1995, Medicaid provided health and long-term care for over 36 million low-income, elderly, and disabled Americans—about 14 percent of the population—at a cost of over $120 billion (U.S. DHHS, HCFA 1997c). After expanding considerably in the early 1990s, Medicaid spending and enrollment growth have recently slowed. Between 1988 and 1995, the number of Medicaid beneficiaries grew 58 percent, from 22 million to nearly 35 million. In part, the recession increased welfare and thus Medicaid enrollment. But much of this growth occurred between 1992 and 1994 and resulted largely from federal and state expansions in coverage of low-income pregnant women and children. In recent years enrollment growth has leveled off. From 1992 to 1994, the number of beneficiaries grew 7.6 percent per year; the growth rate was only 1.8 percent between 1994 and 1995 (Kaiser Family Foundation 1997).

Women are more likely to have a publicly funded source of insurance: 11 percent of women aged 18 to 64 are covered through the public sector while only seven percent of men are covered in such a fashion (IWPR 1994, 7). In 1995, 16 percent of females were enrolled in Medicaid as compared to 10 percent of males (U.S. DHHS, HCFA 1997d). This coverage also differs by marital status: only 6 percent of married women with spouses present are receiving public insurance while 11 percent of all other women receive public insurance (IWPR 1994, 12). Also, African-American women are much more likely to be enrolled in Medicaid than white women (U.S. DHHS, PHS 1993).

In 1995, about 60 percent of Medicaid recipients were female and 36 percent were male (U.S. DHHS, HCFA 1997b). Women and their children form the largest group of recipients—nearly 70 percent—of those receiving Medicaid (U.S. DHHS, HCFA 1997a). And although adults and children in low-income families make up nearly three-fourths of the beneficiaries, they account for only 26 percent of Medicaid spending. The elderly and the disabled account for nearly three-quarters of spending because of their intensive use of acute and long-term care services. And although Medicaid has been expanded to increase coverage for the low-income population, it covers less than one-half of poor Americans.

One problem with Medicaid is that many doctors do not accept Medicaid patients. For example, in 1985, four out of ten physicians who provided obstetrical services did not accept Medicaid clients for both payment and liability reasons (Alan Guttmacher 1985). A study in the 1970s showed that 45 percent of physicians refused to accept Medicaid patients (McBarnette 1988). In New York, the Medicaid maximum fee is so low that specialist care for the poor is almost unavailable (McBarnette 1988). Thus, many women who are enrolled in Medicaid do not get adequate care.

Public Insurance and Women: Medicare

Nearly all people aged 65 and over are enrolled in the Medicare program. In 1996, the plan covered 38.2 million people, some 14 percent of the U.S. population (Moon 1996, 49). And because women compose a larger portion of the elderly, they compose a larger portion of Medicare recipients. In 1996, 22 million women, but only 16 million men, were enrolled in Medicare (U.S. DHHS, HCFA 1996). And because women live longer, the percentage of female Medicare recipients in older age groups is even larger.

Medicare covers hospitalization and, for an extra fee, physician bills. Medicare does not cover long-term care or prescription drugs. This is especially problematical for women who compose three-fourths of the population in long-term care facilities (U.S. Congress, House 1993a). Many nursing home residents have to "spend down" by depleting their resources and then enrolling in Medicaid because Medicaid does cover long-term care in most states (Moon 1993). The elderly also have very high prescription drug costs. In 1992, most Medicare beneficiaries used prescription drugs at an average cost of $604 per user (U.S. Congress, House 1993c). Though the elderly compose 12 percent of the population, they account for 34 percent of total spending on drugs (U.S. Congress, House 1993d). And 75 percent of people under the age of 65 have prescription drug coverage, mainly from private plans, but only 43-46 percent of the elderly have such coverage (U.S. Congress, House 1993c). If the elderly can afford it, they usually purchase another insurance policy or "Medigap" policy that covers items that Medicare excludes. Unfortunately, many cannot afford such a plan.

Though great strides have been made in the reduction of poverty among the elderly in the last 25 years, many elderly still struggle to pay living and medical expenses with very modest incomes. And the likelihood of living on a low income is the greatest for women, minorities, and the eldest of the elderly. Nearly one-quarter of elderly women are poor or near-poor as compared to 12 percent of elderly men, reflecting their lower pay in prior years, increased poverty from widowhood, and longer life that extinguishes savings (Rowland and Lyons 1996). Those with lower incomes report having worse health, more need for health care, and spending a much greater percentage of their income on health-related expenses (Rowland and Lyons 1996).

Uninsured Women

About 14 percent of women have no health insurance (U.S. Bureau of the Census 1996b). Such a statistic tells us how many are uninsured on a particular day; another facet of the problem is to examine how many people do not have insurance *at some point in time* during the year—the number of people who experience gaps in coverage. In the time period 1992-94, 25 percent of women (and 29 percent of men) had no health insurance for at least one month (Bennefield 1996). Lower-income women are among those most severely affected: 26 percent of poor women did not have insurance at some point during 1994 (Bennefield 1995). Furthermore, of the 19 million women who have no health insurance, a disproportionate number are women of color.

Women do not have insurance for various reasons. One reason is that they may work for an employer that does not offer coverage and they cannot afford to purchase insurance on their own. A woman may also be unemployed, either by choice for child-rearing purposes or because she cannot find affordable child care or a job that pays decent wages. Moreover, if she is married, the couple may not be able to afford dependent coverage, and many employers have cut dependent care coverage benefits. Only the poorest of the poor qualify for Medicaid and then not even all who qualify can actually enroll in the program. In the gap between high-priced private insurance and Medicaid is where most of the uninsured women fall.

Women are least likely to have insurance during their prime childbearing years—when under the age of 30—and 70 percent of all births in the U.S. are to women in this age group (IWPR 1994, 11). Babies whose parents have no health insurance are 30 percent more likely to die or be seriously ill at birth (U.S. Congress, House 1992). Many single mothers lack insurance—18 percent of single mothers compared to 11 percent of mothers in two- parent families—and the cost of insurance is the major factor (IWPR 1994, 12). If not offered through an employer (and sometimes even if offered through an employer), premiums can be hundreds of dollars per month and when one considers the problems of affordable child care, lack of child support, and low-paying jobs for many women, it is understandable why many women cannot afford health insurance.

The Employee Benefit Research Institute (EBRI) reports that single individuals and individuals in single-parent families are more likely to be uninsured than married couples with or without children (U.S. Congress, House 1993b). Though 15 percent of the population are uninsured, about 20 percent of single people with children are uninsured. And, of course, women are much more likely to be single parents than men. Looked at in another light, single adults with children lack insurance at a rate of 20 percent, compared with 13 percent of adults in two-parent families (EBRI 1996). And of the uninsured, children make up the highest proportion (26 percent) and people aged 25-34 make up the next highest group (24 percent). It is presumed that many of the younger adults are the children's parents and that the whole family does not have coverage.

Women who are not married or whose spouses are absent from the home are more likely to be uninsured than are women with spouses (IWPR 1994, 11). Married women are most likely to have insurance because they have very high rates of indirect employer-based coverage. And married women with spouses absent and separated women are even more likely to be uninsured than divorced or never-married women: 24 percent of the former have no insurance as compared to 19 percent for divorced and 22 percent for never married women (IWPR 1994). It is thought that separated women have lost their prior forms of insurance and have not yet made the transition to another form.

The uninsured also differ by race. Regarding Hispanic women, 32 percent are uninsured, as compared to 20 percent of African-American, 12 percent of white, and 18 percent of other raced (Asian, American Indian, etc.) women (IWPR 1994, 16). Also, women without a high school diploma are the least likely to have insurance; nearly 28 percent of women who have not completed high school have no insurance (IWPR 1994, 18). And as family income decreases, so does the likelihood of having insurance, leaving one in three women with incomes below $15,000 without insurance. Obviously, Medicaid does not adequately fill the gap left by private insurance.

The uninsured are concentrated disproportionately in low-income families. In 1995, 47 percent of the uninsured were in families with annual incomes under $20,000 (EBRI 1996). In 1995, 33 percent of the uninsured were below the poverty line. Of course many of those living below the poverty line are enrolled in Medicaid, which accounts for the lower percentage of the uninsured in the poorest of the poor.

Fifty-three percent of the uninsured live in households headed by full-time, full-year workers. Also, nearly one-half of all uninsured workers were either self-employed or working in firms with fewer than 25 employees in 1991 (EBRI 1996). In conclusion, the uninsured woman is most likely to be low-income, single, minority, young, and employed but working for an employer who does not offer coverage.

Health Care Insurance: Basic Benefits

If one has health insurance, a very important issue is the type of services and procedures the insurance plan will cover. More specifically, if viewed from the perspective of women, it is important to know whether plans cover female preventive services such as mammograms and Pap smears and reproductive needs such as contraception, abortions, and prenatal and maternity care. Do women have health care needs that are not usually labeled or deemed as health care needs and thus not covered? Many women report that they do not get the care they need—is it because their insurance will not cover the services they need?

Preventive Services for Women

Many women do not get preventive services such a mammograms, Pap smears, clinical breast exams, or complete physical exams and Hispanic and African-American women are more likely not to get these services than white women (Commonwealth Fund 1993). The cost of the services is the main reason why women did not receive them. Another one-quarter of women say that their physicians never discussed it with them, and one-fifth of women state that their insurance does not cover preventive services (Commonwealth Fund 1993). Interestingly, women enrolled in Health Maintenance Organizations (HMOs) are more likely to receive preventive services, but more than one-half of all HMOs impose cost sharing on these services (U.S. Congress, Senate 1994a, 52).

The National Cancer Institute and American Cancer Society recommend that women aged 40-49 receive annual clinical breast exams and mammograms at one to two year intervals. For women aged 50 and above, they should receive annual exams and mammograms. But in 1993, almost one-half of women aged 50 and above had not received a mammogram in the past year (Commonwealth Fund 1993). Of course, income, race, and education greatly affect whether one receives such services. Moreover, twenty percent of private policies do not cover mammograms (U.S. Congress, Senate 1994).

According to a 1990 survey, 30 percent of women with private insurance do not have coverage for Pap smears. The National Cancer Institute recommends that all women who are sexually active or have reached the age of 18 have an annual Pap test and pelvic exam. But 35 percent of women have not had a Pap smear in the last year, and poor women are twice as likely not to get annual Pap smears as higher income women (Commonwealth Fund 1993). In fact, Medicaid does not cover Pap tests and mammograms as preventive measures, only as diagnostic tools, and this prevents poor women from going to their doctors for regular tests (U.S. Congress, House 1993).

Clinical breast exams, mammograms, and Pap smear tests are very important for the early detection and prevention of cancer in women. Since the introduction of the Pap test, the national death rate for cervical cancer has declined by 75 percent. Regular mammograms can reduce breast cancer mortality 30-35 percent in women aged 50-69 (U.S. Congress, House 1993). All of these tests are low-cost preventive measures that are proven to be extremely effective in preventing death among women, but many women are not receiving them.

Reproductive Care

Over one-half of all pregnancies are unplanned and one-half of these are terminated—resulting in 1.4 million abortions in 1994 (Alan Guttmacher Institute 1996a). There are approximately 20 million women living in the U.S. that have had an abortion. No method of contraception is 100 percent effective: almost one-half of the women who suffer unplanned pregnancies are using contraception. In 1993, two-thirds of fee-for-service plans and 70 percent of HMOs covered abortion but usually only if "medically necessary." Abortion coverage is carried by companies such as Aetna, Blue Cross/ Blue Shield, Kaiser Permanente, Principal Financial Group, and Travelers, but many place restrictions on coverage. One-quarter of fee-for-service and one-fifth of HMOs require the certification of a specific medical indication other than the pregnancy to qualify for coverage (U.S. Congress, Senate

1994). About 10 percent of plans do not cover abortions under any situation. Sterilization procedures are covered by 85 percent of plans.

Funding for Title X of the Public Health Services Act, the program that funds more than 4,000 clinics that serve 4-5 million women and girls, has steadily declined (AAUW 1995). The Planned Parenthood of New York reports that Federal family planning programs have been cut 66 percent from 1980 to 1990. The "Gag Rule," instituted by President Reagan, disallowed any information or discussion about abortion in federally funded clinics, but this was lifted in 1992 by President Clinton. Many women, and especially young, minority, poor women that are more likely to be uninsured, go to publicly financed clinics for family planning information (McBarnette 1988). Furthermore, since the passage of the Hyde Amendment in 1976, abortion is not covered by Medicaid except in cases of rape, incest, or if continuation of the pregnancy would endanger the woman's life. States may choose to cover abortions under provisions of the bill, but without federal reimbursement. As has been the case since 1994, 17 states use their own funds, either voluntarily or under state court order, to pay for abortions for low-income women.[3]

Approximately one in four women in their childbearing years have no health insurance for maternity care (U.S. Congress, House 1992).[4] Prenatal care is crucial for the women's health and the health of the baby. The Office of Technology Assessment (OTA) estimates that the health care system saves $14,00 to $30,000 for every low birth weight baby averted by prenatal care (U.S. Congress, House 1993a). Early prenatal care is less likely to be received by minority women, and thus they are more likely to have low birth weight babies, have their babies die, or to die themselves of pregnancy-related diseases (U.S. Congress, Senate 1994, 83).

In the last decade, the Medicaid program has increased its coverage for pregnant women and infants. It has phased-in coverage for poor, pregnant women even if they would not normally qualify. But these women are only covered for their term of pregnancy and 60 days postpartum and only for pregnancy-related care. For many poor women, coverage ends with the pregnancy; 15 percent of the women leaving Medicaid do so because of childbirth (Davis 1996a).

Muller (1990) states that workers in the U.S. have usually had some type of maternity benefit but what this benefit actually covers has varied. In the late 1970s, only about 70 percent of workers had coverage for a normal pregnancy. When a normal pregnancy was covered, the number of hospital days covered was shorter than for other types of stays and/or limited to a lump sum (86). About three-fifths of those with benefits were insured for the full, customary and usual physician fee; 12 percent had partial coverage; and the rest were limited to less than $500. Many plans also institute a waiting period for maternity benefits (Muller 1990).

In 1995, reports were made of managed care organizations hustling new mothers out of hospitals in less than 24 hours—dubbed "drive-through deliveries." In response, some states passed legislation mandating minimum stays, and in 1996, Congress passed the Newborns' and Mother's Health Protection Act that mandates insures to cover minimum hospital stays of 48 hours. Importantly, it does not command that women stay in the hospital for 48 hours.

Contraception for women is excluded from many health insurance plans. Nearly one-half of large-group plans do not cover any contraceptive method and only 15 percent cover all five major reversible prescription methods: IUD, diaphragm, implant, injectable, and the pill (Alan Guttmacher Institute 1994). Oral contraceptives, one of the most commonly used methods, are covered by only one-third of large-group plans. And this is *not* because plans do not cover prescription drugs—quite the contrary. Nearly 97 percent of fee-for-service plans cover prescription drugs. Moreover, about 97 percent of such plans also cover medical devices but only 20 percent cover IUDs, diaphragms, or Norplant.

During the 1995–1996 legislative term, measures to require contraception coverage were proposed, but not enacted, in seven states (California, Hawaii, Illinois, New York, Oregon, Virginia, and Wisconsin). All of the proposed bills would have required that private insurance policies cover contraceptive services and supplies, generally with the same cost-sharing requirements as for other covered services. Despite the cost-effectiveness and social benefit of preventing unplanned pregnancies and the inequitable prescription drug policies that drive contraceptive costs beyond the reach of many women, most of the measures saw no action (Sollom 1997).

Since 1993, 12 states have sought federal permission to establish family planning expansion programs under Medicaid. Five states have received approval (Delaware, Illinois, Maryland, Rhode Island, and South Carolina). Of the five approved programs, all but Delaware's have linked their family planning provisions to the Medicaid expansions enacted in the 1980s to establish eligibility for poor pregnant women. These four states have received permission to extend eligibility for family planning services to as long as five years postpartum (well past the normal 60-day postpartum termination date), and to further expand their income criteria. The program in Delaware utilized a different approach. The state received permission to extend Medicaid coverage for family planning services for two years following the termination of regular Medicaid benefits *for any reason* (Sollom 1997).

Abuse and Violence Against Women

Domestic violence is a major medical and public health problem in the United States even though it is not usually thought of as such. Important concerns for women are treatments for and mental health complications that stem from societal violence, domestic violence, rape, and childhood abuse. Violence is the leading cause of injury to women and domestic violence is the number one cause of emergency room visits for women (estimates are that 20-30 percent of ER visits are for injuries from domestic violence). And 16 percent of pregnant women report abuse by their partners. Medical expenses are greater and physician visits more frequent for victimized women than non-victimized women on a ratio of two to one.

A recent troubling trend has been uncovered regarding insurance companies and women who have suffered abuse. Many insurance companies deny health insurance (along with other types of insurance such as life and disability) to victims of domestic violence because the woman is now a "bad risk." Some companies consider domestic violence to be a pre-existing condition, akin to a disease. And because of heightened awareness of the problem in our society, more women are reporting abuse to legal and medical officials and thus the abuse is more often becoming part of a medical record that can be reviewed by insurance companies.

Mental Illness

Women suffer from depression twice as much as men, and are more likely to experience anxiety disorders, particularly those related to rape, sexual abuse, and other trauma (U.S. Congress, Senate 1994, 98).[5] Also because of domestic violence, counseling services for the treatment and prevention of domestic violence are extremely important. The average indemnity insurance plan offered by employers only covers about 40 percent of the expenses associated with mental health care, and the typical HMO plan pays 25-30 percent. If mental health care is covered at all by insurance, it is almost always covered at a significantly lower rate and with more restrictions on the number of allowable visits, higher co-payments, and lower levels on the total dollars reimbursed (U.S. Congress, House 1993a). For inpatient mental health services, only 13 percent of private insurance has coverage equal to that for physical illness (EBRI 1997a).

Since elderly women have extremely high rates of depression and other mental disorders, the coverage of mental health services by Medicare is very important. Unfortunately, Medicare provides very limited mental health benefits. Recipients must pay 50 percent of all costs for outpatient care by a physician psychiatrist, clinical psychologist, or clinical social worker (U.S. Congress, House 1993a).[6] Medicare does not cover prescription drugs and tranquilizers are commonly prescribed for women: 44 percent of women under the age of 75 are prescribed tranquilizers (compared to 35 percent of men), and 6 percent of women over the age of 75 are prescribed such drugs (compared to 38 percent of men in the same age group) (Muller 1990, 119).

Long-term Care

Long-term care is another important health care issue for women. Women live longer and thus are in greater need of long-term care benefits. They compose about 75 percent of nursing home residents, as well as those living in the community with limitations in their daily activities (U.S. Congress, Senate 1994). Furthermore, women provide long-term care to family members. Presently, over 80 percent of the care needed by the elderly is provided by family members, approximately three-quarters of whom are women (U.S. Congress, House 1993a; AARP 1989). Currently, a woman can expect to spend 18 years caring for an elderly parent (U.S. Congress, Senate 1994), and most of these women are in their mid-forties, and more than one-half are employed outside the home. Many women in this position do not care for another by choice. One-third of primary caregivers report that the responsibility has fallen to them because they are the only ones who live close to the recipient. Another one- quarter say they are the primary caregiver because they have no choice—no one else will do it (AARP 1989).

Caregivers spend their own money to provide services for whom they are caring. This money goes for such things as transportation, telephone bills, special diets and medicines, doctor's fees, cleaning services, hospital care, home health aides, and in-home nursing care, and the like. Caregivers also report that they have to take time off from work, adjust their work schedules, reduce the number of hours they work, take leaves of absence, and even quit their jobs (AARP 1989; OWL 1989).

The reason long-term care is such a problem is because most insurance plans do not cover it. Information from over 1,000 major employers and their benefit plans (both HMOs and indemnity plans) show that almost none provide long-term care benefits (U.S. Congress, House 1993a). Medicare has no long-term care coverage and, as discussed above, many elderly have to "spend down" so they can enroll in Medicaid because it does cover nursing home care (Moon 1993).[7] Presently, long-term care is funded by Medicaid, individuals, and their families. Private insurance plans rarely offer long-term care coverage.

Separate, private long-term care plans are offered by some insurance companies, but the premiums are so high that few can afford such plans. The Health Insurance Association of America reports that in 1994, a long-term care plan would cost $1,538 for a 65 year old and $5,095 for a 79 year old (HIAA 1997). The average purchaser of a long-term care policy does so at the age of 70, but only 10 to 20 percent of the elderly can afford such a plan. Unfortunately, the people who need it the most—the very old—cannot afford long-term care insurance.

Other Issues of Concern

Whether women are insured or not, the rising costs of health care severely affect them. With insurance premiums, physician and hospital fees, and patient's out-of-pocket expenses escalating, the burden increasingly falls onto lower-income groups who now have to devote a disproportionate percentage of their income to health care. The typical indemnity plan offered by medium-to-large size employers entails an annual $200 per individual deductible; after the deductible is met, the plan will pay 80 percent of covered expenses; and the plan has an annual out-of-pocket limitation of $1,500. In addition, employee contributions range from $0 to over $50 per month for individual coverage and $0 to over $150 per month for family coverage (U.S. Congress, Senate 1994a). Though many people would be lucky to have such coverage, many people can not afford the cost sharing mechanism of the typical plan—$200 of their own money before the insurance even takes effect.

Many plans do not offer such generous benefits, and many women might not have any insurance at all. Many poor do not have the money to devote to health care; their income barely covers housing, food, and child care. Again, since a disproportionate number of women fall into lower-income groups, the impact of rising health care costs becomes, partially, a gender equity issue.

Women of reproductive age pay nearly 70 percent more out-of-pocket expenses than men (U.S. Congress, Senate 1994). Females have higher medical bills and pay 1.43 times what men pay for medical care (Muller 1990, 7). But women still have many unmet needs despite the fact that they visit the doctor more and put more money into the health care system.

Another important issue for women is that they are much more likely to be dissatisfied with their physician and are more likely to change their doctor. The most often noted reason is because of communication problems. Women feel as if they are "talked down to" and "treated like a child" and many report having been told that a medical condition was "all in their head" (Commonwealth Fund 1993). Furthermore, five percent of women report having a doctor who made offensive sexual remarks or inappropriate advances.

Many women do not get the care they need because they frequently cancel their own appointments when child care is not available, or when they must care for other family members. Also, the location of health care facilities is an issue. Health care facilities need to be relatively close to home so that they are easily accessible. "If getting medical care means traveling across town with children, many women opt to stay home" (U.S. Congress, House 1993a, 13).

People lack access to primary health care because of their economic situation, health status, or geographic proximity to primary care providers. The location of and number of primary care physicians is important. The U.S. lacks a sufficient number of primary care doctors but has an abundance of specialized physicians, resulting in inadequate primary care for many people. Furthermore, primary care physicians need to be accessible to patients. Even though most underserved people live in urban areas, rural areas have tremendous problems with accessible doctors and hospitals. Rural counties are three times more likely to be medically underserved than urban counties.

Also, women's health care is fragmented in that they have to go to a gynecologist, internist, and primary care doctor to get their basic health care needs met. Women's overall health care lacks continuity of treatment because they never receive comprehensive care (Clancy and Massion 1990; Wallis 1994). Furthermore, some research has shown that general practitioners, and especially male ones, are less likely to provide Pap smears and breast exams. With regards to insurance plans that make one designate a primary physician, many women have a hard choice of deciding whether to designate their gynecologist, if they even are allowed to do so, or their general practitioner. Some have advocated the creation of a "women's health" speciality within the medical field to address these very problems. If created, an important issue would be having such doctors and services covered on insurance plans.

In summary, women use the health care system more and need more health care than men. Women live longer, have more acute symptoms, experience more chronic conditions, suffer more disability days, and log more physician visits even when pregnancy related conditions are excluded (U.S. DHHS, NIH 1992). Women have less income and are less able to pay for medical care, but have more out-of-pocket expenses. Women also have more complaints about their doctors. Given the scope of dissatisfaction with the health care system it is not too surprising that many women feel that it is not organized to meet their health care needs.

PROBLEMS AND ISSUES

In this section, problems for women regarding insurance, access, and benefits will be examined. As I have argued, many policies are designed with males as the standard. The structure of our insurance system and its connection to employment, the Medicaid program providing health care for the poor, the benefits contained in standard insurance packages, and the exclusion of long-term care from most private plans and Medicare are a few important components of the present system that reflect this problem. Such a focus on the male body and life is incorrect and unjustified, and leads to policies that disadvantage, are at least not beneficial for, women. In the end, many of women's health care needs are not met.

Private Insurance: the Male Employee and Dependent Wife

Since the 1950s, insurance has been obtained mainly through and paid for by one's employer. Women obtained their insurance by being classified as a dependent on their husband's policy, as were the children. This is a system that is based on the assumption of a nuclear family which consists of a male being a full-time wage earner and a woman being a full-time homemaker. Such women have little access to any resources independent of their husbands and as such they are "dependent" on the male to provide for their health care needs by obtaining health care insurance through his work.

This organization of access to insurance is very problematical. Women cannot receive insurance in their own right under such a system and they have no independent resources. They are defined as being entitled to health care only in so far as they remain dependent on men. Under such an arrangement, women are not entitled to health care by virtue of their own merits or their own work and effort. Insurance is provided to employees, and often only the higher-paid and higher-status employees, which are more often male. But even if employees are female, they are less likely to have insurance as a benefit; women are more often in the lower-paid, lower-status, and part-time jobs.

The assumption is that women will obtain insurance through their husbands who are the central figures for the distribution of health resources. The assumption is that she will be dependent on her husband for such benefits. A man deserves health insurance because he works. A woman, since she does not "work," or if she does work, it is less important work than her husband's, has to rely on him, his employer, and the continuation of the marriage for insurance and thus health care. As one author stated, "For men, they created retirement plans, medical benefits, profit sharing and gold watches. For women, they created Mother's Day" (Miller 1990, 134).

Another problem is that as the costs of health care and insurance have risen, insurance companies and employers have tried many ways to control or reduce their costs. One of these is to discontinue paying for dependent coverage. This puts the many women who have such insurance at risk of losing their coverage if they cannot afford the premiums.

The male employee as an ideal model also posits uninterrupted work throughout one's career years, and such an employee would also have uninterrupted health care insurance. But women who work outside the home commonly interrupt their careers for child bearing and child rearing reasons. So if insurance is tied to employment, this puts women at risk. And for all of the above described reasons, when insurance is tied to employment, women's independence is compromised, their efforts at home and in the workplace are unrecognized and unrewarded, and their access to insurance and thus to health care are at risk. In such a structure, women lose.

Medicare: Health Care for the Retired Male

The rationale behind Medicare suffers similar faulty reasoning. Established in 1965, it is considered a social insurance program, not a public assistance program, the difference between the two being that people "deserve" the benefits granted under social insurance programs because they have earned them. Such benefits are contributory, work-related, and available to beneficiaries as a right by virtue of their employment throughout their lives. Part A of Medicare that covers hospital bills is financed by deductions from worker's paychecks, just as Social Security is financed. Part B that covers hospital bills is financed partially by the enrollees' contributions and partly by federal government general tax revenue. In both cases, the idea is that the elderly deserve the social insurance because they, meaning men, have worked hard throughout their lives and deserve the help as they retire and grow older. One generation of workers pays for and supports the earlier generation of workers. And even the idea of retirement is modeled on a male framework—the idea that one is employed and works and then retires and does not work anymore. As the cliché goes "a woman's work is never done." Women do not get to retire from their jobs as homemakers.

Medicaid: Woman as Poor, Dependent Mothers

Women may also receive public insurance—Medicaid—if they receive AFDC, but they receive AFDC because they have children to care for, have no employed male in the house to provide for them, and are themselves poor. Again, the presence of a man is central to deciding whether a women receives benefits. These women may or may not be employed, but if they are, they make little money. In such circumstances, women can receive public insurance or public assistance. There are other ways one can receive Medicaid, but being an AFDC recipient is the most common.[8]

As noted above, many more women are enrolled in Medicaid than men. When one receives Medicaid, they are "needy," "unable to take care of themselves," "incapable," "poor," "indigent," and so forth. Medicaid is part of our ugly welfare system. As Linda Gordon (1994) notes about the term "welfare:"

> What once meant prosperity, good health, and good spirits now implies poverty, bad health, and fatalism. A word that once evoked images of pastoral contentment now connotes slums, depressed single mothers and neglected children, even crime. Today "welfare" means grudging aid to the poor, when once it referred to a vision of a good life. (1)

The common thinking is that such people are somewhat substandard. The women enrolled in Medicaid do not have a husband to be dependent on and thus must be dependent on the state. In either case, the woman is not an independent being able to care for herself and her children; she is not a man—she needs help. And a poor woman can only qualify to be covered by Medicaid if she is a mother, that is, if she is a reproducer.[9]

Basically, we have a two tiered health care system; one for the poor and one for all the rest. As Stan Dorn of the Washington, D.C. based National Health Law Program notes, "Today, low-income families often receive care from a different health care delivery system than that serving the people with higher incomes. Often, these systems are both separate and unequal" (U.S. Congress, Senate 1994c, 33). And Medicaid recipients find it hard to obtain care because many doctors do not want to treat Medicaid patients because of the low reimbursement levels. And this is in contrast to Medicare, which reimburses doctors at their "usual and customary fees," as do private fee-for-service plans.

And Medicaid does not even treat all of the poor. This was always a problem but has grown in the recent past with states trying to control their social welfare program costs by setting various restrictions that do not allow as many of the poor to qualify for AFDC and Medicaid. Somewhere between 40 percent and two-thirds of all poor persons in the United States are ineligible for Medicaid because of categorical or income requirements (Brown 1984; McBarnette 1988). Thus, many poor or low-income women remain uninsured; they do not qualify to be dependent on a man or on the state, so they just have to do without.

Basic Health Care Benefits: Medical Care for the Male Patient

As detailed above, many of women's needs are not covered at all or are not covered in an adequate fashion by typical insurance plans, as well as by Medicare and Medicaid. Many reproductive and maternity services are not covered or have high cost sharing, and contraception is a particularly glaring problem. Female preventive services such as Pap smears, breast exams, and mammograms are not covered at all or only with high cost sharing by many plans. Abortion services, though covered by the majority of plans, have restrictions placed upon them. Also, abortion is not covered by Medicaid except in severe circumstances. Mental health benefits are another important area in which standard insurance plans do not address women's needs. In summary, women's specific diseases and conditions are not adequately addressed by present health care insurance plans.

Many of women's specific health care needs, and the diseases and conditions they encounter, arise from their reproductive capabilities. Men do not have these same needs and thus do not suffer any comparable problem of insurance not meeting their basic needs. Once again, because women are different from men, and different in this case because of their reproductive capabilities, their needs are not met.

Men are more likely to say that their health is excellent or very good (Muller 1990, 13). And though women are more likely to see doctors, men are more likely to see a family practitioner for disease, treatment, and injury reasons, and women are more likely to see a doctor for diagnostic, screening, and preventive reasons (Muller 1990, 15). Health insurance and medical care in general were designed around these male needs—visits to physicians for disease and injury as opposed to visits for preventive measures.

Other issues such as mental health care and specifically counseling for domestic violence, rape, and childhood abuse provide more evidence as to how the system was designed for people who generally do not need such services. The meager insurance coverage that is offered, if at all, is not very useful. Cost-sharing is still very high and most plans that include such benefits place severe restrictions on their use. In conclusion, since many of women's health care needs are different from men's, they are often left unmet.

Invisibility of Women's Work: The Exclusion of Long-Term Care

Long-term care is a blatant example of a health care insurance system that is male-biased. As described above, long-term care is rarely covered under insurance plans except for Medicaid. Most importantly, Medicare, the program that provides care for those over the age of 65, has no long-term care coverage. Furthermore, with the implementation of Medicare's Diagnosis-Related Groups, hospitals have an incentive to release Medicare patients as early as possible and this causes more work for the female caregiver. So women almost always provide care, and the amount they have to provide has been increasing. And because women, and not men, provide such care, it does not appear to be a problem. Since "a woman's place is in the home" any services provided by her are presumed to be part of her job, but, of course, this is a job without pay.

That women's lives are hindered because they are more likely to need health care and because they are more likely to provide care, does not appear to be a problem for the health care system. Men more often receive long-term care from their wives (or other female family members) because women live longer and thus are alive and willing to, are feel compelled to, provide such care. Caring for family members, whether it be children, the disabled, sick, or elderly, is perceived as part of the private realm of the family and thus under women's domain. It is not an appropriate problem for, and thus need not be addressed by, health insurance plans.

Let us look at the situation of long-term care from a different perspective. If men had to spend 18 years of their life caring for a family member (not including children); take time off work; rearrange their work schedules, work part-time, or not at all; go to their job and then go home or to the family member's house and provide for the needy family member, and then take care of their own needs and very possibly other family member's needs; and incur many personal costs from such caring activities, the issue of long-term care might be perceived as a problem. Furthermore, the loss of income, either in part or in full, is a critical issue for women since many are already leading financially constrained lives. As a result of the caring activities, many care-givers experience a significant decrease in the quality of their lives as they spend more money, make less money, and take on more responsibilities. Again, because most men do not suffer the consequences of such burdensome activities, it has not been defined as a problem to which public policies should provide, or at least help provide, a solution. Because women usually provide long-term care and fill the gaps left by insurance, the problem remains invisible.

The Male Doctor: Women's Unhappiness with Physicians

As noted above, women are much more likely to change doctors because they are unhappy with their doctor's conduct: the doctor may be uncommunicative, "talk down to," be demeaning, make inappropriate remarks, or any number of factors. Unfortunately, as health care costs have risen, insurance companies have instituted various restrictions on what and which doctors patients may see. Some plans state one must always see their primary physician first and cannot change their primary physician except at designated times, usually once a year. Under such plans, there are usually a group of "participating" physicians and one must see a doctor on the plan if one wants coverage. If a woman wants a female physician or wants to change their physician, as many do, her choices and ability to do so are limited. In HMOs, one may only see doctors that are part of that HMO and if a woman wants to change plans, it is usually a difficult process. Such restrictions may force a woman to keep seeing a doctor she feels mistreats her, or they may cause a women not to get the care she needs because she does not want to have to visit her physician.

Once again, because women are unhappy with their physicians and their desire to change doctors is greater than men's, limitations on such abilities affect women in greater proportion. With doctors more likely to be male, and patients more likely to be female, the issue of the doctor-patient relationship becomes, at least partially, a gender issue. If male patients are generally happy with their doctors, then the ability to change physicians is not viewed as a problem. When insurance plans institute greater control over which doctors patients may see, women lose once again.

And the problem may not just be women's displeasure with their physicians; their health may be in danger. An article in the *New England Journal of Medicine* reported that female physicians screened their female patients for breast and cervical cancer more often than male physicians. It may be that female physicians are more aware of female health concerns and needs and thus provide better care for female patients. In conclusion, it is important for women to be able to change their physicians if they are unhappy and to have the ability to go to a female physician is they so chose.

In conclusion, many aspects of the insurance system, health care benefits, and overall access to health care have been designed with males as the model. Such a system does not meet many of women's health care needs and their health may suffer because of it. In many ways, women are disadvantaged by the present health insurance system.

HEALTH CARE REFORM

President Clinton was elected in 1992 with the agenda of reforming the health care system. He promptly formed the President's Task Force on Health Care Reform and in September 1993, he introduced the Health Security Act. This was the largest effort at health care reform that any President or Congress had initiated in decades.

The Health Security Act called for universal coverage with employers and employees sharing the costs of premiums for health insurance. It included cost-sharing, community rating, and quality standards. It keep private insurance but "managed the competition" between plans through regional health alliances. It also specified a benefit package that would be available for all that included long-term care and preventive services.

It was not long though before hopes for health care reform were dashed. The plan was criticized as containing "too much big government" and even Democrats couldn't agree on the particulars of the President's plan. In fact, the Health Security Act was so long that hardly anyone could actually read it and understand how this new, complex system would work. Though much momentum was in force for health care reform just a year earlier, by 1994 it was clear that the Health Security Act was doomed.

Within this time period, many other bills were introduced calling for varying degrees of reform. The Wellstone/McDermot plan called for a single-payer system entailing universal coverage and cost controls. Private insurance, Medicaid, and Medicare would be eliminated and replaced by one, government-run insurance plan financed through taxes. Services would be free when delivered and available for all. Cost controls would be implemented through set reimbursement schedules and institutional and global budgets.

Other bills called for more conservative revisions. A bill introduced by Cooper, "The Managed Competition Act," relied on market forces and voluntary participation. It proposed a system of purchasing pools and required a standard benefit package, age-adjusted community rating, portability, quality standards, and limited pre-existing condition clauses. Additional bills called for medical savings accounts (MSAs) that would allow individuals to put money aside, tax-free, to pay the family's medical bills.[10]

Despite the activity about health care reform during the early 1990s, no major governmental reform occurred. But the U.S. health care system has not remained stagnant. Managed care organizations are revamping the U.S. health care system at a pace that governmental reform could never imagine. Presently, about one-half of the insured are enrolled in either a health maintenance organization (HMO) or a preferred provider organization (PPO). And many ideas for reforming the system propose to increase enrollment in managed care organizations. Furthermore, Medicaid has enacted many changes in the last few years and although the changes vary state-to-state, most states have either required or encouraged enrollment in managed care.

In the next section, these various reforms will be discussed, along with two other commonly proposed ideas for reforming the health care system: universal coverage and a standard benefits package. Many proposals call for all people to be insured (universal coverage) and for a standard basic benefits package so that all can have access to quality care and equitable benefits. Since these changes are already occurring or are proposed to solve our health care problems, an evaluation of these reform ideas—proposed and enacted—and the implications of them for women needs to be undertaken. Therefore, after these health care trends are discussed, the chapter will conclude with the application of the gender justice framework to the current trends and reform proposals. Will they implement or further justice for women?

The Managed Care Revolution

The most important and profound reform presently occurring in the health care system is the demise of fee-for-service care and the growth of managed care.[11] Enrollment in HMOs in 1995 was up 16 percent from 1994 (Daniels, et al. 1996). Businesses have taken the lead with nearly 75 percent of all Americans with employer-based insurance enrolled in some type of managed care plan (Gonen 1997). In fact, the impetus for managed care came from employers, with government following, as a mechanism to gain control of and reduce the skyrocketing costs of health care. Medicare and Medicaid are starting to encourage participants to enroll in managed care, but Medicaid programs are moving toward requiring enrollment in such organizations. The elderly appear to be resistant to these changes and little coercive mechanisms are presently planned.

As managed care becomes the dominant form of financing and delivering patient care, it can be expected to influence the entire health care system. Managed care is challenging hospitals and physicians to increase their efficiency and monitor their costs with greater vigilance. For people without a regular source of care or who use emergency rooms for routine care, it provides an entry into the health care system. Managed care focuses on primary and preventive care, but at the same time can provide an array of services often needed by patients with chronic illnesses.

At its worst, however, managed care can become a mechanism for cutting costs without regard for access and quality. Financial incentives reward plans and providers who offer fewer and less expensive services, raising the danger of substandard care. For patients without the skills or resources to navigate the system, it may create new barriers to care. For patients who use and need more medical services, managed care may not serve them well.

There are three important ways that managed care is restructuring health care. First, risk is being shifted from insurance to doctors and hospitals (Daniels, et al. 1996, 140). This changes many incentives about whom to insure and the type and quality of care they receive. Secondly, the distinction between insurance and health care is being blurred since managed care combines these two activities into one organization. HMOs were initially started by physicians, but now the managed care industry is run by the insurance industry. Large insurers control 45 percent of the managed care market and for-profit corporations own two-thirds of all HMOs. Third, managed care is bringing the information revolution to medicine because managed care institutions generate large databases of patient information (140).

Women and Managed Care

Managed care holds the potential to improve health care for women. If managed care plans emphasize preventive services, and if they do so with minimal cost-sharing, they could greatly help women obtain Pap smears, breast exams, mammograms, and pelvic exams, for example. But if women have less choice about their doctors in managed care plans—because women are more likely to be dissatisfied with their physicians—this may hinder many women's desire to actually visit the doctor. Moreover, because women, on average, use medical services more often than men, they may be viewed as more costly and thus not good candidates for managed care plans. Furthermore, women may not get the care they need.

The majority of HMO members are female, and women in their childbearing years (aged 15-44) are more likely than women of any other age group to be enrolled in managed care organizations. Thus, how managed care organizations cover prenatal care, childbirth, post-partum care is very important. In 1996, the public became aware of "drive through deliveries" in which women were being forced to leave the hospital within 24 hours after giving birth. The Newborns' and Mothers' Health Protection Act was promptly passed that forces insurance companies to allow women to stay a minimum of 48 hours following an uncomplicated childbirth. Though this legislation should solve the problem, the early dismissal of women did not speak well for how managed care organizations, when left to their own accord, will treat women.

The coverage of contraception by managed care organizations is another important issue. All forms of managed care organizations cover various contraceptive methods more often than indemnity plans. For example, HMOs are substantially more likely to cover all types of reversible contraception than traditional plans. About 86 percent of HMOs cover IUDs but only 25 percent of conventional insurance plans do so. Rates for abortion services for HMOs are about the same as conventional insurance programs (Alan Guttmacher Institute 1994).

Cost sharing for all services, and specifically for women's reproductive services, is another important matter. The number of HMOs that ask members to pay a fee for services at the time of delivery has increased since the late 1980s (GHAA 1995), and higher cost sharing is associated with decreased use. One form of cost sharing is the monthly premium paid by the employee. HMO members who receive insurance through their employers paid a higher monthly premium than did those who chose indemnity plans, but since few HMOs have deductibles or coinsurance provisions, the total cost to the enrollee is actually lower (Bernstein 1996). HMOs typically charge a copayment for primary care visits, but most do *not* charge an additional copayment for women's ob/gyn services. Moreover, many HMOs waive the copayment for prenatal care, though some charge copayments for hospitalization, including childbirth, that can total a few hundred dollars.

Use of services and quality of the services in managed care plans is also important. "Gag Orders" imposed by plans on what physicians can discuss with their patients—ostensibly to prevent patients from gaining knowledge about and thus choosing higher cost alternative treatments—have been criticized by the public. But initial research has shown that women enrolled in HMOs are more likely to have had a mammogram, Pap test, and clinical breast exam than women in conventional insurance plans (Bernstein 1996). Though more research needs to be performed, initial studies show that people enrolled in HMOs are more satisfied with their health care than people in fee-for-service plans. HMO enrollees are more satisfied with time spent filling out forms, are less satisfied with the overall quality of care and access to speciality care, and show no difference with regard to time spent waiting and the length of time between appointment and visit (National Research Corporation as reported in Bernstein 1996). The level of satisfaction varies substantially by managed care and HMO type and thus more research needs to be done to untangle the connection between level of satisfaction and plan type.

Another matter for women is if they can appoint an ob/gyn physician as their primary care doctor or if they can self-refer to one if such a doctor is not their primary care provider. Over 60 percent of women prefer a family physician or a general practitioner to be their primary care provider if they can only designate one doctor, 19 percent prefer a gynecologist, and 10 percent an internist. But most women also oppose requirements that they get a referral from their primary general practitioner before being able to see a gynecologist (Gallup Organization 1993). Unfortunately, the managed care model of one primary care physician that serves as a gatekeeper to all other care may not be compatible with the structure of the present system and women's needs. Women need and prefer to go to two or three physicians for their basic, primary, preventive care.

Other issues have arisen with regard to women and hospital care. In 1997, reports of women being forced to leave the hospital too soon after a mastectomy were publicized. Since Medicare pays for one-third of all mastectomies, the Health Care Financing Administration issued a policy that forbids doctors, hospitals, and insurers to limit the number of days women may remain hospitalized after mastectomies, or to require that the surgery be performed on an outpatient basis. Once again, such actions by managed care organization do not speak well for how they choose to treat women.

Revamping Medicaid

The Federal government has recently enacted far-reaching changes in the Medicaid program. And because Medicaid is jointly run by the federal and the state governments, various states are enacting their own additional changes in the program. As with private insurance, Medicaid has seen a substantial portion of its population enroll in managed care. As of 1995, 36 states have mandated managed care enrollment for some or all of their Medicaid beneficiaries and almost one-quarter of all Medicaid recipients were enrolled in such plans (U.S. DHHS, HCFA 1997e). So in addition to the general concerns about women and managed care organizations, with the enrollment of the poorer and less healthy population of Medicaid, additional concerns arise about the ability of such organizations to meet the health care needs of these people.

The federal government has passed regulations increasing the coverage of lower-income pregnant women, infants, and children. States must cover pregnant women, infants, and children up to age 6 if the family's income is below 133 percent of the poverty line, and states may choose to cover families whose income is above that level. Medicaid enrollment has increased because of these expansions in eligibility and picked up children and women who would have otherwise been uninsured. Furthermore, in 1996 the welfare program of Aid to Families with Dependent Children (AFDC) was dismantled and new state-run programs called Temporary

Assistance to Needy Families (TANF) were formed in its place. It was initially thought that Medicaid would be included in this overhaul, but it was not. Besides a few minor changes, those that qualified for Medicaid before the change in the welfare program will still qualify after states implement their new programs.

Proposed Reform: Universal Coverage

A commonly proposed reform measure is universal coverage. Of course, universal coverage is a proposal that anyone could agree with if costs were not a concern, and thus the important issue becomes how the universal coverage will be achieved. In other words, who will pay for it? Proposals that call for market-driven solutions, as did the Copper bill, do not guarantee universal coverage but many single-payer proposals, as well as the Clinton Health Security Act (HSA), do call for universal coverage. Under the HSA, all people would be enrolled in a health plan, either through their employer (with the employer paying 80 percent of the premium for the family) or on their own (with subsidies for lower income families). All plans and enrollments would be managed by a regional health alliance—a new middle entity.

The HSA's universal coverage proposal will be used as the basis of analysis of how women will fare under universal coverage measures. Because it relied on and yet revised the present system of insurance through employment, as well as incorporating managed care, such a plan takes a more politically feasible approach to instituting universal coverage than single payer proposals. The HSA guarantees health care insurance coverage for every person regardless of work status. Though insurance is still mainly provided through employers, one does not have to depend on employment to have affordable coverage. People can enroll through regional health alliances and still get the benefit of participating in a group plan. This coverage is provided and paid for in a variety of ways.

Under the HSA, if one is employed full-time or at least 30 hours per week, the employer contributes 80 percent of the average premium for the average health plan for that worker and their family. For employees that work between 10 and 30 hours per week, employers contribute on a pro-rated basis. An employer may pay more if they desire. Individuals pay the other 20 percent of the average premium of an average plan, but if they chose a cheaper health plan, they save money and if they chose a more expensive variety, they pay more. For self-employed and unemployed individuals with no family member working, they pay the full cost of the premium unless eligible for governmental assistance. Medicaid recipients would enroll in one of the basic health plans like everyone else, but would have their premium paid for by the Federal Government if they are at or below the poverty level. Medicare would, at least initially, stay separate.

Proposed Reform: A Basic Benefits Package

When discussing universal coverage and access to health care, it is important to think of the issue, to what does one have access? Thus a basic benefits package is important to consider. What types of services are covered? Are there deductibles and co-payments? Are preventive services emphasized and is access to specialized care easily obtained?

The HSA contains a clearly defined basic benefits package. The package is fairly comprehensive and aroused many concerns about abortion and mammography screening, to name a few. Since the HSA has a clearly defined package and because its writers appeared to pay close attention to women's needs, it will be used as the basis of analysis of a proposed benefits package.

The HSA guarantees a comprehensive benefits package for women with no lifetime limit. It includes services that are deemed "medically necessary or appropriate." Hospital services, health professional services, primary and preventive services, prescription drugs, mental health and substance abuse services, medical equipment, hospice care, and dental care and eyeglasses for those under 18 years of age are included as basic benefits. The HSA includes mammograms for women over the age of 50 at two year intervals. (Exceptions are made for women under 50 who have family risk factors, but these account for only a small percentage.) The basic package provides for Pap smears and pelvic exams for sexually active women and for those over the age of 18. After three normal exams have been done, the HSA provides coverage for Pap smears at three year intervals and annual pelvic exams for women under the age of 40. For women aged 40-64, Pap smears are available every year. Women may receive exams more often if they are "at risk for fertility-related illnesses" (U.S. Congress, Senate 1994, 96). More frequent screening would be subject to the cost-sharing requirements of the individual's plan.

Regarding reproductive, prenatal, and maternity services, the HSA includes coverage for a full range of pregnancy-related services. It includes prenatal care and one postpartum visit with no cost-sharing or deductibles required. Delivery care is provided although it may have a cost-sharing component, depending on the plan. The HSA covers prescriptive contraceptive devices. Other family planning services are supposedly provided, but the Act itself does not specifically list them. "Pregnancy-related services" are offered and the President has said that this includes abortion services. Included is a "conscience clause" that allows doctors or hospitals to refuse to provide such services. The bill specifically excludes coverage for in vitro fertilization services. Reproductive health care service choices are left to the patient and her physician.

Under the HSA, women at risk for "fertility related infectious illnesses" can receive annual screenings for chlamydia and gonorrhea. When additional testing is necessary, it will be provided with cost-sharing. On problem is that other dangerous diseases such as syphilis, which are only sexually transmitted, are excluded (U.S. Congress, Senate 1994, 96).

The HSA also includes coverage for long-term care with an emphasis on home- and community-based services. It creates a new joint state and federally financed community-based program for persons with significant functional impairments. It bases need on severity of disability rather than age or income but does ask for income-related co-payments. The states have the option of participating and it places caps on what the federal government will spend. It does not create a new entitlement to long-term care like other health services, but establishes state-run or supported community- and home-based services. Nursing home care is excluded. It also gives states the option of increasing the amount of income one can keep before qualifying for Medicaid's long-term care plan. Eligibility is limited and no specific comprehensive plan is provided.

GENDER JUSTICE AND HEALTH CARE REFORM

Principle of Self-Determination

Self-Development

The first criterion of gender justice developed in Part One is the principle of self-determination and it includes three components: self-development, recognition, and democratic freedom. The principle of self-development involves assessing a policy's ability to help women develop their capacities and abilities. Policies may need to address past constraints on women's ability to develop themselves, if appropriate, and remove past hindrances if possible.

The goal of health insurance and access to medical care is to improve the health of women and, ultimately, to save their lives. The uninsured people and people without access to medical care have their activities and thus their lives limited more, and have a higher chance of dying from illnesses. This is clearly applicable to physical illness but is also true of mental illness. If a person is depressed, their activities and lives are limited; they may even feel suicidal. So, in a general fashion, to assess whether the trends and reforms contribute to the ability of women to develop their capacities and abilities is to assess whether they contribute to women's health and well-being by giving them access to health care services—more specifically, access to the health care services that *women* need. The healthier a woman is, both mentally and physically, the better situated she is to develop herself as a human being. This raises issues of who will receive insurance or access under managed care, Medicaid reforms, and universal coverage, and what type of services women will receive in a basic benefits package

Managed care appears to increase the accessibility of health care for women since the majority of enrollees in managed care are female. This may be because it costs less than other types of insurance and thus women are better able to afford it. In any event, greater accessibility is certainly positive and increases women's health and thus ability to develop themselves. Furthermore, initial research shows that managed care organizations cover more contraceptive and family planning services, and women enrolled in them are more likely to have had preventive tests and exams. And since most organizations do not charge extra for ob/gyn services, this also increase a woman's access to needed services. Though there are some problems with managed care as discussed above, overall, the revolution in managed care appears to be increasing access for women and thus increasing their chance of leading a healthy life and developing their abilities.

With regard to Medicaid and managed care, the initial results are not so positive. Managed care appears to have mixed results regarding access to preventive services for low-income women. Whereas some research found an improvement in access, others found no change. An Arizona study found that women in managed were just as likely to receive a Pap test and mammogram as women in other Medicaid arrangements (Collins and Simon 1996). A 1994 Kaiser Family Foundation survey of Medicaid beneficiaries in California found that preventive service rates were the highest among women enrolled in fee-for-service arrangements; over one-half of the women over the age of 40 in traditional Medicaid had received a mammogram in the past year while only 40 percent of HMO members had received one (Collins and Simon 1996). Similar findings were reported for Pap tests, pelvic exams, and breast exams. As Medicaid continues to enroll more recipients, research regarding the provision of services for these low-income women needs to be undertaken.

Concerns arise about the ability of managed care organizations to effectively treat lower-income populations with increased health care needs. Theoretically, these are exactly the populations that managed care would want to shy away from because they would be less healthy, have increased needs, be costly to treat, and be less profitable. Reports have shown that many Medicaid managed care programs are rife with mismanagement and violations. In Florida where some 360,000 Medicaid recipients have been enrolled in managed care, egregious quality of care problems and mass marketing fraud have been found (Dallek 1996). Similar reports have come from Montgomery County, Ohio where over 40 percent of women in three HMOs had no or inadequate prenatal care, access to primary care declined and emergency room visits increased, and over 40 percent of the Head Start children lacked many required medical exams (Dallek 1996). Though some states have successfully started Medicaid managed care programs, it is unclear if managed care can effectively serve the less healthy populations. Thus, it is unclear whether such changes will help women gain access to needed services, improve their health, and thus be better situated to develop themselves.

But Medicaid, with its recent expansionary measures, has increased its enrollment. Most of the expansion has been for children, but pregnant women have also obtained more coverage. Over 40 percent of pregnant women and infants are now covered by Medicaid. But childbirth is also a common reason why many women leave Medicaid. And though increased coverage of pregnant women is to be applauded, the resulting situation that low-income women only deserve health care if reproducing is misguided. Moreover, states that are experimenting with managed care are enrolling more recipients. Regarding self-development, these expansionary measures are positive in that they are providing health care for women who would have otherwise been uninsured, thus increasing justice. But the same reforms are reinforcing a view of women as reproducers and perpetuating a view that women only deserve health care because of their roles as mothers and not in their own right as women. This is not increasing justice for women.

One of the ethical principles behind the HSA is that every American citizen and legal resident should have access to health care without financial barriers and that the system should avoid the creation of a tiered system; the new system should provide care based only on differences of need, not individual or group characteristics (White House Domestic Policy Council 1993). Such a principle is, of course, very positive for women. Regarding the sexes, it is stating that health care should be provided *as* it is needed and *because* it is needed, not because one is male or because one has the ability to pay for it. The specific implementation of this tenet is that every person will obtain coverage through a health plan that provides a nationally defined set of benefits. Every person is to enroll in a health plan of their choice and pay a certain portion of the premiums with some subsidies provided for low-income people. Problems such as the exclusion of pre-existing conditions are eradicated. Nearly universal coverage is achieved and the problem of lower-income women is addressed in that they will receive help with premium and cost-sharing payments. Women will always have coverage even if they separate, divorce, change jobs, or become unemployed, either by choice or by necessity.

This is very beneficial for women because they will no longer be dependent on a spouse for coverage. Women will be able to obtain health insurance coverage in their own name and in their own right, and they will have the insurance even if they leave a job. Even though insurance is partially paid for by employers, one's coverage is not dependent on staying at the place of employment. Women can continue their insurance if they need to leave the job market for a period of time. This proposed system moves much further toward meeting women's needs by removing the past constraints on obtaining coverage and by reducing women's prior dependence on their husbands for coverage.[12]

Access to medical care is one important concern but the next question becomes to what does one have access? The basic benefits to which all women will be entitled has some very positive aspects, but some components are controversial. As noted before, the HSA guarantees a comprehensive benefits package for women with no lifetime limit and includes a wide range of services; also, there is no cost-sharing for preventive services. But one controversial area is the coverage for mammograms. The HSA includes mammograms for women starting at the age of 50, at two year intervals, with exceptions for women under the age of 50 who have family risk factors. Many groups and doctors have claimed that this is insufficient.

The American Cancer Society and 10 other national organizations recommend routine mammograms (one-to-two year intervals) for women aged 40 to 49 and annual clinical exams. For women aged 50 and above, both clinical exams and mammograms should be performed on an annual basis (U.S. Congress, Senate 1994). Then there was some research that questioned the usefulness of mammograms for women under the age of 50, and with the publication of the Health Security Act and the lowered mammogram coverage, the National Cancer Institute (NCI) was questioned about this matter. The NCI issued two proclamations. "There is a general consensus among experts that routine screening every 1 to 2 years with mammography and clinical breast examination can reduce breast cancer mortality by about one-third for women ages 50 and over." They continued to state that experts do not agree on the role of routine mammographies for women aged 40 to 49. The second proclamation was issued in February 1994 and stated, "Inasmuch as cancer research is the primary mission of the National Cancer Institute, the NCAB [National Cancer Advisory Board] recommends that the NCI not involve itself independently in the setting of health care policy" (U.S. Congress, Senate 1994, 90). In other words, the NCI, an organization supported by U.S. tax dollars and that has the most current and comprehensive information about breast cancer, *chose* not to state what would be best for the women of the United States in order to help prevent 46,000 deaths per year. Previously, the NCI had issued guidelines for breast cancer screening.

Breast cancer is the most common cancer among women (180,000 diagnoses per year) and one in eight women will develop it. It is surpassed only by lung cancer in cancer-related deaths of women, and 90 percent of lung cancer diagnoses have a known cause—smoking—and thus can be prevented (U.S. Congress, Senate 1994). Breast cancer has no known cause; women are at the mercy of early detection measures in order to prevent death from the disease. Nearly 22 percent of breast cancer cases occur before the age of 50, and 78 percent of the cases occur at ages 50 and above. Without disputing the fact that more older women develop cancer, one has to wonder how many younger women have the disease but because of inadequate screening, it is not detected. Early detection is the key to prevention of death from breast cancer and studies show that many women, who do not have adequate medical care because of poverty or lack of insurance, die from the disease. Also, the earlier it is discovered the less tissue has to be removed, if any at all, thus reducing deformity. In designing a national benefits package, the inclusion of proper breast cancer screening is extremely important. It is a good case study of how well the women of the United States are treated in terms of their health care needs.

The frequency of Pap smears and pelvic examinations is another significant area. The National Cancer Institute recommends that women over the age of 18 or who are sexually active receive an annual pelvic exam and Pap smear until three consecutive tests have been found; then the test may be performed less frequently. The American Medical Women's Association agrees and adds that for the Pap smear, "less frequently" should be every three years, but the pelvic exam should still be done every year. The HSA only covers Pap smears *and* pelvic exams at three year intervals after normal ones have been found, and then annual Pap smears for women aged 40 to 64. Furthermore, under the HSA, the only exceptions are for women "at risk of fertility-related illnesses," which excludes known risk factors such as HIV, tobacco use, or multiple sexual partners (U.S. Congress, Senate 1994). More frequent screening would be subject to the cost-sharing requirements. And why the discontinuation at age 65? There is no medical reason to discontinue Pap smears and pelvic exams at the age of 65. Though the HSA provides better coverage than many women previously had, it still falls somewhat short of medical standards.

Regarding reproductive, prenatal, and maternity services, the HSA includes coverage for a full range of pregnancy-related services. It includes prenatal care and one postpartum visit with no cost-sharing or deductibles. Delivery care is provided although it may have a cost-sharing component, depending on the plan. The HSA also covers prescriptive contraceptive devices, but this is not made explicit. This is a particular deficit of the plan; such services should be explicitly covered. Other family planning services are supposedly provided, but the Act itself does not specifically list them. "Pregnancy-related services" are offered and the President has said that this includes abortion services. Included is a "conscience clause" that allows doctors or hospitals to refuse to provide such services. This may not be a problem unless many hospitals and doctors chose to exercise this option, and many doctors are presently making that choice because of ant-abortion protesters. So, in any definition of a basic benefits package, abortion services need to be explicitly stated as being part of the benefits package and a guarantee that each plan will have some providers for such services needs to be included. Having the "right" to abortion may not be enough; the actual availability of the service needs to be guaranteed. The benefit package is very positive in that reproductive health care service choices are left to the patient and her physician.

Under the HSA, women at risk for "fertility related infectious illnesses" can receive annual screening for chlamydia and gonorrhea. When additional testing is necessary, it will be provided with cost-sharing. One problem with this provision is that other dangerous diseases such as syphilis, which are only sexually transmitted, are excluded. Mental health benefits, though recognized as important and included in the plan, have limitations and high cost-sharing. The HSA covers inpatient, residential, and outpatient treatment but has limitations on the number of days and on the number of visits, and requires that recipients pay $25 per visit. This puts mental health counseling outside the reach of many low-income women.

In conclusion, a universal coverage provision such as the one contained in the HSA, does remove barriers for many women regarding their ability to access the health care system. The enactment of universal coverage would greatly enhance a woman's ability to get medical care, thus greatly increasing her chances of living a healthy life and being able to develop her abilities. Such a provision increases justice for women in terms of health care. The benefit package included in the HSA is a considerable improvement for women in terms of reproductive care, but some problems remain. The package does *not* provide the best and most inclusive breast cancer screening that it could, thus reducing its effectiveness in this very important area. All of the reproductive and family planning services are subject to deductibles and cost-sharing, except prenatal and postpartum care, even though lower-income women may receive help through Federal subsidies. Also, regarding contraceptive drugs, women may have to meet deductibles under both the family planning medical visit portion of the Act *and* for the drugs prescribed, while also having to make copayments for those services; this results in high cost-sharing measures for women because of their reproductive needs. Thus, women are being hindered because, one, the responsibility for family planning mainly falls on their shoulders, and two, they have extra health care costs because of it.

Overall, the basic benefit package is very broad and requires the coverage of services that are "medically necessary or appropriate." This is broader than present insurance plans that use a standard of "medically necessary." The provision of universal coverage guarantees that all women will have insurance, which means access to health care services, and then the plan defines a fairly broad basic benefits package. Generally, women's health care would be improved under such arrangements; these provisions specifically address the prior constraints on women's ability to obtain quality and affordable health care, even though there are some problems with the benefits. The enactment of universal coverage and the provision of such a benefit package would lead to improved health for women which, in turn, should contribute to women's ability to develop themselves, as question one asks. Justice for women would be improved if such proposals were enacted.

Recognition

The second criterion of the principle of self-determination is recognition. Thus, the question to ask is "does the policy contribute to the ability of women to express their experiences and have them recognized and legitimated?" With regard to insurance, access, and benefits, important issues include women's ability to communicate and be heard by their medical care providers and the ability to change providers if they are dissatisfied. A related concern for women is the ability to choose the type (ob/gyn, internist, etc.) of provider they will see—to choose the type of provider with which they feel most comfortable.

As was described above, more women than men are unhappy with their physicians and many feel patronized by their doctors; managed care limits the choices women have with regard to their medical providers. This is not a good combination. Some research has shown that women in HMOs are more likely to rate their physicians as fair or poor on aspects about the patient-physician relationship, such as time spent with patient, explanation of symptoms, and talking down to the patient (Collins and Simon 1996). Though placing limitations on providers helps keep costs down and this is beneficial for women, this same control on physician choice limits the positive impact of managed care. If women are uncomfortable with their doctors, they are more likely not to go, no matter how cheap it is.

"Gag Orders" are policies issued by managed care organizations that prohibit medical providers from discussing certain conditions and treatments, tests, or therapies for the condition. Many states have passed laws prohibiting such orders though no federal law has been enacted. Such orders negatively affect a woman's ability to have her experiences recognized and legitimated; her experience may be deemed "off limits" for the physician. These orders obviously negatively affect all recipients and given the fact that many women already have communication problems with their physicians, these orders further hinder communication.

Also with regard to managed care and the ability of women to express themselves and have their experiences legitimated, another important aspect is the need to have a choice of health care professionals. Clearly, managed care limits women's choices. Less than one-half of HMOs allow women to choose an ob/gyn as their primary care physician; about 35 percent do not allow this but give women some direct access to an ob/gyn for an annual exam. For most other needs, the majority of plans require prior authorization (Alan Guttmacher 1996b) and women do not support such a process. And though approval might make sense for some medical services so that unnecessary or excessive utilization can be avoided, for many of women's reproductive concerns such as obtaining contraception or handling an unplanned pregnancy, approval does not make sense. Such decisions do not need a medical determination and the need for authorization can impede access to care and compromise a woman's independency and control over her own reproductive concerns. On the positive side, though the choices are limited, a substantial number of managed care organizations have incorporated some flexibility. And even though physician and treatment choice may be limited, for many women that would otherwise be without insurance, managed care is certainly an improvement.

Overall, managed care does not contribute to the ability of women to have their experiences recognized; in fact, managed care reduces this aspect of self-determination. Managed care is restricting justice for women in this manner.

Democratic Freedom

The institution of gender justice in society requires that women gain more control over the determination of their actions and an important aspect of this is to increase the participation of women in the powerful policy-making structures. So, we should ask "does the policy further the ability of women to participate in determining their actions?"

With regard to managed care, as already discussed, women's choices are limited and thus women's ability to determine their own actions is more limited. This would be true for private recipients of managed care as well as Medicaid recipients in managed care organizations. Moreover, the dissemination of information on various plans so that one can make an informed decision about which plan to join has been widely discussed in the U.S. but little progress has been made. Since managed care organizations typically amass large databases of patient and treatment information, dissemination of information about the health of the people in the plan or "report cards" could easily be accomplished. This would help women, as well as men, to make more informed choices about their health care plans. Overall, managed care reduces, or does nothing to further, women's freedom.

Regarding universal coverage provisions, the provision of health insurance allows *all* women to get health care when they need it, and this certainly gives many women more control over their actions than they had previously. Lack of insurance and payment is no longer a constraint. And it is interesting to note that the HSA gives consumers a choice of plans with which to enroll and the ability to leave one plan and go to another, as well as providing report cards about plans. This would be very good for women and would help provide a system that allows women to have more control over their lives.

Another important aspect is the benefits and who gets to decide what benefits will be included and thus what health care women will receive? The HSA calls for the establishment of the National Health Board to administer the new system and recommend what benefits should be added and deleted from the basic package as technology, treatments, and information changes. And though the HSA sets the qualifications and membership of the National Health Board, gender is not mentioned. Women have no guarantee that they will be included in this important task.

Regarding abortion, the President is to be congratulated for not setting limits on abortions. The choice is left to a woman and her physician and this is very important for women. And the plan specifically goes against established Medicaid regulations. And though the present regulations about abortion as set by *Roe vs. Wade* are still the law, the HSA does not limit the services of abortion according to the trimester approach; it gives patients and their doctors the ability to decide what is "medically necessary and appropriate." This is to be highly commended. It gives women and her physician control over one of the most important matters facing a woman—whether to bear a child or not. And the definition of covered services being those that are "medically necessary or appropriate" allows latitude for a women and her doctor to decide about many courses of action.

In summary, with regard to managed care, women's freedom is curtailed. With regard to universal coverage and a basic benefits package as defined by the HSA, the plan is to be applauded for the wide decision-making power it gives a woman and her doctor. But the new powerful institutions that will decide many matters about the health care system under the HSA do not guarantee the participation of women.

Principle of Equality of Gendered Consequences

The second principle of the gender justice framework is the principle of equality of gendered consequences. The question we want to ask of public policies is "in the actual consequences of outcomes, do women achieve a lived-out equality or parity with men with respect to the policy's goals?"

If we regard the goal of all health care policies as the provision of health services, regarding managed care, concerns regarding gendered consequences are whether women and men are being enrolled in managed care in similar rates and if women end up paying the same amount as men for care. First, more women than men enroll in managed care but it is unclear exactly why this is. Because it is generally cheaper, it may be more affordable for women. And because women use more medical services, managed care may be a way for women to get their care without having to pay more. Though we do not have enough knowledge about this issue, we do know some things. Most managed care organization charge a copayment for primary care visits and if women go more often, they would pay more. But many waive the copayment for women's reproductive and prenatal services and this is very positive. So women may pay slightly more than men because of copayments but as along as these are kept low, the gap will be small. So women are most likely treated better under managed care on this note than under traditional indemnity insurance.

Regarding universal coverage, since the HSA was not passed, the actual consequences of the policy cannot be analyzed. But the Institute for Women's Policy Research (1994) made some projections on what effects they think the policy would have. They use the 1991 Current Population Survey to estimate how many women would become directly insured under the HSA. They estimate that 29 million or 50 percent of working women aged 18 to 64 would be affected by the mandated employer coverage and gain access to direct coverage through their employers. Among newly eligible female employees, 27 percent would gain new coverage while 46 percent would switch from indirect coverage to direct coverage. The remaining would switch from other types of coverage, including public plans and other private plans. About half of the newly eligible women would be employed in retail trade or service industries. The many women who would switch from public plans and indirect coverage through a spouse and obtain direct coverage would rid themselves of the vulnerability of losing public assistance or coverage through their spouse by divorce, separation, death, or cancellation of such a benefit.

Regarding the currently uninsured workers who would gain access to employer coverage if something like the HSA was enacted, about 30 percent earn less than $10,000, another 25 percent earn between $10,000 and $20,000, and about 13 percent earn between $20,000 and $30,000 (EBRI 1996). So the HSA would particularly benefit low-income working women. For the nonworking married women, the mandate that employers cover employees and their dependents is beneficial. Employers would be required to pay 80 percent of the premium for the family. And since about 20 percent of the uninsured are single parents, this would also be beneficial for working single mothers; employers would pay 80 percent of the premiums for them and their children.

From these projections of mandated employer coverage, many more women would have direct insurance coverage and this would be very beneficial. No longer would many women have to rely on their spouses for health insurance. Women would have coverage that was secure—coverage that was their coverage no matter if they divorced, became unemployed, or widowed. This would help meet their health care needs by providing continual access to the system. Regarding the simple issue of whether one has insurance or not, a type of equity would be reached between men and women if universal coverage was enacted.

But another area of concern is the extra money that women may still have to pay because they will visit the doctor more often and need more care in general. Under the HSA, even with the low-cost sharing plan there are charges of $10 per outpatient visit, $25 per emergency room visit, $5 per prescription drug, and $25 per psychotherapy visit. It is helpful that lower-income women can receive subsidies to help with these cost-sharing and premium payments, but women will still most likely have more out-of-pocket expenses. Thus, the benefit package as provided by the HSA does not impose a lived-out parity between men and women though it would be an improvement over present conditions.

Principle of Diversity

As noted in Part One, a gender justice framework needs to acknowledge the diversity of women and make sure that policies address their assorted needs. Thus, the question to ask becomes "does the policy recognize the diversity of women—age, class, race, ethnicity, sexual orientation, disability status, etc.—and address their differing needs?"

This topic is very important for women's health care needs. Some minority and lower-income women have had less access to the health care system. The absence of bilingual physicians and staff at health care institutions can make treatment for some populations problematic. Older women covered under Medicare have different needs, insurance, and thus problems than a young women covered under a private policy might have. A woman of age 25 is not too concerned about breast cancer but is more concerned about reproductive care.

Lesbian women have particular health care concerns and they face greater barriers to health care. The primary barriers identified by lesbians are related to the consequences of discovery of their sexual orientation, which include unwanted identification of sexual orientation, negative responses from health care providers, stereotyping, and inappropriate care because of assumptions about heterosexuality (Horton 1995). With the increase of managed care and restrictions on choice of providers, this can have severe implications for lesbian women

Not much research has been done regarding managed care's ability to handle diverse populations. This has been mentioned with regard to the Medicaid population's lower health status, but what about their ability to handle lesbian women and women from different cultures? Once again, if physician choice is limited, this has severe implications for these populations.

Some studies have been done regarding the enrollment of the disabled Medicaid population in managed care. The disabled usually need extensive services and access to specialized providers and do not appear to be good candidates for managed care. States that are experimenting with these programs are finding that the issue is very complex and that significant efforts are needed to ensure quality of care.

One crucial issue for older women is long-term care. As discussed before, women give care and then because they live longer, they need long-term care themselves. This is one particular issue upon which the HSA is very weak. The HSA does not include long-term care as a basic benefit. It helps states set up community- and home-based long-term care program but the amount of money states will be given will be limited. Though it is a start and progress from the present state, this will not address the need of long-term care. Furthermore, nursing home care is excluded.

Geographical locations of people are important for health care. Rural areas have a hard time attracting doctors and thus access to care is limited for many rural residents. One problem that the HSA addresses is that health plans might not want to participate in alliances that encompass disadvantaged areas; this could be a new type of "cherry picking" in that health plans find the lowest risk areas in which to offer insurance and skip the high risk ones. The HSA authorizes states to offer incentives to insure that health plans enroll disadvantaged groups and provide appropriate outreach services for them. The White House Domestic Policy Group recognized the barriers to care that are faced by low-income and lower educated individuals, minority groups, inner-city and rural residents, the homeless, individuals who lack a stable residence, adolescents, HIV infected individuals, substance abusers, and the mentally ill. Of course, universal coverage will significantly improve access to care but will not remove all of the barriers. Lack of providers in different rural and low-income areas, language and cultural barriers, transportation and hours of service, and lack of understanding among consumers still impose constraints on access.

NOTES

1. The public programs of Medicaid and Medicare were instituted in 1965. Medicaid serves the poor and Medicare serves those aged 65 and older and the disabled. About ten percent of all Medicare beneficiaries are disabled. There are many differences in the benefits and administration of the two programs, as well as in how the two programs are perceived by the public.

2. For all men and women, 13 percent of women and 9 percent of men report not getting the needed care within the last year, but of the uninsured, 36 percent of women but only 23 percent of men report not getting needed care (Commonwealth Fund 1993).

3. The Hyde Amendment, passed in 1976 and every session thereafter, does not allow any federal money to be used for abortions except to save the life of the mother. At various times and again in 1993, the amendment also allows Medicaid to pay for abortions in the case of rape or incest. Muller (1990) notes that virtually no federal payments for abortions have been made. States can provide abortion services as part of their Medicaid program but receive no reimbursement from the federal government for such services. The majority of states (about 30) do not provide any services, some pay for abortions if severe fetal deformity is expected, and some are under court order to provide funding (Muller 1990, 181). The states that do cover abortions include Alaska, California, Connecticut, Hawaii, Idaho, Illinois, Maryland, Massachusetts, Minnesota, Montana, New Jersey, New Mexico, New York, Oregon, Vermont, Washington, and West Virginia (Sollom 1997).

4. This number has most likely improved in the last few years from expansions in Medicaid coverage for pregnant women and infants that are discussed below.

5. Depression is a complex condition because it is unclear how much of it is truly depression in women and how much is a misdiagnosis by physicians, but nevertheless, mental health benefits are very important for women.

6. In 1993, outpatient mental health benefits for Medicare were capped at the lesser of $562.50 or 62.5 percent of actual service costs (Moon 1993, 232).

7. The Medicare Catastrophic Act of 1988, that was repealed a year later, had provisions that helped with long-term care. It improved the benefits for skilled nursing facilities and hospice benefits, provided an unlimited duration of home health care, offered home respite care. It also included coverage for prescription drugs.

8. AFDC was abolished by the Personal Responsibility and Work Opportunity Reconciliation Act of 1996 (P.L. 104-193). Now states receive block grants and devise their own plans for providing assistance to needy families—Temporary Assistance to Needy Families (TANF). Now, to qualify for Medicaid, one must meet the old AFDC requirements not the new state welfare requirements.

9. Many elderly women qualify for Medicaid and such coverage makes no distinction about reproducer status. About 8 percent of Medicaid enrollees are aged 65 and over.

10. On July 1, 1997 the Health Insurance Portability and Accountability Act went into effect. The law, among many things, includes a provision for experimental medical savings accounts that will run for four years. Under the program, self-employed people and company employees who have health insurance with high deductibles ($1,500 to $2,250 for individuals, $3,000 to $4,500 for a family) can open a tax-free medical savings account. Workers can contribute 65 percent of their deductible for individual policies, and 75 percent for a family plan. Earnings and withdrawals for medical expenses are not taxable. The government will allow 750,000 of these accounts to be opened (Chartrand 1997).

11. The term "managed care" is confusing because it refers to a wide variety of health care plans. Health maintenance organizations (HMOs) and preferred provider organizations (PPOs) are the two main types of managed care organizations. HMOs can be group, staff, network, or independent practice associations (IPAs), or some combination of these. PPOs are usually groups of physicians that are designated "providers" and in which the insurance company has contracted specific reimbursement levels. Services for the patient are cheaper if they see a designated provider. Also, the term "managed care" commonly refers to the financing mechanisms that plans use to take in money and by which services are paid, hence the common notion of managing costs. Herein, I will use the term "managed care" to refer to the many types of health care and insurance plans that are not fee-for-service or indemnity based. When referring to a specific type of managed care plan, such as an HMO, specific terminology will be used.

12. Some features of this proposal were actually enacted in the Health Insurance and Portability Act of 1996.

CHAPTER 8

A Gender Just Health Care System for Women

This book has proposed a framework for analyzing public policies according to issues of gender and justice. The goal of a gender just policy should be to reach a society in which "women as a group are not disadvantaged in controlling their destiny." This goal involves many principles, but they are all based upon the fact that no one should gain or lose from the arbitrary distinction of their sex. We have no control over what sex we were born. But we can control the consequences that society inflicts on certain members because of their sex—it is not the sexual difference that is important, it is the difference that difference makes.

The first step in the process of instituting gender just policies is to show or convince others that women are disadvantaged and do not have their needs met by many present public policies. In this work, it has been shown how policies regarding medical research on women and on women's health issues have been based on a male paradigm that views women in light of their similarities to or differences from men but never in terms of women's own health care concerns. Not surprisingly, such policies have not met women's needs and many of these policies disadvantage women. The health care insurance system—the system that allocates what, if any, health care women will receive—was discussed and it was shown how many aspects of this system are based on a male model.

The next step in the process of instituting gender just policies is to devise and articulate a new guiding framework. A new framework that is *not* based on the male model but concerns itself with women's needs is required and was developed in Part One herein. Self-determination is one very important aspect of justice for women and is a principle that any public policy should address. Self-determination was broken down into the components of self-development, recognition, and democratic freedom. The other two principles deemed important for gender justice were equality of gendered consequences and diversity. A set of questions, based on these principles, was developed and it was argued that these should be asked of public policies in order to analyze how well they institute gender justice. The questions are a start toward a new framework for gender justice.

The new NIH and FDA policies, as well as issues of managed care, revisions in Medicaid, universal coverage, and a standard benefits package were analyzed according to the framework of gender justice. The new policies enacted at NIH, and to a lesser degree at the FDA, are positive improvements for women. Many of the important issues described above are addressed, in some degree, by the new policies, and thus the gender justice of medical research has been greatly improved. Women and minorities are now required to be included and the diversity of women is taken into account. Regarding the topics being studied by NIH, women are not so lucky. Many more trials like the Women's Health Initiative need to instituted.

Managed care has increased the gender justice of the health care system in some ways and reduced it in others. Positive factors include the increased accessibility of the health care system for women and better coverage and provision of reproductive and preventive services. With regard to choice of physician and type of primary care physician, as well as notions of freedom, managed care is not so positive. Thus, under managed care, women's self-development is increased, but managed care receives a disfavor able assessment with regard to the recognition of women's experiences and democratic freedom. Though it does not institute equality with regard to gendered consequences from differential use of the health care system by men and women, managed care is an improvement from indemnity, fee-for-service insurance plans.

Medicaid's recent expansion in eligibility requirements has improved access for pregnant women but this does little to help women develop themselves. In fact, it only helps women develop themselves as mothers. Universal coverage and a standard benefits package as proposed by President Clinton's Health Security Act, if enacted, would improve access to health care insurance and services for women. No longer would women be dependent on their spouse or Medicaid to get medical care because everyone would have a right to health care. But some of women's needs are not addressed by the HSA. Mammogram screening needs to be improved until more definitive evidence is found about women under age 50. Because women use the health care system more, any system that requires cost-sharing and payments-per-visit will disadvantage women. In summary, if something similar to the HSA was passed, it would greatly improve health care for women, meet many more of their health care needs, and increase access to the health care system.

Policies regarding medical research have been implemented by NIH and the ORWH. They have already instituted change and improved the situation for women. This is to be applauded. But the health care system has not been reformed and still disadvantages women. Managed care has helped *and* hindered women. Changes in Medicaid have increased coverage for some women, mainly pregnant women. Though enactment of universal coverage and a benefits package similar to the one proposed in the HSA would increase justice for women, there is not much hope for any such reforms in the near future.

A GENDER JUST HEALTH CARE SYSTEM

A gender just health care system would provide all women and men with health care coverage for physical as well as mental services. Thus, universal coverage would be enacted. Such a system would not charge women more because they use they system more nor because of their reproductive needs. It would provide a wide range of choice with regard to medical provider use and type. Such a system would provide better training for doctors with regard to patient communication and dealing with and providing care for diverse groups of people. A gender just health care system would have more input from men and women regarding its design and management, and would provide health data or report cards about various plans so that people could make more informed choices.

So how do we move from here to there?

If managed care's restrictions on choice continue, a medical specialty focused specifically on women's health will be needed so that women can designate such physicians as their primary care physicians. But the ability to switch doctors will need to be allowed in case one is unhappy with their choice. Governmental policies should be enacted to force managed care organizations to publish their data on their plan and participants. The data is available but without some help from government, health care groups may not take the trouble to publish it. Quality of care should be better watched by state governments for the sake of all, but specifically for Medicaid managed care enrollees. And more regulation of the insurance and managed care plans may need to be enforced such that they all provide a standard benefits package. This will also help consumers to judge various plans because they will have common factors. That way women would not pay more because they go more.

The health care system should help women live a healthy life so they can pursue their life plans. And it should not penalize women by making them pay more for basic health care. Copayments and deductibles need to be eliminated and the loss rolled into the monthly premium that persons enrolled in managed care pay.

Bibliography

Ackerman, Bruce. 1980. *Social Justice in the Liberal State*. New Haven: Yale University Press.

Aditta, R. and S. Cavarak. 1980. *Science and Liberation*. Boston, MA: South End.

Agich, George J. and Charles Begley. 1986. *The Price of Health*. Dordrecht, Holland: D. Reidel.

Alan Guttmacher Institute. 1985. "Paying for Maternity Care." *Family Planning Perspectives*, 17(3):103-11.

———. 1994 "Uneven & Unequal: Insurance Coverage and Reproductive Health Services." New York: Alan Guttmacher Institute.

———. 1996a. "Facts in Brief: Induced Abortion." URL http://www.agi-usa.org/pubs/fb_abortion2/fb_abort2.html [1997, September 3].

———. 1996b. "Issues in Brief: Reproductive Health Services and Managed Care Plans: Improving the Fit." URL http://206.215.210.5/pubs/ibl.html [1997, June 25].

Allison, Lincoln, ed. 1990. *The Utilitarian Response: The Contemporary Viability of Utilitarian Political Philosophy*. Newbery Park, CA: Sage.

American Association of Retired Persons (AARP). 1989. "Working Caregivers Report: National Survey of Caregivers Final Report." March. Washington, D.C.: AARP.

American Association of University Women (AAUW). 1992. *How Schools Shortchange Girls*. Washington, DC: AAUW.

———. 1993a. *Hostile Hallways*. Washington, DC: AAUW.

———. 1993b. "National Health Care Reform: Position Paper." December. Washington, DC: AAUW.

———. 1995. "Family Planning Bill Introduced." *Action Alert* 15(3):4.

Ameswith, Katherine. 1990. "Our Bodies, Their Selves." *Newsweek*, December 17, 60.

Auerbach, Judith D. 1992. "The Emergence of the Women's Health Research Agenda: Some Preliminary Analysis." Paper presented at the Annual Meeting of the Association for Public Policy Analysis and Management, Denver CO, Oct. 29-31.

Baier, Annette. 1987. "The Need for More Than Justice." In *Science, Morality, and Feminist Theory*, eds. Marsha Hanen and Kai Nelson. Calgary, Alberta: University of Calgary.

Barber, Benjamin. 1977. "Justifying Justice: Problems of Psychology, Politics, and Measurement in Rawls." In *Reading Rawls*, ed. Norman Daniels. New York: Basic Books.

Barrett, Michele. 1991. "Words and Things: Materialism and Method in Contemporary Feminist Analysis." In *Destabilizing Theory*, eds. Michele Barrett and Anne Phillips. Stanford, CA: Stanford University Press.

Barrett, Michele and Anne Phillips, eds. 1991. *Destabilizing Theory*. Stanford, CA: Stanford University Press.

Barry, Brian. 1973. *The Liberal Theory of Justice*. New York: Oxford University Press.

Bartlett, Katharine T. 1991. *Feminist Legal Theory*. Boulder, CO: Westview.

Bartman, Barbara. 1996. "Women's Access to Appropriate Providers Within Managed Care: Implications for the Quality of Primary Care." *Women's Health Issues* 6(1):45-50.

Bayer, Ronald, Arthur L. Caplan, and Norman Daniels, eds. 1983. *In Search of Equity*. New York: Plenum.

Bayles, Michael D., ed. 1968. *Contemporary Utilitarianism*. Garden City, NY: Doubleday.

Becker, Mary E. 1992. "Prince Charming: Abstract Equality." In *Feminist Jurisprudence*, ed. Leslie Friedman Goldstein. Lanham, MD: Rowman & Littlefield.

Benhabib, Seyla. 1987. "The Generalized and Concrete Other." In *Feminism as Critique*, ed. Seyla Benhabib and Drucilla Cornell. Cambridge: Polity Press.

———. 1992. *Situating the Self*. New York: Routledge.

———. 1992a. "The Debate Over Woman and Moral Theory Revisited." In *Situating the Self*, Seyla Benhabib. New York: Routledge.

———. 1992b. "The Generalized and the Concrete Other." In *Situating the Self*, Seyla Benhabib. New York: Routledge.

Benhabib, Seyla, Judith Butler, Drucilla Cornell, and Nancy Fraser. 1995. *Feminist Contentions*. New York: Routledge.

Bennefield, Robert. 1995 (November). "Current Population Reports. Household Economic Studies. Health Insurance Coverage: 1994." Washington, D.C.: Census Bureau.

———. 1996 (May). "Current Population Reports. Household Economic Studies. Who Loses Coverage and for How Long?" Washington, D.C.: Census Bureau.

Bennett, Maisha. 1988. "Afro-American Women, Poverty and Mental Health: A Social Essay." In *Women, Health, and Poverty*, eds. Cesar Perales and Lauren Young. New York: Hayworth.

Berlin, Cheston, Jr. 1987. "The Use of Drugs During Pregnancy and Lactation." Proceedings of the National Conference on Women's Health, sponsored by FDA and Public Health Service Coordinating Committee on Women's Health Issues. Public Health Reports (supp. to July-August 1987):53-54.

Berney, Barbara. 1990. "In Research, Women Don't Matter." *The Progressive* Oct.:24- 27.

Bernstein, Amy. 1996. "Women's Health in HMOs: What We Know and What We Need to Find Out." *Women's Health Issues* 6(1):51-59.

Bertin, Joan E. 1989. "Women's Health and Women's Rights: Reproductive Hazards in the Workplace." In *Healing Technology: Feminist Perspectives*, eds. Kathryn Ratcliff, Myra Marx Feree, Gail Mellow, et al. Ann Arbor, MI: University of Michigan.

Bien-Aime, Taina. 1990. "The Woman Behind the Blindfold: Toward a Reconstruction of Rawls' *Theory of Justice*." *Review of Law and Social Change* XVIII:1125-1149.

Birke, Lynda. 1986. *Women, Feminism, and Biology*. New York: Methuen.

Bock, Gisela and Susan James, eds. 1992. *Beyond Equality and Difference*. New York: Routledge.

Bodenheimer, Thomas. 1977. "Health Care in the United States: Who Pays?" In *Health and Medical Care in the U.S.: A Critical Analysis*, ed. Vicente Navarro. Farmingdale, NY: Baywood.

Bodenheimer, Thomas, Steven Cummings, and Elizabeth Harding. 1977. "Capitalizing on Illness: The Health Insurance Industry." In *Health and Medical Care in the U.S.: A Critical Analysis*, ed. Vicente Navarro. Farmingdale, NY: Baywood

Boneparth, Ellen, ed. 1982. *Women, Power and Policy*. New York: Pergamen.

Boralevi, Lea Campos. 1987. "Utilitarianism and Feminism." In *Women in Western Political Philosophy*, eds. Ellen Kennedy and Susan Mendus. New York: St. Martin's.

Boumil, Marcia and Stephen C. Hicks. 1992. *Women and the Law*. Littleton, CO: Fred B. Rothman.

Brandt, Richard B. 1968. "Toward a Credible Form of Utilitarianism." In *Contemporary Utilitarianism*, ed. Michael D. Bayles. Garden City, NY: Doubleday.

Brittan, Samuel. 1990. "Choice and Utility." In *The Utilitarian Response*, ed. Lincoln Allison. Newbury Park, CA: Sage.

Brown, Richard E. 1984. "Medicare and Medicaid: Band-Aids for the Old and Poor." In *Reforming Medicine: Lessons of the Last Quarter Century*, eds. Victor W. Sidel and Ruth Sidel. New York: Pantheon.

Budge, Ian. 1990. "Can Utilitarianism Justify Democracy? Benthamism as a Positive Theory." In *The Utilitarian Response*, ed. Lincoln Alison. Newbery Park, CA: Sage.

Bullough, Vern L. And Bonnie Bullough. 1982. *Health Care for the Other Americans*. New York: Appleton-Century-Crofts.

Calhoun, Cheshire. 1988. "Justice, Care, Gender Bias." *The Journal of Philosophy* LXXXV:451-463.

California Federal Savings and Loan Association et al v. Mark Guerra et al. 479 U.S. 272, 1987.

California Federal Savings and Loan Association et al v. Mark Guerra et al.. 479 U.S. 272. 1987. Amici Curiae, Supreme Court of the United States, October term, 1985, No.85-494.

Campaign for Women's Health. 1993. "A Model Benefits Package for Women in Health Care Reform." Washington, D.C.: Campaign for Women's Health.

Campbell, Alastair V. 1978. *Medicine, Health and Justice*. New York: Churchill Livingston.

Caplan, Arthur. 1983. "How Should Values Count in the Allocation of New Technologies in Health Care?" In *In Search of Equity*, eds. Ronald Bayer, Arthur L. Caplan, and Norman Daniels. New York: Plenum.

Card, Claudia, ed. 1991. *Feminist Ethics*. Lawrence: University Press of Kansas.

Chartrand, Sabra. 1997 (June 29). "A New Era for Health Insurance Coverage." *New York Times, Cybertimes*. URL http://nytimes.com/ [1997, September 4].

Chodorow, Nancy. 1978. *The Reproduction of Mothering*. Berkeley, CA: University of California Press.

Churchill, Larry R. 1987. *Rationing Health Care in America*. Notre Dame, IN: University of Notre Dame Press.

Clancy, Carolyn and Charlea Massion. 1992. "American Women's Health Care: A Patchwork Quilt with Gaps." *JAMA* 268(14):1918- 1920.

Cohen, Susan M., Ellen O. Mitchell, Virginia Olesen, Ellen Olshansky, and Diana L. Taylor. 1994. "From Female Disease to Women's Health: New Education Paradigms." In *Reframing Women's Health*, ed. Alice J. Dan. Thousand Oaks, CA: Sage.

Collins, Karen Scott and Lois Simons. 1996. "Women's Health and Managed Care: Promises and Challenges." *Women's Health Issues* 6(1):39-44.

Commonwealth Fund. 1993. *The Commonwealth Fund Survey of Women's Health*. New York: Commonwealth Fund.

Conrad, Peter and Rochelle Kern, eds. 1990. *The Sociology of Health and Illness*. New York: St. Martin's.

Coole, Diana. 1988. *Women in Political Theory: From Ancient Misogyny to Contemporary Feminism.* New York: Weatsheaf.

Corea, Gina, Renate Duelli Klein, et al. 1987. *Man-Made Woman.* Indianapolis: Indiana University Press.

Cott, Nancy F. 1990. "Historical Perspectives: The Equal Rights Amendment Conflict in the 1920's." In *Conflicts in Feminism*, eds. Mariane Hirsch and Evelyn Fox Keller. New York: Routledge.

Cotton, Paul. 1990. "Examples Abound of Gaps in Medical Knowledge Because of Groups Excluded from Scientific Study." *JAMA* 263(8):1051-52.

————. 1992. "Women's Health Initiative Leads Way as Research Begins to Fill Gender Gaps." *JAMA* 267(4):469-73.

Council on Ethical and Judicial Affairs, AMA. 1991. "Gender Disparities in Clinical Decision Making." *JAMA* 266(4):559-62.

Craig vs. Boren. 429 U.S. 190, 1976.

Dallek, Geraldine. 1996 (December). "Learning the Lessons of Medicaid Managed Care." *Families USA.* URL http://epn.org/families/medaid/html [1997, September 4].

Dan, Alice J., ed 1994. *Reframing Women's Health.* Thousand Oaks, CA: Sage.

Daniels, Norman. 1977a. "Equal Liberty and Unequal Worth of Liberty." In *Reading Rawls*, ed. Norman Daniels. New York: Basic Books.

———— ed. 1977b. *Reading Rawls.* New York: Basic Books.

————. 1983. "Health Care Needs and Distributive Justice." *In Search of Equity*, eds. Ronald Bayer, Arthur L. Caplan, and Norman Daniels. New York: Plenum.

————. 1985. *Just Health Care.* New York: Cambridge University Press.

————. 1988. *Am I My Parents' Keeper?* New York: Oxford University Press.

Daniels, Norman, Donald Light, and Ronald Caplan. 1996. *Benchmarks of Fairness for Health Care Reform.* New York: Oxford University Press.

Davis, Angela. 1990. "Sick and Tired of Being Sick and Tired: The Politics of Black Women's Health." In *The Black Women's Health Book*, ed. Evelyn White. Seattle, WA: Seal.

Davis, Karen. 1996a. "Medicaid: The Health Care Safety Net for the Nation's Poor." URL http://www.cmwf.org/senfi2.html [1997, June 16].

————. 1996b. "Managed Care and Patients at Risk. President's Message from the 1996 Annual Report." URL http://www.cmwf.org/96arpres.html [1997, September 4].

Day, John. 1990. "Justice and Utility in Health Care." In *The Utilitarian Response*, ed. Lincoln Alison. Newbery Park, CA: Sage.

DeBruin, Debra. 1994. "Justice and the Inclusion of Women in Clinical Studies: A Conceptual Framework." In Institute of Medicine, Division of Health Sciences Policy, Committee on the Ethical and Legal Issues Relating to the Inclusion of Women in Clinical Studies. *Women and Health Research*, Volume 2, eds.

Mastroianni, Anna, Ruth Faden, and Daniel Federman. Washington, D.C.: National Academy Press.

Di Stefano, Christene. 1991. *Configurations of Masculinity*. Ithaca, NY: Cornell University Press.

Diamond, Irene, ed. 1983. *Families, Politics, and Public Policy*. New York: Longman.

Dickman, Robert L. 1983. "Operationalizing Respect for Persons." In *In Search of Equity*, eds. Ronald Bayer, Arthur L. Caplan, and Norman Daniels. New York: Plenum.

Diggs, B.J. 1968. "Rules and Utilitarianism." In *Contemporary Utilitarianism*, ed. Michael D. Bayles. Garden City, NY: Doubleday.

Donner, Wendy. 1991. *The Liberal Self*. Ithaca, NY: Cornell University Press.

Dresser, Rebecca. 1992. "Wanted Single, White, Male for Medical Research." *Hastings Center Report* Jan.-Feb.:24-29.

Dworkin, Roland. 1977. "The Original Position." In *Reading Rawls*, ed. Norman Daniels. New York: Basic Books.

Eisenstein, Zillah R. 1988. *The Female Body and the Law*. Berkeley: University of California Press.

Elshtain, Jean Bethke. 1981. *Public Man, Private Woman*. Princeton: Princeton University Press.

———— ed. 1982. *The Family in Political Thought*. Amherst, MA: University of Massachusetts Press.

————. 1986. *Meditations on Modern Political Thought*. New York: Praeger.

Ely, John Hart. 1978. "Constitutional Interpretivism: Its Allure and Impossibility." *Indiana Law Journal* 53:407.

Employee Benefit Research Institute (EBRI). 1996. "Sources of Health Insurance and Characteristics of the Uninsured," November. URL http://www.ebri.org/pdfs/1196ib.pdf [1997, September 2].

————. 1997a. "Issues in Mental Health Care Benefits: The Costs of Mental Health Parity," February. URL http://www.ebri.org/pdfs/0297ib.pdf [1997, September 2].

————. 1997b. *EBRI Notes, Executive Sumary* 18(5), May. URL http://ebri.org/notesx/ 0597note.htm [1997, September 2].

————. 1997c. *EBRI Notes, Executie Summary* 18(6), June. URL http://ebri.org/notesx/ 0697note.htm [1997, September 2].

English, Jane. 1977. "Justice Between Generations." *Philosophical Studies* 31:91-104.

Fee, Elizabeth. 1977. "Women and Health Care: A Comparison of Theories." In *Health and Medical Care in the U.S.: A Critical Analysis*, ed. Vicente Navarro. Farmingdale, NY: Baywood.

———— ed. 1982. *The Politics of Sex in Medicine*. Farmingdale, NY: Baywood.

Feinberg, Joel. 1977. "Rawls' and Intuitionism." In *Reading Rawls*, ed. Norman Daniels. New York: Basic Books.

Fisk, Milton. 1977. "History and Reason in Rawls' Moral Theory." In *Reading Rawls*, ed. Norman Daniels. New York: Basic Books.

Flanagan, Owen and Jackson, Kathryn. 1987. "Justice, Care, And Gender." *Ethics* XCVII:622-687.

Flax, Jane. 1992. "Beyond Equality: gender, justice and difference." In *Beyond Equality and Difference*, eds. Gisela Bock and Susan James. New York: Routledge.

Frontiero vs. Richardson. 411 U.S. 677, 1983.

Fuchs, Victor R. 1974. *Who Shall Live?* New York: Basic Books.

Gallop, Jane, Mariane Hirsch, and Nancy K. Miller. 1990. "Criticizing Feminist Criticism." In *Conflicts in Feminism*, eds. Mariane Hirsch and Evelyn Fox Keller. New York: Routledge.

Gallup Organization. 1993. "A Gallup study of women's attitudes toward the use of ob/gyn for primary care." Princeton, N.J.: Gallup Organization.

Galston, William. 1980. *Justice and the Human Good*. Chicago: University of Chicago Press.

Gatens, Moira. 1992. "Power, Bodies and Difference." In *Destabilizing Theory*, eds. Michele Barrett and Anne Phillips. Stanford, CA: Stanford University Press.

Geduldig vs. Aiello. 417 U.S. 484, 1974.

Gelb, Joyce and Marian Lief Palley. 1987. *Women and Public Policies*. Princeton, NJ: Princeton University Press.

Gibbard, Allan. 1990. *Utilitarianism and Coordination*. New York: Garland.

Gibbins, John R. 1990. "Utilitarianism, Conservatism, and Social Policy." In *The Utilitarian Response*, ed. Lincoln Alison. Newbery Park, CA: Sage.

Gilligan Carol. 1982. *In a Different Voice*. Cambridge, MA: Harvard University Press.

Ginzberg, Eli. 1977. *The Limits of Health Reform*. New York: Basic Books.

Goldstein, Leslie Friedman, ed. 1992a. *Feminist Jurisprudence: the Difference Debate*. Lanham, MD: Rowman & Littlefield.

————. 1992b. "Can this Marriage Be Saved: Feminist Public Policy and Feminist Jurisprudence." In *Feminist Jurisprudence*, ed. Leslie Friedman Goldstein. Lanham, MD: Rowman & Littlefield.

Goldzieher, J.W., L. Moses, E. Averkin, C. Scheel, and B. Taber. 1971a. "A Placebo-controlled Double-Blind Crossover Investigation of the Side Effects Attribute to Oral Contraceptives." *Fertility and Sterility* 22(9):609-23.

————. 1971b. "Nervousness and Depression Attributed to Oral Contraceptives: A Double-Blind, Placebo-Controlled Study." *American Journal of Obstetrics and Gynecology* 22:1013-20.

Gonen, Julianna. 1997. "Health Plans and Purchasers: Managing Women's Primary Care." *Briefing Paper*, May(2). Washington, D.C.: Jacobs Institute of Women's Health.

Goodin, Robert E. "Government House Utilitarianism." In *The Utilitarian Response*, ed. Lincoln Alison. Newbery Park, CA: Sage.

Gordon, Linda. 1982. "The Politics of Birth Control, 1920-1940: The Impact of Professionals." In *The Politics of Sex in Medicine*, ed. Elizabeth Fee. New York: Baywood.

————. 1994. *Pitied But Not Entitled: Single Mothers and the History of Welfare, 1890-1935*. New York: The Free Press.

Grav, Lois. 1988. "Illness-Engendered Poverty Among the Elderly." In *Women, Health, and Poverty*, eds. Cesar Perales and Lauren Young. New York: Hayworth.

Green, Karen. 1986. "Rawls, Women and the Priority of Women." *Australasian Journal of Philosophy* supp. to 64:26-36.

Grimshaw, Jean. 1986. *Philosophy and Feminist Thinking*. Minneapolis: University of Minnesota Press.

Gross, Elizabeth. 1987. "What is Feminist Theory?" In *Feminist Challenges*, eds. Carole Pateman and Elizabeth Gross. Boston, MA: Northeastern University Press.

Group Health Asssociation of America (GHAA). 1995. *HMO Industry Profile, 1994*. Washington, D.C.: GHAA.

Gutman, Amy. 1980. *Liberal Equality*. New York: Cambridge University Press.

————. 1983. "For and Against Equal Access to Health Care." In *In Search of Equity*, eds. Ronald Bayer, Arthur L. Caplan, and Norman Daniels. New York: Plenum.

Hamilton, Jean. 1990. "When Medical Research is for Men Only." *Business Week*, July 16:33.

Hanmer, Jalna. 1987. "Transforming Consciousness: Women and the New Reproductive Technologies." In *Man-Made Woman*, ed. Corea, Gina, Reante Duelli Klein, et al. Indianapolis: Indiana University Press.

Harding, Sandra. 1991. *Whose science? Whose knowledge? Thinking from Women's Lives*. Ithaca, N.Y.: Cornell University Press.

Hare, R. M. 1977. "Rawls' Theory of Justice." In *Reading Rawls*, ed. Norman Daniels. New York: Basic Books.

Hart, H.L.A. 1977. "Rawls on Liberty and its Priority." In *Reading Rawls*, ed. Norman Daniels. New York: Basic Books.

Haslett, C.W. 1987. *Equal Consideration*. Cranbury, NJ: Associated University Press.

Hayunga, Eugene, Karen Rothenberg, and Vivian Pinn. 1996. 1996. "Women of Childbearing Potential in Clinical Research: Perspectives on NIH Policy and Liability Issues." *Food, Drug, Cosmetic and Medical Device Law Digest* 13(1):7-11.

Health Insurance Association of America (HIAA). 1997. "Consumer Information, Guide to Long-Term Care." URL http://www.hiaa.org/consumerinfo/guideltc.html [1997, June 30].

Held, Virginia. 1991. "A Review of *Justice, Gender, and the Family.*" *Political Theory* 19:299- 303.

———. 1993. *Feminist Morality: Transforming Culture, Society, and Politics.* Chicago: University of Chicago Press.

———. 1995. "The Meshing of Care and Justice." *Hypatia* 10(2):128-132.

Hill, Jr., Thomas. 1987. "The Importance of Autonomy." In *Women and Moral Theory*, ed. Eva Feder Kittay and Diana Meyers. Totowa, NJ: Rowman & Littlefield.

Hirsch, Mariane and Evelyn Fox Keller. 1990a. "Practicing Conflict in Feminist Theory." In *Conflicts in Feminism*, eds. Mariane Hirsch and Evelyn Fox Keller. New York: Routledge.

——— eds. 1990b. *Conflicts in Feminism.* New York: Routledge.

Hochschild, Arlie with Anne Machung. 1989. *The Second Shift: Working Parents and the Revolution at Home.* New York: Viking.

Hodgson, D.H. 1967. *Consequences of Utilitarianism.* London: Oxford University Press.

Hoffman, J.C. 1982. "Biorhythms in Human Reproduction: The Not-So-Steady States." *Signs: Journal of Women in Culture and Society* 7(4):829-844.

Horton, Jacqueline A. 1995. *The Women's Health Data Book*, 2nd Edition. Washington, D.C.: Jacob's Institute of Health.

Huckle, Patricia. 1982. "The Womb Factor: Pregnancy Policies and Employment of Women." In *Women, Power and Policy*, ed. Ellen Boneparth. New York: Pergamen.

Institute for Women's Policy Research (IWPR). 1994. *Women's Access to Health Insurance.* Washington, D.C.: IWPR.

Institute of Medicine (IOM), Division of Health Sciences Policy, Committee on the Ethical and Legal Issues Relating to the Inclusion of Women in Clinical Studies. 1994. *Women and Health Research*, Volumes 1 and 2, eds. Mastroianni, Anna, Ruth Faden, and Daniel Federman. Washington, D.C.: National Academy Press.

Jaggar, Alison M. 1983. *Feminist Politics and Human Nature.* Totowa, NJ: Rowman & Littlefield.

———. 1995. "Caring as a Feminist Practice of Moral Reason." In *Justice and Care*, ed. Virginia Held. Boulder, CO: Westview.

Jaschik, Scott. 1990. "Report says NIH Ignores Own Rules on Including Women in its Research." *Chronicle of Higher Education* June 27:A27.

Johnson, Tracey and Elizabeth Fee. 1994. "Women's Participation in Clinical Research: From Protectionism to Access." In Institute of Medicine, Division of Health Sciences Policy, Committee on the Ethical and Legal Issues Relating to the Inclusion of Women in Clinical Studies. *Women and Health Research*, Volume 2, eds. Mastroianni, Anna, Ruth Faden, and Daniel Federman. Washington, D.C.: National Academy Press.

Jones, James. 1981. *Bad Blood: The Tuskegee Syphilis Experiment*. New York: The Free Press.

Jones, Vida Labrie. 1990. "Lupus and Black Women: Managing a Complex Chronic Disability." In *The Black Women's Health Book*, ed. Evelyn White. Seattle, WA: Seal.

Kaiser Family Foundation. 1994. "Uninsured in America: Straight Facts on Health Care Reform." April. Washington, D.C.: Kaiser Family Foundation.

———. 1997. "Medicaid Enrollment and Spending Growth." URL http://www.kff.org/kff/admin/index.html [1997, June 30].

Kane, Penny. 1991. *Women's Health*. New York: St. Martin's.

Kaufert, Patricia A. and Sonja M. McKinlay. 1985. "Estrogen-replacement Therapy: the Production of Medical Knowledge and the Emergence of Policy." In *Women, Health and Healing*, eds. Ellen Lewin and Virginia Olesend. New York: Tavistock.

Kelman, Sander. 1977. "The Social Nature of the Definition of Health." In *Health and Medical Care in the U.S.: A Critical Analysis*, ed. Vicente Navarro. Farmingdale, NY: Baywood.

Kendrigan, Mary Lou. 1984. *Political Equality In A Democratic Society*. Westport, CT: Greenwood.

———. 1991. *Gender Differences: Their Impact on Public Policy*. Westport, CT: Greenwood.

Kenner, Charmian. 1985. *No Time for Women*. Boston, MA: Pandora.

Kingdon, Elizabeth. 1991. *What's Wrong with Rights?* Edinburgh, Great Britain: Edinburgh University Press.

Kinney, E.L. 1981. "Underrepresentation of Women in New Drug Trials: Ramifications and Remedies."*Annals of Internal Medicine*, 95(4):495-99.

Kirp, David L., Mark G. Yudof, and Marlene Strong Franks. 1986. *Gender Justice*. Chicago: University of Chicago Press.

Kittay, Eva Feder. 1995. "Taking Dependency Seriously: The Family and Medical Leave Act Considered in Light of the Social Organization of Dependency Work and Gender Equality." *Hypatia* 10(1):8-29.

———. 1997. "Human Dependency and Rawlsian Equality." In *Feminists Rethink the Self*, ed. Diana T. Meyers. New York: Westview.

Kittay, Eva Feder and Diana T. Meyers, eds. 1987. *Women and Moral Theory.* Savage, MD: Rowman & Littlefield.

Klein, Renate. 1989. *Infertility: Women Speak Out about their Experiences of Reproductive Medicine.* London: Pandora.

Kohlberg, Lawrence. 1981. *The Philosophy of Moral Development.* San Francisco: Harper and Row.

Kymlicka, Will. 1990. *Contemporary Political Philosophy.* New York: Oxford University Press.

LaRosa, Judith, Belinda Seto, Carlos Caban, and Eugene Hayunga. 1995. "Including Women and Minorities in Clinical Research." *Applied Clinical Trials* 4(5):31-38.

Lauver, Diane. 1994. "Factors Related to Secondary Prevention Behaviors for Breast Cancer." In *Reframing Women's Health,* ed. Alice J. Dan. Thousand Oaks, CA: Sage.

Law, Sylvia A. 1984. "Rethinking Sex and the Constitution." *Univ. of Pennsylvania Law Review* 132:955-1040.

Legato, Marianne. 1991. *The Female Heart.* New York: Avon.

Lewin, Ellen and Virginia Olesen, eds. 1985. *Women, Health and Healing.* New York: Tavistock.

Littleton, Christine A. 1987a. "Reconstructing Sexual Equality." *California Law Review* 75(4):1279-1337.

———. 1987b. "Equality and Feminist Legal Theory." *Univ. of Pittsburgh Law Review* 48:1243-1289.

Longino, Helen E. and Evelyn Hammonds. 1990. "Conflicts and Tensions in the Feminist Study of Gender and Science." In *Conflicts in Feminism,* eds. Mariane Hirsch and Evelyn Fox Keller. New York: Routledge.

Lowe, Marian and Ruth Hubbard. 1983. *Women's Nature.* Elmsford, NY: Pergamon.

Lyons, David, 1965. *Forms and Limits of Utilitarianism.* London: Oxford University Press.

———. 1977. "Nature and Soundness of the Contract and Coherence Arguments." In *Reading Rawls,* ed. Norman Daniels. New York: Basic Books.

MacIntyre, Alasdair. 1981. *After Virtue.* Notre Dame, IN: University of Notre Dame Press.

———. 1988. *Whose Justice? Whose Rationality?* Notre Dame, IN: University Notre Dame Press.

MacKinnon, Catharine. 1987. *Feminism Unmodified.* Cambridge, MA: Harvard University Press.

———. 1989. *Toward a Feminist Theory of the State.* Cambridge, MA: Harvard University Press.

Mahar, Maggie. 1993. "The Truth about Women's Pay." *Working Women* April:52.

Mahowald, Mary Briody. 1993. *Women and Children in Health Care.* New York: Oxford University Press.

Manzel, Paul T. 1983. *Medical Costs, Moral Choices.* New Haven, CT: Yale University Press.

McBarnette, Lorna. 1988. "Women and Poverty: The Effects of Reproductive Status." In *Women, Health, and Poverty*, eds. Cesar Perales and Lauren Young. New York: Hayworth.

McBride, Angela and William Leon McBride. 1994. "Women's Health Scholarship: From Critique to Assertion." In *Reframing Women's Health*, ed. Alice J. Dan. Thousand Oaks, CA: Sage.

Messing, Karen. 1982. "Do Men and Women Have Different Jobs Because of their Biological Differences?" In *The Politics of Sex in Medicine*, ed. Elizabeth Fee. New York: Baywood.

Meyers, Diana T., ed. 1997. *Feminists Rethink the Self.* New York: Westview.

Michelman, Frank. 1977. "Constitutional Welfare Rights and A Theory of Justice." In *Reading Rawls*, ed. Norman Daniels. New York: Basic Books.

Mill, John Stuart. 1975. *On Liberty.* Ed. David Spitz. New York: W.W. Norton.

Mill, John Stuart and Harriet Taylor Mill. 1970. *Essays on Sexual Equality*, ed. Alice Rossi. Chicago: University of Chicago Press.

Miller, David. 1976. *Social Justice.* London: Oxford University Press.

Miller, Dorothy. 1990. *Women and Social Welfare.* New York: Praeger.

Miller, Harlan B. and William H. Williams, ed. 1982. *The Limits of Utilitarianism.* Minneapolis, MN: University of Minnesota Press.

Miller, Jean Baker. 1976. *Toward a New Psychology of Women.* Boston, MA: Beacon.

Miller, Richard. 1977. "Rawls' Theory of Justice." In *Reading Rawls*, ed. Norman Daniels. New York: Basic Books.

Minow, Martha. 1987. "Justice Engendered." *Harvard Law Review* 101:10-95.

————. 1990. *Making All the Difference. Inclusion, Exclusion, and the American Law.* Ithaca, NY: Cornell University Press.

Moon, Marilyn. 1993. *Medicare Now and in the Future.* Washington, D.C.: Urban Institute.

————. 1996. "What Medicare has Meant to Older Americans." *Health Care Financing Review* 18(2):49-59.

Moreno, Jonathan D. 1994. "Ethical Issues Related to the Inclusion of Women of Childbearing Age in Clinical Trials." In Institute of Medicine, Division of Health Sciences Policy, Committee on the Ethical and Legal Issues Relating to the Inclusion of Women in Clinical Studies. *Women and Health Research*, Volume

2, eds. Mastroianni, Anna, Ruth Faden, and Daniel Federman. Washington, D.C.: National Academy Press.

Mueller, Keith. 1993. *Health Care Policy in the United States*. Lincoln, NE: University of Nebraska Press.

Muller, Charlotte. 1990. *Health Care and Gender*. New York: Russell Sage Foundation.

Narveson, Jan. 1967. *Morality and Utility*. Baltimore, MD: Johns Hopkins University Press.

National Institutes of Health Revitalization Act of 1993. Public Law 103-43, 42 U.S.C. 289.a-1

Navarro, Vicente, ed. 1977a. *Health and Medical Care in the U.S.: A Critical Analysis*. Farmingdale, NY: Baywood.

———. 1977b. "The Industrialization of Fetishism or the Fetishism of Industrialization." In *Health and Medical Care in the U.S.: A Critical Analysis*, ed. Vincente Navarro. Farmingdale, NY: Baywood.

Nechas, Eileen and Denise Foley, eds. 1994. *Unequal Treatment*. New York: Simon and Schuster.

Nelson, William. 1984. "Equal Opportunity." *Social Theory and Practice* 10:157-184.

Noddings, Nel. 1984. *Caring: A Feminine Approach to Ethics and Moral Education*. Berkeley: University of California Press.

———. 1990. "Ethics from the Standpoint of Women." In *Theoretical Perspectives on Sexual Difference*, ed. Deborah Rhode. New Haven, CT: Yale University Press.

Norsigian, Judy. 1994. "Women and National Health Care Reform: A Progressive Feminist Agenda." In *Reframing Women's Health*, ed. Alice J. Dan. Thousand Oaks, CA: Sage.

Nozick, Robert. 1974. *Anarchy, State, and Utopia*. New York: Basic Books.

Nsia-Jefferson, Laurie and Elaine J. Hall. 1989. "Reproductive Technology: Perspectives and Implications for Low-Income Women and Women of Color." In *Healing Technology: Feminist Perspectives*, eds. Kathryn Ratcliff, Myra Marx Feree, Gail Mellow, et al. Ann Arbor, MI: University of Michigan Press.

Nussbaum, Martha and Jonathan Glover, eds. 1995. *Women, Culture, and Development*. New York: Oxford University Press.

Oakley, Ann. 1984. *The Captured Womb*. New York: Basal Blackwell.

Oberman, Michelle. 1994. "Real and Perceived Legal Barriers to the Inclusion of Women in Clinical Trials." In *Reframing Women's Health*, ed. Alice J. Dan. Thousand Oaks, CA: Sage.

Okin, Susan Moller. 1979. *Women in Western Political Thought*. Princeton, NJ: Princeton University Press.

————. 1982. "Philosopher Queens and Private Wives: Plato on Women and the Family," In *The Family in Political Thought,* ed. Jean Bethke Elshtain. Amherst, MA: University of Massachusetts Press.

————. 1989a. "Reason and Feeling in Thinking about Justice." *Ethics* 99:229-249.

————. 1989b. *Justice, Gender, and the Family.* New York: Basic Books.

————. 1990. "Thinking Like a Woman." In *Theoretical Perspectives on Sexual Difference,* ed. Deborah Rhode. New Haven, CT: Yale University Press.

Older Women's League (OWL). 1989. "Failing America's Caregivers: A Status Report on Women who Care." May. Washington, D.C.: OWL.

Olesen, Virginia and Ellen Lewin, 1985. "Women, Health and Healing: A Theoretical Introduction." In *Women, Health and Healing,* eds. Ellen Lewin and Virginia Olesen. New York: Tavistock.

Overall, Christene.1987. *Ethics and Human Reproduction: A Feminist Analysis.* Winchester, MA: Allen & Unwin.

Pateman, Carole. 1988. *The Sexual Contract.* Stanford, CA: Stanford University Press.

————. 1989. *The Disorder of Women.* Stanford, CA: Stanford University Press.

Pateman, Carole and Elizabeth Gross, eds. 1987. *Feminist Challenges.* Boston, MA: Northeastern University Press.

Payne, Sarah. 1991. *Women, Health and Poverty.* New York: Harvester/Wheatsheaf.

Perales, Cesar and Lauren Young, eds. 1988. *Women, Health, and Poverty.* New York: Hayworth.

Perman, Laurie and Beth Stevens. 1989. "Industrial Segregation and the Gender Distribution of Fringe Benefits." *Gender and Society* 3(3):388-404.

Pharmaceutical Manufacturers Association (PMA). 1993. *In Development: New Medicines for Older Americans.* Washington, D.C.: PMA.

Phillips, Anne. 1991. *Engendering Democracy.* University Park, PA: Pennsylvania State University Press.

————. 1992. "Universal Pretensions in Political Thought." In *Destabilizing Theory,* eds. Michele Barrett and Anne Phillips. Stanford, CA: Stanford University Press.

Pregnancy Discrimination Act. 1978. 42 U.S.C, sec. 2000 e[k].

Purvis, Andrew. 1990. "A Perilous Gap." *Time* Fall:66-67.

Putnam, Ruth Anna. 1995. "Why Not a Feminist Theroy of Justice?" In *Women, Culture, and Development,* eds. Martha Nussbaum and Jonathan Glover. New York: Oxford University Press.

Quinton, Anthony. 1973. *Utilitarian Ethics.* New York: St. Martin's.

Ratcliff, Kathryn, Myra Marx Feree, Gail Mellow, et al., eds. 1989. *Healing Technology: Feminist Perspectives.* Ann Arbor, MI: University of Michigan.

Rawls, John. 1958. "Justice as Fairness." *The Philosophical Review* 57.

————. 1971. *A Theory of Justice*. Cambridge, MA: Harvard University Press.

————. 1975. "Fairness to Goodness." *Philosophical Review* 84:537.

————. 1985. "Justice as Fairness, Political Not Metaphysical." *Philosophy and Public Affairs* 14:224.

————. 1993. *Political Liberalism*. New York: Columbia University Press.

Reed vs. Reed. 404 U.S. 71, 1971.

Reeve, Andrew. 1990. "Individual Choice and the Retreat from Utilitarianism." In *The Utilitarian Response*, ed. Lincoln Allison. Newbery Park, CA: Sage.

Regan, Donald, 1980. *Utilitarianism and Co-operation*. New York: Oxford University Press.

Rhode, Deborah L. 1989. *Justice and Gender*. Cambridge, MA: University Press.

————. ed. 1990a. *Theoretical Perspectives on Sexual Difference*. New Haven, CT: Yale University Press.

————. 1990b. "Feminist Critical Theories." *Stanford Law Review* 42:617-638.

————. 1992. "The Politics of Paradigms: gender difference and gender disadvantage." In *Beyond Equality and Difference*, eds. Gisela Bock and Susan James. New York: Routledge.

Richards, Janet Radcliffe. 1980. *The Sceptical Feminist*. New York: Routledge.

Riley, Johnathan. 1990. "Utilitarian Ethics and Democratic Government." In *The Utilitarian Response*, ed. Lincoln Alison. Newbery Park, CA: Sage.

Rodriquez-Trias, Helen. 1984. "The Women's Health Movement: Women Take Power." In *Reforming Medicine: Lessons of the Last Quarter Century*, eds. Victor W. Sidel and Ruth Sidel. New York: Pantheon.

Rosser, Sue V. 1992. "Gender Bias in Clinical Research: The Difference It Makes." In *Reframing Women's Health*, ed. Alice J. Dan. Thousand Oaks, CA: Sage.

Rothenberg, Karen. 1996. "Gender Matters: Implications for Clinical Research and Women's Health Care." *Houston Law Review* 32:1201-1272.

Rowland, Dianne and Barbara Lyons. 1996. "Medicare, Medicaid, and the Elderly Poor." *Health Care Financing Review* 18(2):61-85.

Royak-Schaler, Renee. 1994. "Health Policy and Breast Cancer Screening: The Politics of Research and Intervention." In *Reframing Women's Health*, ed. Alice J. Dan. Thousand, Oaks, CA: Sage.

Ruddick, Sarah. 1980. "Maternal Thinking." *Feminist Studies* 6:342-67.

————. 1989. *Maternal Thinking: Toward a Politics of Peace*. Boston, MA: Beacon.

Ruth, Sheila. 1995. *Issues in Feminism*. Mountain View, CA: Mayfield.

Sandel, Michael. 1982. *Liberalism and the Limits of Justice*. New York: Cambridge University Press.

Sandelowski, Margarete. 1981. *Women Health and Choice*. Englewood Cliffs, N.J.: Prentice- Hall.

Sartori, Giovanni. 1987. *The Theory of Democracy Revisited*, Volumes 1 and 2. Chatham, NJ: Chatham House.

Scanlon, T.T.M. 1977. "Rawls' Theory of Justice." In *Reading Rawls*, ed. Norman Daniels. New York: Basic Books.

Schroeder, Steven. 1994. "The President's Message: Cost Containment." *Annual Report for 1994 for the Robert Wood Johnson Foundation*. Princeton, NJ: RWJ Foundation.

Schur, Edwin M. 1983. *Labeling Women Deviant*. Philadelphia: Temple University Press.

Scott, Joan W. 1990. "Deconstructing Equality - Versus - Difference: Or, the Uses of Poststructionalist Theory for Feminism." In *Conflicts in Feminism*, eds. Mariane Hirsch and Evelyn Fox Keller. New York: Routledge.

Shanley, Mary Lyndon and Carole Pateman. 1991. *Feminist Interpretations and Political Theory*. Cambridge, MA: Polity.

Sher, George. 1975. "Justifying Reverse Discrimination in Employment." *Philosophy and Public Affairs* 19/2:111-21.

———. 1987. "Other Voices, Other Rooms?" In *Women and Moral Theory*, eds. Eva Feder Kittay and Diana T. Meyers. Savage, MD: Rowman & Littlefield.

Sherrod, Pamela. 1990. "Controlling Hypertension." In *The Black Women's Health Book*, ed. Evelyn White. Seattle, WA: Seal.

Sherwin, Sue. 1992. *No Longer Patient: Feminist Ethics and Health Care*. Philadelphia: Temple University Press.

———. 1994. "Women in Clinical Studies: A Feminist View." In Institute of Medicine, Division of Health Sciences Policy, Committee on the Ethical and Legal Issues Relating to the Inclusion of Women in Clinical Studies. *Women and Health Research*, Volume 2, eds. Mastroianni, Anna, Ruth Faden, and Daniel Federman. Washington, D.C.: National Academy Press.

Sidel, Victor W. and Ruth Sidel, eds. 1984. *Reforming Medicine: Lessons of the Last Quarter Century*. New York: Pantheon.

Smart, J.J.C. 1968. "Extreme and Restricted Utilitarianism." In *Contemporary Utilitarianism*, ed. Michael D. Bayles. Garden City, NY: Doubleday.

———. 1973. "An Outline of a System of Utilitarian Ethics." In *Utilitarianism For and Against*, J.J.C. Smart and Bernard Williams. London: Cambridge University Press.

Smart, J.J.C. and Bernard Williams. 1973. *Utilitarianism For and Against*. London: Cambridge University Press.

Smith, John M. 1992. *Women and Doctors*. New York: Atlantic Monthly.

Sollom, Terry. 1997. "State Actions on Reproductive Health Issues in 1996." *Family Planning Perspectives* 29(1):35-40.

Stacey, Margaret. 1985. "Women and Health: The United States and the United Kingdom Compared." In *Women, Health and Healing*, eds. Ellen Lewin and Virginia Olesen. New York: Tavistock.

Stark, Evan, Anne Flitcraft, and William Frazier. 1982. "Medicine and Patriarchal Violence: The Social Construction of a 'Private Event.' " In *The Politics of Sex in Medicine*, ed. Elizabeth Fee. New York: Baywood.

Starr, Paul. 1982. *The Social Transformation of American Medicine*. New York: Penguin.

———. 1994. *The Logic of Health Care Reform*. New York: Penguin.

Steinbock, Bonnie. 1994. "Ethical Issues Related to the Inclusion of Pregnant Women in Clinical Trials (II)." In Institute of Medicine, Division of Health Sciences Policy, Committee on the Ethical and Legal Issues Relating to the Inclusion of Women in Clinical Studies. *Women and Health Research*, Volume 2, eds. Mastroianni, Anna, Ruth Faden, and Daniel Federman. Washington, D.C.: National Academy Press.

Stone, Deborah. 1988. *Policy Paradox and Political Reason*. New York: Harper Collins.

Strelnick, Hal and Richard Younge. 1984. "Affirmative Action in Medicine: Money Becomes the Admissions Criterion of the 1980's." In *Reforming Medicine: Lessons of the Last Quarter Century*, eds. Victor W Sidel And Ruth Sidel. New York: Pantheon.

Tallon, James R., Jr. and Rachel Block. 1988. "Changing Patterns of Health Insurance Coverage: Special Concerns for Women." In *Women, Health, and Poverty*, eds. Cesar Perales and Lauren Young. New York: Hayworth.

Thornton, Merle. 1987. "Sex Equality is not Enough for Feminism." In *Feminist Challenges*, eds. Carole Pateman and Elizabeth Cross. Boston, MA: Northeastern University Press.

Todd, Alexandra Dundas. 1989. *Intimate Adversaries*. Philadelphia: University of Pennsylvania Press.

Tong, Rosemarie. 1989. *Feminist Thought*. Boulder, CO: Westview.

Travis, Cheryl Brown. 1988. *Women and Health Psychology*. Hillsdale, NJ: Lawerence Erlbaum Associates.

Tulloch, Gail. 1989. *Mill and Sexual Equality*. New York: Lynne Rienner.

"U.N. Finds Teen-Age Girls at High Risk of AIDS." *New York Times* July 30, 1993:5.

U.S. Bureau of the Census. 1996a. *Statistical Abstract of the United States:1996*. URL http://www.census.gov/prod/2/gen/96statab/income.pdf [9, September 1997].

———. 1996b. "Health Insurance Coverage 1995." URL http://www.census.gov/hhes/hlthins/cover95/c95tabb.html [3, September 1997].

U.S. Congress. House. Human Resources and Intergovernmental Relations Subcommittee. Committee on Government Operations. 1993. *Standard Health Benefits: The Impact on Women's Health.* 103rd Congress, 1st Session, October 15. Washington, D.C.: U.S. Government Printing Office.

U.S. Congress. House. Select Committee on Children, Youth, and Families. 1992. *Health Care Reform: How Do Women, Children, and Teens Fare? Fact Sheet.* 103rd Congress, 1st Session, May 5. Washington, D.C.: U.S. Government Printing Office.

U.S. Congress. House. Subcommittee on Health. Committee on Ways and Means. 1993a. *Health Care Reform: Consideration of Benefits for Inclusion in a Standard Health Benefit Package.*103rd Congress, 1st Session, March 30. Washington, D.C.: U.S. Government Printing Office.

―――. 1993b. *Health Care Reform: Current Trends in Health Care Costs and Health Insurance Coverage.* 103rd Congress, 1st Session, January 26. Washington, D.C.: U.S. Government Printing Office.

―――. 1993c. *Health Care Reform: Expansion of Medicare Benefits to Include Prescription Drugs.* 103rd Congress, 1st Session, June 22. Washington, D.C.: U.S. Government Printing Office.

―――. 1993d. "Press Release, the Honorable Pete Stark (D., Calif.), Chairman, Announces a Hearing on Health Care Reform: Expansion of Medicare Benefits to Include Prescription Drugs." June 16. Washington, D.C.: U.S. Government Printing Office.

U.S. Congress. House. Subcommittee on Housing and Consumer Interests. Select Committee on Aging. 1990. *Women Health Care Consumers: Short-Changed on Medical Research and Treatment.* 101st Congress, 2nd Session, July 24. Washington, D.C.: U.S. Government Printing Office.

U.S. Congress. Senate. Committee on Finance. 1994a. *Health Care Benefits Package.* 103rd Congress, 2nd Session, March 3. Washington, DC:U.S. Government Printing Office.

―――. 1994b. *Long-term Care and Drug Benefits Under Health Care Reform.* 103rd Congress, 2nd Session, April 19. Washington, D.C.: U.S. Government Printing Office.

―――. 1994c. *Medicaid Issues in Health Care Reform.* 103rd Congress, 2nd Session, March 24. Washington, D.C.: U.S. Government Printing Office.

U.S. Congress. Senate. Subcommittee on Aging. Committee on Labor and Human Resources. 1994. *Women's Health Care in the President's Health Care Plan.* 103rd Congress, 2nd Session, March 9. Washington, D.C.: U.S. Government Printing Office.

U.S. Dept. of Health and Human Services (DHHS). Food and Drug Administration (FDA). 1993. "Guideline for the Study and Evaluation of Gender Differences in the Clinical Evaluation of Drugs." *Federal Register* Vol. 58, No. 139, July 22:39406-39416.

U.S. Dept. of Health and Human Services (DHHS). Health Care Financing Administration (HCFA). 1996. "Table 3, Medicare Enrollment/Demographics." URL http://www.hcfa.gov/ stats/hstats96/blustats.htm#demographics [1997, September 2].

————. 1997a. "Medicaid National Summary Statistics, Table 3. Medicaid Recipients and Vendor Payments by Basis of Eligibility." URL http://www.hcfa.gov/medicaid/ 395.htm [1997, Septmber 2].

————. 1997b. "Medicaid National Summary Statistics, Table 7. Medicaid Recipients and Vendor Payments by Sex." URL http://www.hcfa.gov/medicaid/795.htm [1997, September 2].

————. 1997c. "Medicaid National Summary Statistics, Table 9. Medicaid Recipients as a Percentage of Population by Age." URL http://www.hcfa.gov/medicaid/995.htm [1997, September 2].

————. 1997d. "Medicaid National Summary Statistics, Table 10. Medicaid Recipients as a Percentage of Population by Sex." URL http://www.hcfa.gov/medicaid/1095.htm [1997, September 2].

————. 1997e. "Medicaid Services Information." URL http://www.hcfa.gov/medicaid/mservice.htm [1997, September 13].

U.S. Dept. of Health and Human Services (DHHS). National Institutes of Health (NIH). 1994a. "NIH Guidelines on the Inclusion of Women and Minorities as Subjects in Clinical Research." *Federal Register*, Vol. 59, No. 59, March 28:14508-513.

————. 1994b. "Outreach Notebook for the NIH Guidelines on Inclusion of Women and Minorities as Subjects in Clinical Research." August. Bethesda, MD: NIH.

U.S. Dept. of Health and Human Services (DHHS). National Institutes of Health (NIH). Office of Research on Women's Health (ORWH). 1992. *Report of the National Institutes of Health: Opportunities for Research on Women's Health.* September. Bethesda, MD: NIH. NIH Publication No. 92-3457.

U.S. Dept. of Health and Human Services (DHHS). Public Health Service (PHS). 1985. *Report of the Public Health Service Task Force on Women's Health Issues, Volumes I and II.* May. Hyattsville, MD: PHS. DHHS Pub. No. (PHS):85-50206.

U.S. Dept. of Health and Human Services (DHHS). Public Health Service (PHS). Health Resources and Services Administration. 1990. *Health Status and the Disadvantaged.* Hyattsville, MD: PHS. DHHS Pub. No. (HRSA) HRS-P-DV 90-1.

U.S. Dept. of Health and Human Services (DHHS). Public Health Service (PHS). National Center for Health Statistics. 1993. *Health, United States, 1992.* Hyattsville, MD: PHS. DHHS Pub. No. (PHS) 93-1232.

U.S. Dept. of Health, Education, and Welfare (DHEW). Public Health Service. Food and Drug Administration. 1977. *General Considerations for the Clinical Evaluation of Drugs.* Washington, DC. HEW/FDA-77-3040.

U.S. General Accounting Office (GAO). 1990. "National Institutes of Health: Problems in Implementing Policy on Women in Study Populations." Testimony of Mark Nadel before the Subcommittee on Health and the Environment, Committee on Energy and Commerce, House of Representatives. Washington, DC: Government Printing Office.

———. 1992. *Women's Health. FDA Needs to Ensure More Study of Gender Differences in Prescription Drug Testing.* October. GAO/HRD-93-17.

———. 1996. *Private Health Insurance. Millions Relying on Individual Market Face Cost and Coverage Trade Offs.* November. GAO/HEHS-97-8.

———. 1997. *Employment-Based Health Insurance. Cost Increases and Family Coverage Decreases.* February. GAO/HEHS-97-35.

Wallis, Lila A. 1994. "Why a Curriculum on Women's Health?" In *Reframing Women's Health,* ed. Alice J. Dan. Thousand Oaks, CA: Sage.

Walzer, Michael. 1983. *Spheres of Justice.* New York: Basic Books.

Warshaw, Carole. 1994. "Domestic Violence: Challenges to Medical Practice." In *Reframing Women's Health,* ed. Alice J. Dan. Thousand Oaks, CA: Sage.

Weitzman, Lenore. 1985. *The Divorce Revolution.* New York: The Free Press.

Wenz, Peter S. 1986. "CBA, Utilitarianism, and Reliance Upon Intuitions." In *The Price of Health,* eds. George J. Agich and Charles E. Begley. Dordrecht, Holland: D. Reidel.

Whatley, Mariamne and Nancy Worcester. 1989. "The Role of Technology in the Co-optation of the Women's Health Movement: The Cases of Osteoporosis and Breast Cancer Screening." In *Healing Technology: Feminist Perspectives,* eds. Kathryn Ratcliff, Myra Marx Feree, Gail Mellow, et al. Ann Arbor, MI: University of Michigan Press.

White, Evelyn, ed. 1990. *The Black Women's Health Book.* Seattle, WA: Seal.

White House Domestic Policy Council. 1993. *The President's Report to the American People.* New York: Touchstone.

Wierga D.E. and C. Eaton. 1993. "The Drug Development and Approval Process." In *In Development: New Medicines for Older Americans.* Washington, DC.: PMA.

Williams, Bernard. 1973. "A Critique of Utilitarianism." In *Utilitarianism For and Against,* eds. J.J.C. Smart and Bernard Williams. London: Cambridge University Press.

Williams, Wendy. 1982. "The Equality Crisis: Some Reflections on Culture, Courts, and Feminism." *Women's Rights Law Reporter* 7:175-200.

————. 1985. "Equality's Riddle: Pregnancy and the Equal Treatment/Special/ Treatment Debate." *NYU Review of Law and Social Change* 13:325-80.

Wolgast, Elizabeth H. 1980. *Equality and the Rights of Women*. Ithaca, NY: Cornell University Press.

Yanoshik, Kim and July Norsigian. 1989. "Contraception, Control, and Choice: International Perspectives." In *Healing Technology: Feminist Perspectives*, eds. Kathryn Ratcliff, Myra Marx Feree, Gail Mellow, et al. Ann Arbor, MI: University of Michigan Press.

Young, Quentin. 1984. "The Urban Hospital: Inequity, High Tech, and Low Performance." In *Reforming Medicine: Lessons of the Last Quarter Century*, eds. Victor W. Sidel and Ruth Sidel. New York: Pantheon.

Young, Frank. 1987. "Welcoming Remarks." Proceedings of the National Conference on Women's Health, sponsored by FDA and Public Health Service Coordinating Committee on Women's Health Issues, as published in *Public Health Reports*, supp. to July-August 1987.

Young, Iris Marion. 1990. *Justice and the Politics of Difference*. Princeton, NJ: Princeton University Press.

————. 1992. "Recent Theories of Justice." *Social Theory and Practice* 18(1):63-73.

Zambrana, Ruth. 1988. "A Research Agenda on Issues Affecting Poor and Minority Women: A Model for Understanding Their Health Needs." In *Women, Health, and Poverty*, eds. Cesar Perales and Lauren Young. New York: Hayworth.

Index

DATE DUE